A PLUME BOOK

HER MAJESTY'S SPYMASTER

STEPHEN BUDIANSKY, journalist and military historian, is the author of nine books about history, science, and nature. He publishes frequently in the *New York Times* and the *Washington Post* and currently serves as a correspondent for the *Atlantic Monthly*.

"Fascinating and superbly written. I know just the man who could revivify and unite our country's floundering, sundered intelligence services. Unfortunately, he has been dead for 415 years. Walsingham was 'Wild Bill' Donovan, William Casey, and James Angleton, not to mention the fictional George Smiley of MI6. We can learn from Walsingham, even if we cannot hire him." —*The Wall Street Journal*

"Does this bring to mind a certain masterful, discreet White House policy advisor, dubbed 'the Architect' by Bush? In this time of war, terrorism, and administration leaks, CIA-related and otherwise, it's hard not to relate Tudor-era struggles over faith and empire to contemporary goings-on." —*Los Angeles Times*

"Racy. Tells the tale of Walsingham and his spies with all the bravura of a historical novelist. [Budiansky's] accounts of events and personalities associated with Elizabethan espionage are full of suspense and melodrama." —*The Washington Post*

"Illuminates a new route to appreciating the distinct personality of England's Elizabeth I and the exciting climate found at her court. In this vivid account, Walsingham emerges full-blown as a 'strange and powerful combination' of both Puritan and Renaissance man." —*Booklist* (starred review)

OTHER BOOKS BY STEPHEN BUDIANSKY

HISTORY

*Air Power: The Men, Machines, and Ideas That
Revolutionized War from Kitty Hawk to Gulf War II*

*Battle of Wits: The Complete Story of Codebreaking
in World War II*

NATURAL HISTORY

The Character of Cats

The Truth About Dogs

The Nature of Horses

If a Lion Could Talk

Nature's Keepers

The Covenant of the Wild

FOR CHILDREN

The World According to Horses

Her Majesty's Spymaster

ELIZABETH I, SIR FRANCIS WALSINGHAM,

AND

THE BIRTH OF MODERN ESPIONAGE

Stephen Budiansky

A PLUME BOOK

PLUME

Published by Penguin Group

Penguin Group (USA) Inc., 375 Hudson Street, New York, New York 10014, USA

Penguin Group (Canada), 90 Eglinton Avenue East, Suite 700, Toronto, Ontario,
Canada M4P 2Y3 (a division of Pearson Penguin Canada Inc.)

Penguin Books Ltd, 80 Strand, London WC2R 0RL, England

Penguin Ireland, 25 St. Stephen's Green, Dublin 2, Ireland (a division of Penguin Books Ltd.)

Penguin Group (Australia), 250 Camberwell Road, Camberwell, Victoria 3124, Australia
(a division of Pearson Australia Group Pty. Ltd.)

Penguin Books India Pvt. Ltd., 11 Community Centre, Panchsheel Park,
New Delhi – 110 017, India

Penguin Books (NZ), cnr Airborne and Rosedale Roads, Albany, Auckland 1310, New Zealand
(a division of Pearson New Zealand Ltd.)

Penguin Books (South Africa) (Pty.) Ltd., 24 Sturdee Avenue, Rosebank, Johannesburg 2196,
South Africa

Penguin Books Ltd, Registered Offices: 80 Strand, London WC2R 0RL, England

Published by Plume, a member of Penguin Group (USA) Inc. Previously published in a Viking
edition.

First Plume Printing, August 2006

10   9   8   7

Ⓟ REGISTERED TRADEMARK—MARCA REGISTRADA

The Library of Congress has catalogued the Viking edition as follows:

Budiansky, Stephen.
    Her majesty's spymaster : Elizabeth I, Sir Francis Walsingham, and the birth of modern
espionage / Stephen Budiansky.
        p.   cm.
    Includes bibliographical references.
    ISBN 0-670-03426-6 (hc.)
    ISBN 0-452-28747-2 (pbk.)
        1. Walsingham, Francis, Sir, 1530?–1590. 2. Espionage, British—History—
16th century. 3. Great Britain—Foreign relations—1558–1603. 4. Elizabeth I, Queen
of England, 1533–1603—Relations with cabinet officers. 5. Great Britain—History—
Elizabeth, 1558–1603—Biography. 6. Cabinet officers—Great Britain—Biography.
7. Great Britain—Foreign relations—France. 8. France—Foreign relations—Great
Britain. I. Title.

DA358.W2B83 2005
327.42'0092—dc22   2004061198

Printed in the United States of America
Original hardcover design by Daniel Lagin

To David Alvarez

CONTENTS

LIST OF NAMES

Alençon, Francis, Duke of; Elizabeth's suitor, later Duke of Anjou

Allen, Dr. William, Cardinal; head of English Catholic seminary at Douai and Rheims

Alva, Fernando Álvarez de Toledo, Duke of; Spanish governor of Netherlands, 1567–1573

Anjou, Henry, Duke of; suitor to Elizabeth, later Henry III, King of France

Arran, James Stewart, Earl of; powerful courtier of James VI

Babington, Anthony; Catholic conspirator, executed 1586

Baillie, Charles; Mary's courier, arrested at Dover 1571

Beale, Robert; Walsingham's secretary

Berden, Nicholas; alias of Thomas Rogers, prison informer and spy

Bothwell, James Hepburn, 4th Earl of; third husband of Mary Queen of Scots

Bruno, Giordano; lapsed Dominican friar, philosopher, possible spy

Burghley, William Cecil, 1st Baron; Privy Councilor, Principal Secretary, 1558–72, Lord Treasurer, 1572–98

Camden, William; chronicler of Elizabeth's reign

Campion, Edmund; Jesuit missionary priest, executed 1581

Catlyn, Maliverny; prison informer

Cecil, Robert; son of William Cecil, named Principal Secretary 1596

Charles IX; King of France, 1560–1574

Châteauneuf, Claude de l'Aubespine, baron de; French Ambassador to England, 1585–1589

Chérelles, Jean Arnault de; secretary to Mauvissière and later the French Council

Cockyn, Henry; London bookseller, arrested for aiding Mary

Coligny, Gaspard de, seigneur de Châtillon; Admiral of France, Huguenot leader, assassinated 1572

Courcelles, Claude de; a secretary to Mauvissière

Creighton, William; Scottish Jesuit and conspirator, arrested 1584

Darnley, Henry Stuart, Earl of; second husband of Mary Queen of Scots, murdered 1567

Davison, William; Walsingham's assistant

Drake, Sir Francis; voyager, vice-admiral against the Armada

Edward VI; Elizabeth's half-brother, King of England, 1547–1553

Elizabeth; Queen of England, 1558–1603

Essex, Robert Devereux, 2nd Earl of; Walsingham's son-in-law, executed for treason 1601

Fagot, Henry; pseudonymous informer in the French embassy

Faunt, Nicholas; Walsingham's secretary

Feron, Laurent; secretary, and possible mole, in the French embassy

Fowler, William; Scottish poet, unsuccessful spy on French embassy

Gifford, Gilbert; agent provocateur, carrier of messages to Mary

Glasgow, James Beaton, Archbishop of; Mary's ambassador in Paris

Gregory XIII; Pope, 1572–1585

Gregory, Arthur; Walsingham's expert seal-lifter

Guise, Henri of Lorraine, 3rd Duke of; leader of French Catholic faction, uncle of Mary Queen of Scots, plotter against Elizabeth

Heneage, Sir Thomas; Vice-Chamberlain, friend of Walsingham's

Henry III; King of France, 1574–1589

Henry VIII; Elizabeth's father, King of England, 1509–1547

Howard of Effingham, Charles, 2nd baron; Lord Admiral, commander against the Armada

Howard, Lord Henry; Catholic nobleman, brother of Norfolk

James VI; King of Scotland, 1567–1625, James I of England, 1603–1625

John of Austria, Don; Spanish governor of Netherlands, 1576–1578

Leicester, Robert Dudley, Earl of; courtier and Privy Councilor, leader of Puritan faction

Lennox, Esmé Stuart, seigneur d'Aubigny, Earl of; influential Catholic courtier of James of Scotland, ousted 1582

Lorraine, Charles, Cardinal of; brother of Duke of Guise, uncle of Mary Queen of Scots

Manucci, Jacobo (also sometimes Jacomo or Giacomo); servant and confidential agent of Walsingham

Mary; Queen of Scots, 1561–1567

Mary Tudor; Elizabeth's half-sister, Queen of England, 1553–1558

Mauvissière, Michel de Castelnau, seigneur de; French Ambassador to England, 1575–1585

Médicis, Catherine de; Queen Mother of France

Medina-Sidonia, Alonso Pérez de Guzmán, Duke of; commander of Spanish Armada

Mendoza, Bernardino de; Spanish Ambassador to England, 1578–1584

Moray, James Stewart, Earl of; Mary's half-brother, Regent of Scotland, 1567–1570

Morgan, Thomas; English Catholic exile and conspirator, Mary's agent in Paris

Navarre, Henry of; French Protestant prince, later King Henry IV

Norfolk, Thomas Howard, 4th Duke of; ineffectual conspirator, executed 1572

Ousley, Nicholas; English spy in Spain

Oxford, Edward de Vere, 17th Earl of; courtier

Paget, Charles; English Catholic exile, Mary's agent in Paris

Paget, Thomas, 3rd Baron; Catholic refugee

Parma, Alexander Farnese, Prince of; Spanish governor of Netherlands

Parry, Dr. William; spy and possible Catholic conspirator, executed 1585

Paulet, Sir Amias; ambassador to France 1576–1579, last keeper of Mary Queen of Scots

Phelippes, Thomas; Walsingham's confidential agent and expert decipherer

Philip II; King of Spain, 1556–1598

Pius V; Pope, 1566–1572

Poley, Robert; spy and agent provocateur

Quadra, Álvarez de, Bishop of Aquila; Spanish Ambassador to England, 1559–1563

Ridolfi, Roberto; Florentine banker, papal agent in 1571 invasion plot

Ross, John Leslie, Bishop of; Mary's ambassador in London

Sainte-Aldegonde, Philip van Marnix, baron de; Flemish Protestant nobleman and decipherer

Santa Cruz, Álvaro de Bazán, Marquis of; Spanish admiral

Seymour, Lord Henry; vice-admiral in Armada battle

Sheffield, Lady Douglas; cast-off mistress of Leicester, Catholic-leaning wife of Sir Edward Stafford

Shrewsbury, George Talbot, 6th Earl of; keeper of Mary Queen of Scots

Sidney, Sir Philip; poet, courtier, soldier, Walsingham's son-in-law

Silva, Guzmán de; Spanish Ambassador to England, 1564–1568

Sixtus V; Pope, 1585–1590

Smith, Sir Thomas; Principal Secretary, 1572–1577

Somers, John; Walsingham's secretary

Spes, Guerau de; Spanish Ambassador to England, 1568–1572

Stafford, Sir Edward; English Ambassador to France, 1583–89

Standen, Anthony; English spy in Florence and Spain

Throckmorton, Francis; Catholic conspirator against Elizabeth, executed 1584

Topcliffe, Richard; torturer

Walsingham, Anne Carleill; first wife of Walsingham

Walsingham, Frances; daughter of Walsingham, wife of Sir Philip Sidney, the Earl of Essex, and the Earl of Calnricarde

Walsingham, Sir Francis; ambassador to France, 1570–1573, Principal Secretary, 1573–1590

Walsingham, Ursula St. Barbe; second wife of Walsingham

William; Prince of Orange, leader of Dutch rebellion

Williams, Walter; prison informer and Walsingham factotum

Winchester, John White, Bishop of; officiator at Mary Tudor's funeral

A NOTE ON LANGUAGE, MONEY, AND DATES

In the sixteenth century, the English language was undergoing a rapid transformation from the spoken dialect of provincials to a written medium of serious literature, official transactions, and even the occasional scholarly treatise. The rise of the printing trade had meanwhile begun the evolution toward standardized spelling, but this was a much slower process. Clearly, most writers of English of this period still thought of words as sounds rather than unique written forms: it was not at all unusual for educated writers to spell the same word two different ways in the course of a single letter, or even to spell their own names differently on different occasions.

To a modern reader, such irregular spelling looks irredeemably quaint, if not bizarre. Of course, it did not seem so to a contemporary. I have chosen to modernize the spelling of quoted documents for the most part; though at first blush paradoxical, I think doing so brings us closer to the men and women who wrote these words, by stripping away the haze of picturesque quaintness that the passage of time has artificially interposed, and allowing us to receive their words more as a contemporary would have.

The language itself can still be a challenge, however, as many words have changed their meaning over time, some radically. A few explanations may be in order: although *intelligence* begins to appear at this time in its modern sense, *advertisement* is frequently used to the same general effect, with the particular meaning of information or warning; *entertain* can mean to employ or pay; a *practice* is a scheme or deception; a *plat* is a dramatic scenario and thus by extension a stratagem or plan; *jealous* connotes simple suspicion; *discover* means to reveal or expose; *family* usually refers to one's immediate household, including servants.

———————— ❧ ❧ ————————

Equating the value of money between two very different eras is strictly speaking impossible, since along with overall inflation the relative worth of different items alters considerably from one era to another: In sixteenth-century England, for example, a printed book like Foxe's *Acts and Monuments* could cost as much as a good horse. But as a *very* rough guide, an Elizabethan pound can be taken to be the equivalent of £250 or $400 in modern terms.

Perhaps a better sense of how the Elizabethans themselves gauged the value of money may be had by reference to a few contemporary benchmarks. A farm laborer earned £5 a year; a school headmaster or a shipmaster £20; a large landholding lord, or a lawyer at the pinnacle of his profession, £1,000. A pound would buy a cow, a plain cloth coat, or a gun; £150 kept the young Earl of Oxford, an extravagant fop, supplied with clothing for a year; £10,000 bought a great London mansion.

A crown was an English silver coin worth a quarter of a pound; more loosely, the term could refer to any of a number of similar continental coins, such as the French écu, that all had about the same value as an English crown.

A mark was a unit of account equal to two-thirds of a pound.

———————— ❧ ❧ ————————

In late 1582 (October in Spain, December in France), most of the Catholic countries adopted the Gregorian calendar. England retained the "Old Style" or Julian calendar. From that point on (until England finally rejoined the rest of the world in 1752), dates in England and the rest of Europe differed by ten days: January 1 in England was January 11 on the Continent. Since my focus is England, I have used Old Style dates throughout. The English calendar had another peculiarity at this time—namely, that for official purposes the new year was deemed to begin not on January 1 but, rather, not until Lady Day, March 25. To avoid confusion, I have followed the modern convention in rendering dates that fall between January 1 and March 25; thus a date that a contemporary might have denoted 10 February 1569 (or, sometimes, 10 February 15$\frac{69}{70}$) is given as 10 February 1570.

1572: Murder in Paris

I

AN ILL-FITTING SHOE

fterward, when the Seine flowed with corpses and thousands were dead, there were some who said that if only the assassin had not bungled his job in the first place all of the subsequent trouble might have been avoided.

But at the crucial instant, as the Admiral entered the rue des Fossés-Saint-Germain late on a bright summer's morning on his usual route from the Louvre, he had bent down to adjust an ill-fitting shoe, or perhaps to consult more closely a letter he was reading, or perhaps just to spit; and the arquebus balls that struck him merely carried away a right index finger and ploughed a furrow in his left forearm up to the elbow.

A party of the Admiral's men ran to the house from which the shots had come and broke down the front door; they rushed in just in time to hear, through a back door that stood swinging open, the sound of clattering hoofs as the would-be assassin made good his escape on a horse that, subsequent investigation would reveal, had been left saddled and bridled in the cloister of Saint-Germain-l'Auxerrois just to the rear. The still-smoking arquebus lay on a bed in a chamber on the ground floor.

In view of the bewilderingly contradictory royal statements that would emanate from the palace in the ensuing days—righteous indignation one day, bloodthirsty approval the next—the initial reaction of his Most Christian Majesty Charles IX to the news that Gaspard de Coligny, seigneur de Châtillon, Admiral of France, adviser to the King, had been shot in broad daylight not a hundred paces from the Palace of the Louvre at least had the virtue of petulant frankness. The twenty-two-year-old King cursed, smashed his tennis racket, screamed, "What, nothing but trouble?" and went off to sulk.

The royal surgeon, having snipped off the mangled end of Coligny's severed finger and painfully extracted the copper ball from his arm, declared his patient out of danger.

A medical diagnosis: not a political one.

Later in the day, the King, his composure recovered, made the grand gesture of calling upon the wounded Admiral at his lodgings on the rue de Béthisy, to pay his respects in person. The King swore he would see justice done. In a letter dispatched to his ambassador in London the same day, he hastened to reassure his English allies that "this wicked act stems from the enmity between Coligny's house and that of the Duke of Guise," nothing more. That the Admiral was the military hero of the Protestants in the late, terrible civil wars of religion, that the Guises were the most powerful and vehement Catholic party, was not to be considered. The Edict of Pacification that had ended the war two years before was to continue to be "observed in all points," including the Catholic state's extraordinary concession of toleration of Protestant worship. A feud between two families would not be permitted to reopen wounds so recently healed. He, the King, had given an order that "they shall not drag my subjects into their quarrels."

All very fine and magnificent, but the subjects had their own ideas. Throughout that sweltering August, Paris—Catholic, ruined, hungry, poor—had filled with strutting Huguenot noblemen, many openly carrying arms, many wearing the austere, dark, somber clothing of Calvinist believers, in its own way just as ostentatious and maddening as if they had flaunted their wealth and newly recovered status with a brilliant display of silk, lace, and jewels. Their coming was to seal a final act of religious reconciliation, the wedding of their Protestant Prince of Navarre with the Catholic King's sister. Instead, it had brought every fanatic out of the woodwork. "God will not suffer this execrable coupling!" Franciscan preachers screamed, prophesying torrents of blood, urging the mob to grasp salvation by slaughtering the heretics.

The ceremony itself, a carefully orchestrated compromise of the two faiths, picked at all the old scabs, reminded everyone of the incendiary insults that had been traded for decades, the single words and gestures that had the power to flash into white-hot hatred and violence in a second; the leaves of the Protestant Bible that had been stuffed into the mouths of Huguenot corpses by a Catholic mob in Provence, the desecration of the host in Tournai ("God of paste!" mocked the Protestant mob as they crumbled and trampled the wafers), or the murder of a hapless baker guarding the holy wafers inside a church in Paris; the rumors of sexual orgies that the Protestants practiced after their nocturnal psalm-singing, or the hundreds of concubines said to be kept for the pleasure of the priests and canons in Lyon; the "vermin" of heresy, the "vile filth" of the mass.

Two bishops had refused outright to assist in a marriage that the Pope himself had condemned as "an insult to God and a danger to souls." The Cardinal of Bourbon, pressured to preside, finally agreed, on condition that it was understood he would bless the union not in his capacity as a priest but merely as uncle of the bridegroom. Two Italian prelates ("rather dubious characters," the Spanish Ambassador observed) were found to assist. The marriage itself would be consecrated not inside a church but on a dais set up on the porch of Notre Dame; when mass was said inside the cathedral beforehand, Navarre and the Protestants would absent themselves.

That compromise had not, however, anticipated the Catholic mobs that gathered outside Notre Dame to heckle and taunt the waiting Protestants when they withdrew to avoid being present during the mass they so abhorred: "We will make you go in!" the mob shouted over and over.

The four days of official festivities following the wedding had been a succession of more subtle and courtly taunts. The King's brother Henry, the twenty-year-old Duke of Anjou—"Monsieur," he was always called—arranged a series of elaborate pageants and tournaments that somehow always ended in the humiliation of the Huguenot lords. At the Petit-Bourbon, the King and his noble guests enacted The Mystery of the Three Worlds; the Protestants found themselves held "prisoner" by Tartarus and his devils for an hour while their ladies, cast as nymphs in Paradise, danced and held hands with the angels, Monsieur, and his royal brothers. The night before the attempted assassination of Coligny, Monsieur staged yet another tournament; this time the Protestant lords were cast as infidel Turks, duly trounced by the King and his brothers—dressed as Amazons, women warriors, no less.

The wedding guests seethed; the Catholic zealots of Paris seethed; the city's vast army of beggars, thieves, and cutthroats that emerged each night from the "Court of Miracles" seethed. And then the hero of the Protestant church militant was shot from ambush in broad daylight on a busy street in the heart of Paris, but not, alas, killed outright.

———————— ~⊙⊙~ ————————

The Admiral was shot late on the morning of Friday, the 22nd of August 1572, at the end of the week of the wedding festivities. By the following day, the judicial investigation ordered by the King had, to the surprise of absolutely no one, inculpated the Duke of Guise. The house from which the shot had been fired belonged to a Guise retainer, the Canon Villemur, former tutor of the Duke himself. Villemur was away on a journey, but the supervisor of the Guise household had appeared a few days before to introduce to Villemur's housekeeper a man who would be staying there in the Canon's absence. This was the man who was seen galloping off in a gray cloak leaving a smoking arquebus and a heavy purse of money behind him.

Rumors swirled through the city that Saturday. The Huguenots were planning to avenge themselves. The Catholics were preparing to appoint their own captain-general if the King did not act to neutralize the threat. Monsieur, traveling forth in his coach to see for himself the reports that Paris was on the brink of riot, was greeted by crowds chanting the names of famous Catholic victories in the recent civil wars.

An order went out from the palace forbidding citizens to take up arms. A royal guard of fifty French and Swiss arquebusiers was commanded to protect the wounded Admiral against any further outrages. The governors of the provinces were instructed to maintain order.

But as night closed over Paris, with the shadows came whispers of other, stealthy preparations. The district captains of the town militia were to have a man in every house armed, with a white scarf tied to his left arm and a torch at the ready, prepared to assemble when the tocsin sounded. The gates of the city were shut, the keys secured. The boats across the Seine were quietly gathered, artillery moved into place before the Hôtel de Ville, the seat of the Paris city government.

More ominously, the King's guard at the Louvre were to let none of Navarre's retinue leave.

Strangest of all, when the royal guard that had been charged with the Admiral's safety arrived to take up their position in the rue de Béthisy, they were under the command of one Captain Cosseins—an old and sworn personal enemy of Coligny's.

———— ❧❧ ————

Francis Walsingham had been England's ambassador to the Court of Charles IX for nineteen months. It was the first foray for this rather ascetic, undoubtedly Protestant, and notably clear-thinking gentleman of forty into the perils and complexities of high office. He had not had a particularly happy time of it.

"My private life hath made me utterly unacquainted with that skill that the dealings in Prince's affairs requireth," Walsingham confided to a friend. His embassy had been a maximum of tedium and a minimum of results; daily the English Ambassador had to negotiate a labyrinth of courtly dissimulation. The nominal alliance between France and England, and the nominal peace between France's warring factions, wound in and out through religious, and party, and family intrigue that would have confounded Machiavelli himself. For months on end, Walsingham had painstakingly pursued negotiations for a marriage between his mistress Elizabeth the Queen of England and one of the French King's younger brothers—first Monsieur, then the eighteen-year-old Duke of Alençon. At every turn there were diplomatic and political pitfalls. In Paris, the Papal Nuncio and the Spanish Ambassador were constantly intriguing behind Walsingham's back to break up any projected liaison between the Protestant Queen of England and the Catholic royal house of France. So, too, for his own reasons, was one of Walsingham's own superiors on the Privy Council, the Earl of Leicester: if any native English nobleman had hopes of carrying away the prize himself, it was Leicester, ever the Queen's favorite courtier. Back in London, the Earl was simultaneously assuring both the Queen and the French Ambassador, with the same insinuating confidence to each, that if only each would hold firm the other would be sure to give way on the remaining points of contention holding up the intricate negotiations.

Walsingham, Protestant Puritan that he was, had sought to wend a careful way through his own labyrinth of private and public allegiances by scrupulously declining to express his own opinion of the Queen's projected marriage to a Catholic, by doing not one iota more or less than he was instructed. Everyone around the Court in Paris tried to get him to tip his hand as to what he truly thought of the matter, and to all he presented the same impassive face. "My general answer," he carefully explained to Leicester, "is that I left my private passions behind me, and do here submit to the passions of my Prince, to execute whatsoever she shall command me, as precisely as I may. And as for her marriage, whensoever it shall please God to incline her to that change I should forget my duty towards her and my country if I should not like very well thereof."

But then there was the maddening factor that it had never been clear whether the Queen herself, a past master at diplomatic dissimulation, wanted the negotiations to succeed or not. To her dutiful ambassador she sent one contradictory hint after another. It might have been subtle politics, for as long as the hope for a marriage was alive the French would remain friendly, and the irksome advisers at home who kept urging upon her the need to marry, and produce an heir, and so safeguard the royal succession, would be silenced; a good strategy if at heart she had no intention of marrying.

But then at times it seemed that she was merely uncertain herself, or that she was enjoying her prerogative to act like a woman, and a queen, and coyly keep everyone guessing. Either way, her poor ambassador was frequently left bewildered. In late July 1572, Elizabeth had sent Walsingham a letter instructing him to tell the French King that the twenty-year age difference between her Majesty and the young Alençon made a marriage impossible. Four days later, she sent a second letter stating that she believed the age difference might well be overcome—and instructing Walsingham to show the King both of these mutually contradictory letters at the same time.

"I see your negotiation shall be full of perplexities," William Cecil, Elizabeth's Principal Secretary, sympathized.

Meanwhile, the job of ambassador was destroying Walsingham, financially and physically. The expenses of the office, which he was expected to cover mostly from his own private income as a landowning gentleman, were crippling: like "to bring me to beggary," he said. In March 1571, after a mere two months at the post, Walsingham had written Cecil—Lord Burghley, as he had just become—beseeching his Lordship to save him from the financial ruin that already seemed a certainty.

"Your Lordship knoweth that necessity hath no law," Walsingham began, by way of apology for broaching so unseemly a topic; but her Majesty's allowance of £10 per week was not enough to cover even the minimal costs of maintaining his household, though he spent less on food and kept fewer horses than his predecessor. He had brought £800 of his own money with him; already he had less than £300 left.

Things had only gotten worse since. A year into his job, Walsingham told Burghley he had so far spent £1,600 beyond his income in meeting his ambassadorial expenses; he had been forced to sell some land and borrow £730 against his future salary. Now his expenses were running £200 a month, "notwithstanding my diet is thin, my family reduced to as small a proportion as may be, and my horse being only twelve."

The ambassador's health had been a trial to him, too. An attack of the stone the previous autumn had left him unable to pass water, almost despairing of his life, begging to London to send a replacement

before he was beyond "the reach of cure." For two months he had re-
cuperated under the care of physicians in Paris. On other occasions
he had tried to take matters into his own hands and cope with this re-
curring ill, and its associated griping colics, by dosing himself with
copious quantities of one dubious physic or another that left him out
of commission for days.

And so each month that passed added another £160 to the ambassador's debts, and the perplexities of serving a ruler who had long
since perfected the fine art of calculated bafflement deepened, and
so the night of Saturday the 23rd of August 1572 found Mr. Ambassador Walsingham, his wife and four-year-old daughter, his reduced
establishment of servants and his twelve horses, and a young visiting
Englishman by the name of Philip Sidney ensconced at the English
ambassador's lodgings on the Quai des Barnardins, across the Seine
and upriver from official Paris. It was the eve of the feast day of
Saint Bartholomew: Bartholomew, who had the distinction in the
Gospels of being enumerated among the Apostles of Jesus and then
never being mentioned again; though later tradition had it that he
met his end by being flayed alive, and so the more enthusiastic mar-
tyrologists of the Catholic Church were ever wont to depict him
carrying his own skin.

───────── ❧ ☙ ─────────

It was at four in the morning when the unexpected sound of the ringing bells of the church of Saint-Germain-l'Auxerrois, halfway between the Louvre and the rue de Béthisy, broke the still of the
ominous night.

By dawn the clash of other bells, punctuated now by gunfire and
the unmistakable bruit of a city in full riot, could be heard at the ambassador's residence, coming from across the river.

The first reports to arrive were reassuring. The King was acting
quickly to suppress the disorder. The Admiral was being safely
guarded by the King's own men.

But there soon came rather more tangible and contradictory evidence: terrified Englishmen pounding on the door, seeking sanctuary

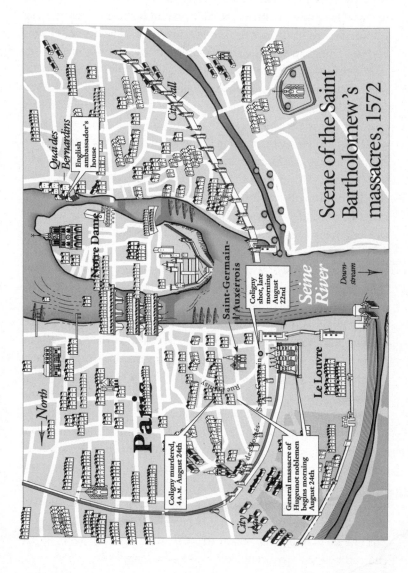

Scene of the Saint
Bartholomew's
massacres, 1572

Quai des
Bernardins

English
ambassador's
house

City Wall

Notre Dame

Saint-Germain-
l'Auxérrois

Coligny shot, late
morning August
22nd

Seine River

Down-
stream

North

Paris

Le Louvre

Rue Saint-Germain

Rue des Fossés

Coligny murdered,
4 A.M. August 24th

General massacre of
Huguenot noblemen
begins morning
August 24th

City Wall

from the ravening mob, a mob whose fury had only grown as the day went on. And then, disguised as a groom, came Coligny's own lieutenant, François de Beauvais, seigneur de Briquemault. He had made his way over rooftops, across the river, God alone knew how. The tale he bore completely altered the complexion of things. This was no riot; it was a systematic massacre, and it had begun in the dead of the night with the horrific murder of Coligny himself.

The story was soon everywhere. Shortly before four o'clock in the morning, Cosseins and his men had suddenly pounded on the door of Coligny's house, demanding to be admitted in the name of the King. They instantly stabbed one of the Admiral's gentlemen who had been guarding the door from the inside, cleared the stairway with a volley of arquebus fire, then rushed the stair and burst into the Admiral's bedchamber. Two of the Duke of Guise's henchmen rushed in along with Cosseins's Swiss: they finished off the Admiral with a pike thrust through his body.

The Duke himself, who had come to make sure the job was done right this time, shouted up from the street below to throw the body out the window. He briefly surveyed the lifeless form of his dead adversary lying on the street in front of him, then kicked it in the face. One of his men cut off the head to take back to the Louvre. And then the crowd of hundreds of street urchins that had instantly gathered to cheer the proceedings set upon what was left, hacking off the hands and genitals and dragging the remainder on a macabre tour through the city that would continue for the next three days.

Troops of Guise's men and the King's guard then fanned out through the surrounding streets to hunt down other Protestant lords who lodged nearby. The ringing of the bells of Saint-Germain-l'Auxerrois had been the signal for a simultaneous massacre of the King's guests at the Louvre to begin. Swiss guards went from room to room, methodically seizing the Huguenots, disarming them, and pushing them into the inner courtyard of the palace, where they were run through with pikes and added to a growing pile of corpses.

And then the mob and the city militia began; methodical, too, but far less discriminating. "The sword being given to the common people," as Francis Walsingham would later describe it, they went from house to house through the city's commercial quarter dispatching any Huguenots they found; all the better if their victims were booksellers or binders or printers who had helped spread heretical ideas, better still if they were goldsmiths or jewelers or bankers to whom the opprobrium of heresy was added the attraction of movable wealth.

Some of the victims were taken to the Seine bridges and thrown into the river. Others plunged in themselves as a last resort to escape the mob, only to be set upon by particularly determined pursuers in boats, who pushed them under until they drowned.

And everywhere the words that Guise had uttered upon viewing his dead rival's body were repeated, to reassure any who might hesitate with legal scruples before giving vent to long-simmering passions of religious bloodlust: "It is the King's command."

For three days, the city's gates remained locked as the slaughter continued its course. When the mob's ardor threatened to wane, on the morning after Saint Bartholomew's feast, a convenient miracle occurred. A Franciscan declared that an old dead hawthorn tree in the Catholic cemetery of the Holy Innocents had suddenly come to life, putting out green leaves and a profusion of flowers. It was not lost on the mob that this was the same cemetery to which Coligny had forced the authorities a half-year earlier to move an offensive cross that had marked and celebrated the spot of the hanging of a Huguenot family. The first attempt to remove the cross had set off a riot; in the end, the King's artillery had had to seal off the street and carry out the job.

Now God himself had sent an unmistakable sign of his approval for the revenge that his faithful had taken against such blasphemy. Word of the miracle spread with the speed that only profound idiocy can. The crowds that thronged to venerate the miracle were not in the least shaken in their faith by the refusal of a guard of soldiers to let them close enough to see the tree for themselves.

God's command had now overtaken the King's command; not that anyone short of a student of Machiavelli, human desperation, or human madness could have made much sense of the King's commands by this point. On the Sunday afternoon, he had ordered the city's magistrates to restore order and disarm the mob. The official story issued for envoys abroad continued to claim that "all this happened through a private quarrel long fostered between these two houses": the house of Guise had feared a revenge attack by Coligny's followers and so had struck first; the King, as much as he would have liked to prevent the more widespread killing, "had much ado to employ my guards and other forces to maintain my security within my castle of the Louvre" and, alas, had been powerless to prevent it.

By Tuesday, the palace had performed an impressively complete about-face. The King went forth to address the Parlement of Paris in a grand procession, and declared that the massacre of the Huguenots had been necessary to thwart a vile conspiracy hatched by Admiral Coligny and his followers. They and the members of their sect were plotting nothing less than a coup d'état. "All that has been done in Paris has been done not only with my consent, but at my command," the King proclaimed. The lords who had been the executors of his will were not to be impugned, now or later, for their actions.

The President of the Parlement heartily congratulated the King and quoted, in Latin, the words of Louis XI, whose reign a century before had earned him the name Louis the Cruel: "He who cannot dissimulate cannot rule."

The next day, the King drew up an order informing "all gentlemen and others of the so-called reformed religion that it was his mind and purpose that they shall live under his protection, with their wives and children in their houses, in as much safeguard as they did before." The governors of the provinces were not to permit any persecution of the Protestants, upon pain of death for the offenders. The Edict of Pacification would be strictly respected. Except, that is, for its major provision, the toleration of Protestant worship, which was hereby suspended.

At the same moment, the Papal Nuncio, Bishop Antonio-Maria Salviati, was reporting the widespread belief that the French Court was planning to reimpose Catholic unity on the entire nation. The following day, the King took part in a great jubilee and procession proclaimed by the Catholic Church to celebrate the extermination of the Huguenots. The King and his court stopped at the miraculous hawthorn to pray, and then proceeded to the gibbet at Montfaucon, where, by order of the Parlement, what was left of the Admiral's corpse had at last been reclaimed from the mob and hung up by the feet, as a traitor. Some members of the King's royal party were offended by the smell of the four-day-old remains, but the King, according to his personal historiographer, quoted the Roman emperor who had on a similar occasion declared, "The smell of a dead enemy is sweet and delightful."

Some of the Court's gyrations no doubt reflected a desire to prevent a complete fissure of relations with England, even as it attempted to ride the wave of popular passion. On Wednesday, the 27th of August, the King had written his ambassador in London to pass on his assurances that "Le seigneur de Walsingham" had been "meticulously looked after in his home during this trouble." The King had indeed sent a guard to the English Ambassador's house: this time they had actually done their job of guarding.

The same day, Francis Walsingham cautiously dispatched to London a "bearer" to whom he entrusted an oral account of the horrors of the past four days; to Burghley he explained, in a short note a few days later, that London could well guess why he forbore to commit any such account to writing while things remained so dangerous and volatile. As one observer in the English embassy recorded, the King's visit to Montfaucon was "a spectacle what showeth what good nature is in the King."

If it was true that the King had not been the author of Coligny's murder, he was nonetheless showing signs of becoming completely unhinged by the orgy of slaughter that had followed. "The King is now become so bloody that it is impossible to stay his thirst to quench the same in innocent blood," the English embassy's record noted. Strange tales, probably untrue, but who could say for certain, told of a deranged Charles standing on a balcony of the Louvre with an arquebus, taking aim at those who did not drown quickly enough as they floated by the palace on the river.

More royal gyrations followed. Orders from the King to the provinces at first appeared to encourage stern measures against Protestants there, too; but then, on the 30th, he issued yet another order, canceling all previous such orders and strictly forbidding further attacks. But amid such utter confusion, the zealots in the provinces took heart, and anti-Protestant rampages spread to a dozen other cities. Though in Paris the worst of the violence had by now spent itself, small eruptions continued for weeks. Walsingham could not set foot from his door without a large escort of the King's guards; even so he was taunted and threatened on the streets wherever he went. His wife and daughter, whom he sent home at the earliest possible moment when it at last seemed safe to do so, narrowly missed witnessing two Englishmen being hacked to death at one of the gates of the city as they departed.

It was also several days after calm had apparently returned to the capital that Briquemault was forcibly seized from his place of refuge in the English Ambassador's house.

A month later, in filth and chains, Briquemault was brought forth with another of Coligny's old aides to the front of the Hôtel de Ville, where both were hanged. They were accompanied on the gibbet by a straw effigy of the Admiral; his own remains were unavailable to participate in the occasion as they had finally been cut down and secretly buried in the night by some brave soul who had at last grown revolted by the display at Montfaucon.

While the King celebrated at a lavish banquet within the Hôtel de Ville, the mob, glad to have one more opportunity to relive the fading excitement of Saint Bartholomew's Day, overset the gallows and tore the corpses to pieces.

2

LESS PERIL AS ENEMIES

Those who had escaped the terror of the mob in the refuge of the English Ambassador's house were seared with a memory that would stay with them throughout their lives. Near the end of Walsingham's life, an English Doctor of Physic, Timothy Bright, wrote him a dedication recalling the time "now sixteen years past, yet (as ever it will be) fresh with me in memory," when "your Honor's house at that time was a very sanctuary, not only for all of our nation, but even to many strangers then in peril . . . who had all tasted of the rage of that furious tragedy, had not your Honor shrouded them" by "that right noble act."

Others would commemorate the events rather differently. The embalmed head of Coligny was duly delivered to His Holiness Pope Gregory XIII in Rome, who duly celebrated a Te Deum. The Pope was beside himself with praises for the French King, who by "his destruction of heretics, the enemies of Christ," had truly earned the right to his traditional title, Most Christian. A papal medal was struck for the occasion: on one side was the Pope's image, on the other an angel bearing a cross superintended the slaying of Coligny. In the Sala Regia, the royal hall next to the Sistine Chapel, the pontiff had a series of frescoes painted depicting the death of Coligny and his followers in gruesome detail. The completed paintings stood alongside images of another late triumph of Christian arms against infidels, the victory of Spanish and papal naval forces over the Turks at Lepanto.

Although the Pope would later regret the shedding of innocent blood alongside that of the guilty when he learned the complete details of the popular massacres that had taken place in Paris and the provinces, he did not regret the salutary effect of the slayings in convincing the remaining heretics to return to the fold. Tomasso Sassetti, a courier and informant who often supplied the English Ambassador with gleanings from his Florentine acquaintances in and around the French Court and from Italian travelers lately arrived in Paris, reported that the priests were reaping a great harvest of souls among the survivors. The churches were packed; emblems of Catholic piety everywhere appeared on caps and clothing; during the mass, when the priest raised the host, there was now a great show of "beating on breasts and a fluttering of lips" among those who just days earlier had affected to despise the vile superstition of such Catholic rites.

In the stunned quiet that settled on Paris the first week of September, the diplomatic community and its surrounding netherworld—Court hangers-on, knowing men of business, garden-variety household informers—teemed with rumors and theories. Sassetti had been in Lyon during the uprising in Paris, but on his return to the capital, on the 9th of September, he began at once to work his network of contacts, "persons who had been eyewitnesses and others at Court who, even if they are Catholics, make it their occupation to displease neither one side nor the other."

In four days, he wrote a sixty-four-page reconstruction of the events that had precipitated the massacre. Men who worked for the ambassadors of Spain, Venice, and Rome were peddling their versions, too. They were all the usual blend of scraps of undigested truth and innuendo; every possible permutation of Machiavellian conspiracy was bruited; yet all were agreed, Catholic and Protestant alike, that the King's official version of events was nonsense. There had never been any Protestant conspiracy to seize the throne. What there had been was the craftiness and ruthlessness of the Queen Mother, Catherine de Médicis, who had long been viewed as the real power behind the throne of her weak son.

Of course, she had long been whispered to have gone about poisoning her rivals, too; but, then, they always said that about Italians. But now even those who were bursting with approval for the murder of the heretics agreed that it had been the culmination of Catherine's well-laid schemes. Some said the plot had been in the works for years; the Venetian envoy heard that during the long negotiations for the Navarre marriage the Queen Mother had eagerly given way on all points—just as long as it was always agreed that the wedding would take place in Paris, thereby making sure that Coligny and his men would fall into her trap. Some believed Catherine was simply jealous of the influence the Admiral had gained over her son; others, that she feared Coligny would push France into a catastrophic war with Spain if he was not removed; still others said she had an even more audacious and horrific plot in mind, to induce a final, all-out clash between Guise and Coligny, in which the leading men of both sides would be exterminated, and so remove once and for all a source of strife in the kingdom, and the challenge to royal power that the nobility of both factions represented.

The Protestants were prepared to believe the worst such tales of treacherous premeditation, just as they would turn Coligny into a saint who mouthed pieties in his death throes; there was no crime too monstrous to blame on Catherine.

But Walsingham, zealous Protestant and all, had no time for histrionics, and Sassetti's account, which there was little doubt reflected his employer's information and views, was far more icily logical in its indictment of the Queen Mother. Sassetti argued that she was indeed likely to have been behind the initial assassination attempt on Coligny; when it failed, and the risk of exposure and Protestant reprisals threatened, Catherine had persuaded the King that he had no choice but to give the Duke of Guise and the royal guard the command to finish the deed, doing away with Coligny's top henchmen at the same time. The larger killing spree, however, could not have been premeditated, Sassetti argued; for one thing, there was the obvious chaos and confusion that had characterized it; for another, even on the very eve of the massacres, Guise and his men had had to send hurriedly to the armorers of the city for weapons, though the Protestants had for weeks been known to be well supplied with arms and horses. When events had spun out of control, not to be checked even by royal command, the King had been forced to pretend it had all been done on his order to avoid the shame of admitting himself powerless—and to reap what residual benefit he could with the Catholic side for what he could not prevent anyway.

Walsingham had professed himself two years earlier "utterly unacquainted with that skill that the dealings in Prince's affairs requireth," but now, faced with a trial that would have tested the skill of any man, he was pure steel and ice: if his job demanded that he look evil in the eye, he would do so, and conceal his feelings and his knowledge of the truth, and extract what he could in the way of information and advantage, and smile if he had to while he was at it. Many of his good friends were dead; the survival of his very religion was in peril; the French King and Queen Mother were stained with the blood of the massacres; but the ambassador had his job to do.

At the first possible moment, on the 26th of August, he had sent a messenger to the Queen Mother thanking her for his safety and that of his fellow Englishmen in "this last tumult," then quickly coming to the point: he had heard "divers reports made of the late execution"; he would be "very loath to credit reports" without having their Majesties "send me the very truth thereof, to the end that I might accordingly advertise the Queen's Majesty my Mistress." In reply, the Queen Mother assured Walsingham that the French Ambassador in London had already supplied Queen Elizabeth with a report on the "late accident" here. A delicate diplomatic fencing match, just as dangerous but far more refined, now began where the cruder methods of the Paris mob left off: Catherine de Médicis had cut better men than he to ribbons in the past.

On the 1st of September, conducted by a guard of a dozen gentlemen-at-arms, Walsingham was at last summoned to an audience at Court. Walsingham listened impassively while the King repeated his story that the Admiral had been part of a conspiracy which it had been necessary to strike against at once, without awaiting the formality of legal proceedings. The King would provide his mistress a copy of the judicial examination he had subsequently ordered, which would affirm Coligny's guilt.

Walsingham informed the King that three Englishmen had been killed in the riots. The King said he would make "exemplary justice" of the offenders if they could be produced. Walsingham replied to this piece of royal fatuity by blandly noting that it would be rather difficult to identify the perpetrators at this point, "the disorder being so general." Beyond that, however, the English Ambassador held his peace, saying nothing more for now about the "late accident."

In England, the first news of the massacres had arrived with Protestant refugees fleeing for their lives from Dieppe. The news caught up with the Queen and her court on a great royal progress that, since July, had taken her through a succession of towns in the Midlands; she at once canceled the day's hunting, sent her musicians and dancers home, and ordered an end to the gaieties, fireworks displays, and entertainments that had marked her travels. The French Ambassador, who had hurried west from London to offer reassuring words of France's continued goodwill toward England, was left waiting at Oxford for three days before the Queen would consent to see him. When he was allowed at last into her Majesty's presence on the 8th of September, he found himself confronted by the entire court, dressed in mourning and silent.

The French Ambassador's earnest explanations of the dastardly Protestant plot that had been foiled were greeted coolly. That story was already known in England to contradict the first story put out by the French King, namely that the murder of Coligny and his men had been the work of the Guises "in the manner of sedition"—in other words, against the King's wishes. Elizabeth replied that she feared for the King's reputation and honor that he should have allowed the murder of a wounded man under royal protection. She trembled at the vengeance God in heaven would take should his Majesty fail to make every reparation in his power for the lives of the innocent women and children who had perished. Nevertheless, the King was an honorable man; Elizabeth assured the ambassador that she was inclined to accept his explanations. She also ordered the forts on the south coast readied for defense and the fleet sent into the Channel.

The Queen's desire to prevent an outright break in relations, yet to exploit her great grief over the massacre of her coreligionists as a diplomatic bargaining lever, required a deftness and subtlety on the part of her ambassador in Paris that the delays of communication across the Channel taxed to the limit; so, too, did the competing views of the other powerful men of the government. Burghley wrote to Walsingham that if it were up to him he would be recalled at once in protest. Leicester wrote a letter dripping with the religious sanctimony that he had recently acquired, having allied himself politically with the Puritan forces in England: all moral outrage, and obfuscation on the matter of practical measures. Although the massacres "doth make all Christians look for a just revenge," this "lamentable tragedy" nonetheless had to be looked upon as the Lord's doing, Leicester preached: "to pinch us in the meantime with the scourge of correction by the sufferance of his people to be murdered, but our sins deserve this and more."

The Queen, for her part, hinted she might go along with Walsingham's revocation as ambassador, but first she wished him to clarify what had been the French King's role in the massacres: and, more important, ascertain what the significance of recent French naval movements were.

But couriers bearing Walsingham's reports and his instructions from the Queen and Council kept crossing paths. It was not until the 9th of September that reports providing the full details of the massacres, and the peril in which Walsingham's own life had been, arrived in England; it was not until a week after that that the Queen's and Burghley's letters instructing the English Ambassador on what course to take with the French arrived in Paris. And so, when Walsingham was summoned on the 10th of September to return to the French Court for another audience with the King and Queen Mother, he was left in the most precarious position an ambassador who had once sworn to leave his "private passions behind" him could be in: he would have to rely completely on his own devices, instincts, and native wits.

◦◦◦

The Queen Mother was most disturbed and perplexed: or so she had insisted in summoning the English Ambassador to that second meeting between them since the massacres, now two weeks past. A nice feint. She had heard, she continued, that Monsieur Walsingham was not inclined to continue his friendly feelings toward the King her son. She had hoped the ambassador would continue to lend his support to her efforts to bring the match between his mistress and her youngest son to the long-hoped-for conclusion. Perhaps he would come to the palace and explain the reasons for his "scruple touching the King's and her sincere meaning"?

Walsingham came; this time he wasted no time showing his steel. There were three reasons, he told Catherine, that he entertained doubts whether the French were in earnest in their protestations of amity and desire to bring about the marriage. First was "the violating of the late Edict and the present severity used against those of the Religion." Next was the "strange dealing" of the French in the negotiations over the first proposed match, between Elizabeth and Anjou. And, finally, there were the "certain discourses" now everywhere heard around Court of French dreams of "conquest of England and Ireland."

Queens were not generally spoken to this way, but Catherine was as cool and unfazed as the ambassador; she also was well aware that the real issue was the Saint Bartholomew's massacres, and so she ignored the last two points the ambassador had raised and went at once to the heart of the matter. France and England had signed a defensive alliance; that treaty, she said, was made not with the Admiral or any other faction but with the French Crown; differences of religion had not prevented its being signed, nor would they prevent its being respected.

That was true, Walsingham acknowledged, but "the chiefest causes that moved the Queen my Mistress to make account of the

Amity of this Crown was that the King suffered certain of his subjects to enjoy, by the virtue of this Edict, exercise of the same Religion her Majesty professed." And he went on, "Surely, Madame, I fear that this late severity executed herein will make all the princes of the Religion to repute the same a general denunciation of war against them, which I fear will prove as bloody as ever war that happened, whereof the benefit would chiefly grow to the Turk."

Catherine suggested that the English had been misled to have thought of the Admiral as a friend to their cause in any case. She produced a discourse found with the Admiral's will, a letter of advice to the King written a number of months before, in which the Admiral urged the Crown to pursue a policy of apportioning equal mistrust to the Queen of England and the King of Spain, the better to ensure the safety of the French Crown. Walsingham examined the document for a moment. It merely showed, he calmly riposted, that the Admiral was a faithful servant of his master the King; such loyalty and devotion were virtues his mistress always respected.

Walsingham again pressed Catherine on the abandonment of the Edict's toleration of freedom of worship for the Huguenots; and so the thrust and parry began in earnest.

"They shall enjoy the liberty of their conscience," Catherine insisted.

"And the exercise of their religion, too?"

"No, my son will have exercise of but one religion in his realm."

"Then how can it agree, that the observation of the Edict, whereof you willed me to advertise the Queen my mistress, should continue in its former strength?"

Catherine replied that they had "discovered certain matters of late" that made it "necessary to abolish all exercise of the same."

"Why, Madame, will you then have them live without exercise of religion?"

"Even as your mistress suffereth the Catholics of England."

"My mistress never did promise them anything by edict; if she had she would not fail to have performed it."

The bluntest language yet, summoning a blunt answer: "The

Queen, your mistress is to direct the government of her own country, the King his."

"I do not move these questions out of curiosity," Walsingham retorted, "but to render account to the Queen my Mistress of the proceedings."

And so it had ended; a draw perhaps.

A week and a half later, on the 21st of September, the English Ambassador was back for yet another interview. At last the mail had caught up, and for the first time since the massacres he was armed with full instructions from London. Elizabeth had written demanding to know from the French King why, even if the accusations against the Admiral were true, it had been necessary to act outside of the law and kill him in cold blood; after all, he was confined to bed, wounded in his right hand and left arm, under the care of surgeons, surrounded even by the King's own guard; the force that had slain him could just as easily have taken him prisoner and brought him to answer the charges. "The manner of the cruelty used," Walsingham boldly stated, "cannot be allowable in any kingdom or government." His mistress was prepared to order his recall, he informed Catherine: she had heard his very life was in danger.

The Queen Mother replied that there had been no time for the normal machinery of justice to deal with a conspiracy about to be sprung only hours hence; it was a known fact that the Huguenot commander Count Montgomery had amassed in the Faubourg-Saint-Germain a great troop ready to seize power. Walsingham said that surely Montgomery's forty horsemen, only four of whom even had pistols, were no danger to the Crown. The King asserted that if he were to consent to Walsingham's recall he would have to recall his own ambassador in London; such an action would be tantamount to a declaration of war. He the King would ensure that the English Ambassador was adequately protected, but could not grant him his passports to leave.

In parting, the King and the Queen Mother both assured the ambassador of their devotion and friendship to his mistress the Queen of England.

———— ∽⊙ ⊙∾ ————

Another draw; but a draw that had reinforced Walsingham's conviction that to continue England's traditional diplomatic course as if
nothing had happened was madness. The massacres showed that
there could be no true peace with Catholic countries, now or ever,
and it was time for a revolution in policy: not for moral reasons, not
even for the cause of the Protestant religion, but for pure political
practicality.

Elizabeth still hoped to thread a course of temporizing and half-
measures: safety in ambiguity, an ambiguity that kept friends and enemies alike uncertain where they stood amid all of the competing ties
of religion, courtship, and family. As a token of friendship the French
King sent an envoy to ask Elizabeth if she would stand godmother to
his newborn daughter. Elizabeth feigned astonishment at the sugges-
tion: why would the King, who had just persecuted those of her religion, now ask her to be godmother to his child? Many of her advisers
were urging her to break relations altogether. After berating the
French Ambassador in this vein for some time, she majestically declared that she would nonetheless rise above all of these wrongs and all
of this hard counsel and show her love to her brother king by agreeing
to his request. She would send an English nobleman to represent her:
the Earl of Worcester, an English Catholic nobleman at that.

Meanwhile, both sides had resumed the seemingly endless series
of proposals and counter-proposals of the marriage negotiations between Elizabeth and Alençon. Yet Walsingham saw that the time for
such games was over. Though not making so bold as to oppose the
marriage outright, he grew increasingly suspicious of French sincer-
ity; their intention appeared nothing more than to "lull us asleep in
security." He wrote a trusted colleague, Sir Thomas Smith, one of
her Majesty's principal secretaries, "The more I observe of their doings here, the more I increase my jealousy of their evil meaning."

"The best way not to be deceived by them," he added with harsh
simplicity, "is not to trust them." The protestations of friendship
from Catherine and Charles were themselves suspicious, Walsingham

insisted. The Admiral had been fawned over and petted by the King and Queen Mother just two days before he died; likewise, the French Court now never used "fairer speech" or "greater protestations of amity" toward England, such a torrent of kind words at a time when their actions spoke just the opposite. Politics *had* aligned with religion, and the Queen was playing with her very life and crown to ignore that truth:

> If her Majesty stick now to spend or put in execution all those things that tend to her safety, she must not look long to live in repose, nay she must not long look to keep the crown upon her head. The cause of her former quietness proceeded of her neighbors' unquietness, which being removed, she must now make another account.

With the Admiral dead, not only was a distracting "unquietness" removed from the French King's attentions, but the influence of the ultra-Catholic Guises was inevitably increased. The Papal Nuncio and the Spanish Ambassador were every day seen closeted with the King or members of the court.

"Can we think that the fire kindled here in France will extend itself no further?" Walsingham wrote in another letter that autumn. "Let us not deceive ourselves but assuredly think that the two great monarchs of Europe together with the rest of the Papists do mean shortly to put in execution" their aim of exterminating Protestantism altogether.

And amid the outpouring of prose that Walsingham penned in a rush of growing certainty, he pronounced what would become his watchwords for the next two decades: "It may be said that I fear too much. Surely, considering the state we stand in, I think it less danger to fear too much than too little."

In late September, he went so far as to offer his advice to the Privy Council itself, the inner circle of power and administration of the English government; his manner was deferential, his conviction unbending. "Your Honors, by the King and his mother's answers, may see great protestations of amity. I am sorry that I cannot yield that assurance thereof that heretofore I have done." He himself had believed such French expressions of goodwill in the past, but he hoped he might be excused for that mistake; "my error in that belief was common with a great many wiser than myself." But the King's assurances were now inescapably belied by his actions: in persecuting the Protestants, in violating the terms of the Edict, and in giving his ear to the sworn enemies of England. "I leave it to your Honors now to judge what account you may make of the amity of this crown. If I may without presumption or offense say my opinion, considering how things presently stand, I think less peril to live with them as enemies than as friends."

Personally, Walsingham was heartily ready to leave. Elizabeth had quickly backed off from her threat to the French King that Walsingham might be withdrawn, leaving a mere secretary in his place; now she was willing to consider Walsingham's departure on personal grounds, but only if it carried no diplomatic significance, and that meant not until a replacement was found and dispatched.

The months dragged by heavily; Walsingham suffered another bout of his illness; his household continued to hemorrhage money. His wife, back home, was pregnant with their second child. Thomas Smith reported in December that he was working on the Queen as best he could in London: "All your friends have not only been diligent but more than importunate to bring you home, and your wife with tears and lamentations. And the Queen's Majesty seemeth to incline and grant our requests. But when a pin is set fast in a hole, till we have another to thrust that out and tarry there itself, it is hard to get out."

The crux was finding the next willing victim for such a thankless office. "Your successor cannot yet be found; yea, find enough, but we cannot get one that will stick fast," Smith wrote. The first nominee had succeeded in wriggling out of the job: "slipped his head out of the collar," Walsingham sardonically put it. The next pleaded sickness. A third had manfully accepted the commission, bought his horses, engaged his servants; then the Queen had changed her mind. Given the delicacy of the marriage negotiations, she explained, she had decided she could not after all spare a man of Walsingham's experience and discretion.

"You are a wise man," Smith wrote by way of apology, "and can comfort yourself with wisdom and patience."

By February 1573, Walsingham's financial ruin was near total. When the Court removed to Fontainebleau, fifty miles up the Seine from the capital, he reported, "I shall be driven to remain here . . . having neither furniture, money, nor credit."

Finally, on the 19th of March, the Queen signed Walsingham's revocation; two weeks later, his designated replacement was on his way from London. On the 19th of April, Walsingham presented his successor to the King at Court. The King thanked him for his services and presented him a gold chain worth a thousand crowns. Catherine gave him presents for his wife and daughter and a letter in her own hand to Elizabeth, praising his behavior and service while in France.

After a final farcical episode—the King, suddenly fearing that Walsingham's departure presaged a declaration of war by England, had sent a rider flying after the departing ambassador to carry him back to Fontainebleau, and by the time the King was reassured another week had passed—Walsingham arrived in London on the 10th of May.

For his two years and four months in her Majesty's service, he had been richly compensated with broken health, financial ruin, and an unequaled lesson in political reality.

1532-72: Making of a Spymaster

3

A PARTICULAR KIND OF GENTLEMAN

The characteristic that everyone would always later remark upon about Francis Walsingham was, to put it simply, that he knew how to shut up.

Video et taceo, see and keep silent: It was said to be Queen Elizabeth's motto, but it was Walsingham's first, and the truth was that the Queen, for all her diplomatic shrewdness, came out with the most extraordinary things on occasion. No one ever heard Walsingham let a stray word slip. In the perpetual intrigue of the Court, boasts of influence and intimate knowledge of goings-on were the common currency of power. That, or shrill complaints of ill-use, and wounded protests of vanity and merit slighted. In an age of braggarts and swagger and public lamentations, a man with the self-assurance to keep his own counsel stood out.

Not just stood out: was distinctly unnerving. "A man exceeding wise and industrious," William Camden, the great chronicler of the age, called Walsingham, "a most sharp maintainer of the purer Religion, a most subtle searcher of hidden secrets, who knew excellently well how to win men's minds unto him, and to apply them to his own uses."

"As the close room sucketh in most air," wrote a later chronicler, so Walsingham, "this wary man, got most intelligence":

> Dexterous he was in finding a secret, close in keeping it. His converse was insinuating and reserved: he saw every man, and none saw him. It was his first maxim, *Knowledge is never too dear.* . . .
>
> He was no less dexterous to work on humors than to convince

by reason. He would say, he must observe the joints and flex-
ures of affairs; and so could do more with a story than others
could with a harangue. . . .

He said what another writ, *That an habit of secrecy is policy
and virtue.* To him faces spake as much as tongues, and their
countenances were indexes of their hearts. He would so beset
men with questions, and draw them on, and pick it out of
them by piecemeals, that they discovered themselves whether
they answered or were silent. . . . He waited on men's souls
with his eye, discerning their secret hearts through their trans-
parent faces.

He saw every man, and none saw him. Certainly none knew his enemies better. He had early on learned to study them, to know them,
to like them even. "He was a gentleman, at first of a good house and
of better education," noted a contemporary, "and from university
traveled for the rest of his learning." His father had been a London
lawyer; he died in 1534, when Francis was but two. But the family was
left well enough off that as a young man Francis was enrolled at
Cambridge as a "fellow commoner," the higher stratum of fee-paying
students, distinguishing the sons of gentlemen from the lesser sorts
who paid their fees but lacked social cachet, and the even lesser sorts,
those with more brains than money or family, who paid their way
through university waiting on tables.

The usual regimen at Cambridge was Latin leavened with Greek,
Hebrew, and not infrequent beatings for infractions of the college
rules. Students were expected to speak to one another in Latin; in
general they were not expected to apply their brains to much other
than memorization. But King's College, where Walsingham went,
was the most ardently Protestant college in a university that was becoming a bastion of reformist thought, and Walsingham's own tutor
was a leading light among the young reformers: an early exercise in
stretching one's mind amid an otherwise conventional course.

Like many a gentleman's son, Walsingham then went convention-
ally on to study law at Gray's Inn in London. And then he fled

abroad, along with the rest of the zealous Protestants that Cambridge and King's had nurtured in the flowering of reform that ended abruptly with the very unexpected accession of the very Catholic Mary Tudor to the throne in 1553.

Some, like William Cecil, older, established, prudent, with much to lose in lands and offices and little to gain from an overnice fidelity to one religion or another, conformed to the restored Catholic faith. Others, younger, or more ardent, or with less to lose, fled. Eight hundred, mostly gentlemen, merchants, clergymen, chose to save their religion and their skins abroad; three hundred, mostly ordinary people whose stubbornness, zeal, poverty, or inertia led them to try to retain both at home, were burned at the stake during Mary's reign.

Walsingham, young, ardent, prudent, fled: and so began the far less conventional part of his education. He was gone for five years; he became fluent in French and Italian; the foremost linguist among the Englishmen of his day, it was later said. In Padua, he studied Roman civil law. Everywhere, he got to know men of all kinds. "Books are but dead letters," he would advise a nephew years later, when that young man was setting out on his own travel of discovery. "It is the voice and conference of men that giveth them life and shall engender in you true knowledge."

He was speaking to his nephew but he was speaking of his own young self: study Spanish, Italian, French, Latin; practice translating passages from one to another every day; read the lives of Plutarch, the histories of ancient Rome, "books of State both old and new . . . as well profane as holy"; ponder what lessons from past governments might apply to the present. But also take careful note of the "manners and dispositions" of the people one met everywhere.

Of the nobility, gentry, and "learned sort," men of power and influence,

> have their company as much as in safety of conscience and peace of God you may: that you see the inclination of each man the way he is bent, whether it be marshal or counselor, a plain, open nature, a dissembling and counterfeit, whether he be in

credit with his people, and what pension he hath from abroad, how inclining toward the neighbors bordering upon him.

Be "civil and companionable to all" such men; but take no sides and make no commitments.

But also get to know the lesser sort, the "men of experience as the world calleth them," the secretaries, notaries, and agents of princes, the men who in truth control the machinery of government. "Though themselves they have no water," Walsingham advised, they are the "conduit pipes" for the affairs of state and the counsel of princes. Through them one can learn of the daily dealings of the state, "whether they appertain to civil government or warlike affairs"; through them one can influence events.

When Protestantism later returned to England, the convention of the time drew a distinction between those men of affairs who were Puritans and those who the French called *politiques:* those who sought to make the pure religion the test of all policy, and those who counseled caution and compromise when the interests of the state and the realities of politics demanded it. Walsingham was ever a Puritan, a Puritan in fundamental conviction; but his travels had stamped him a very *politique* in method and manner, in knowledge of the world, and in equanimity in dealing with its imperfections.

He liked Italy, and trees. He was later said to have been able to match wits with King James VI of Scotland "with sayings out of Xenophon, Thucydides, Plutarch or Tacitus"; or Henry of Navarre "with Rabelais"; or "the Hollander with mechanic discourses."

He made wry, self-deprecating jokes, jokes about a supposed rumor that he would be hanged for his mishandling of negotiations in the Low Countries, jokes about his supposed perfections as a husband. In the midst of the maddening marriage negotiations with Anjou in France, he had written a friend, Thomas Heneage, about Anjou's character:

> Though he be choleric yet lacketh he not reason to govern and bridle the same. And you know that these natures are the best

natures and commonly prove the best husbands. Or else should not you and I be in the highest degree in such perfection as we are. Yet in this matter we shall do well not to be judged neither by Mrs. Heneage nor Mrs. Walsingham because they are parties.

When he could afford it, he became a patron of the arts and sciences, supporting voyages of discovery, the search for the Northwest Passage, makers of Latin dictionaries, needful poets and writers, Oxford colleges, the study of civil and international law. He engaged in a lengthy correspondence about the Gregorian calendar. He wrote a treatise on how to train soldiers without excessive waste of powder. He was curious about the science of navigation. Robert Hakluyt dedicated the first edition of his collection of tales of discovery to Walsingham, thanking him for his support and encouragement by "letter and speech."

Walsingham's fellow Puritans railed against the evils of the theater; "lascivious writhing," "bawdy fables gathered from idolatrous heathen poets"; "the cause of sin is plays," said one Puritan preacher, with the smug certainty of ignorance that made Puritan preachers ever so tiresome. Walsingham, seeing the possibilities of advancing the Protestant cause through plays with patriotic and historical themes, created a company of actors, the Queen's Men, under the direct patronage, and control, of the Crown. When the prim London authorities tried to limit the new troupe's performances, Walsingham calmly remonstrated with them, and got his way.

A Puritan and a Renaissance man, a strange and powerful combination: a zealot who knew how to keep his mouth shut.

———— ❧❦❧ ————

But a Puritan all the same. "This Walsingham is of all heretics the worst," sputtered the Spanish agent in London. The Queen more than once called him a "rank Puritan"; and there was no doubting what she thought about Puritans, rank or otherwise. They were smug, they were bores, they were nitpickers, and with their constant demands for ever-more Protestant reforms in the Protestant Church of England, the church of which Elizabeth was Supreme Governor and which she considered quite adequately reformed as it was, thank you very much, they were a threat to the very social order and royal supremacy.

The Puritans' direct-pipeline-to-God self-righteousness was an affront in itself. One especially earnest, or foolhardy, Puritan dared deliver to the Queen a book reproving her Majesty for her frequent habit, in her not infrequent moments of anger, of blasphemously swearing: swearing "by that abominable idol the Mass, and often and grievously by God, and by Christ, and by many parts of his glorified body, and by saints, troth, and other forbidden things." An impressive repertoire of oaths, popish and profane: it scandalized the Puritans and perfectly summed up what the Queen felt about the place of religion, which was once a week, orderly, decorous, every Sunday, a piece of smoothly working social machinery ordained by God through the sovereign to an obedient people and that was the end of it. The Queen disliked and distrusted evangelical fervor, was constantly vexed by the endless theological disputes over "trifles," was simply bored by the tedious issues of church administration, so keen a contrast with her quick interest in affairs of state. The Archbishop of Canterbury came to complain about the difficulties of finding learned ministers to fill the thirteen thousand parishes in England. "Jesus!" the Queen exclaimed. "Thirteen thousand!"

But it was probably no more than one of her little jokes that she called Walsingham a "rank Puritan." Walsingham the Puritan was sober, ascetic, formally devout enough; Walsingham the Puritan *politique* had his eyes on a bigger fish than whether ministers of the church should wear vestments, or whether the sign of the cross should be omitted during baptisms. He knew better than to tax the Queen with her oaths, or with the cases of Puritan divines who had fallen afoul of the church hierarchy for their too-zealous preaching. He once advised his fellow Puritans against instituting any change in the service at the English merchants' chapel in Antwerp, pointing out that, though he personally liked the form of prayer they were proposing, reforms must be made with due authority and uniformity, lest chaos reign—and the Queen take offense. "Thank God for what we presently enjoy, having God's word sincerely preached and the Sacraments truly administered," Walsingham cautioned them; "the rest we lack we are to beg by prayer and attend with patience."

But there was never any of the smarmy religiosity of the mock devout in Walsingham's frequent allusions to God; when he spoke of God's will and judgment, or his guiding wisdom and care, it was always more by way of reference to a given, a touching of the stone of underlying faith: faith in the ultimate triumph of rightness, though never a substitute for human judgment and action, or man's obligation to do what needed to be done here and now to serve God's plan on earth. What plainly appealed to Walsingham in Puritanism was its no-nonsense realism, its renunciation of superstition and magic, its seriousness of purpose, its extolling of hard work, its *purity;* sober black garb sat well on a man who wished the world to know he had no time for frippery. He left the hot Gospel zeal to others.

Anyway, the Queen liked making her little demeaning jokes about the men around her and their quirks and personal appearances. Some thought Walsingham "satanic"-looking, but that was hindsight, after his reputation as a master counter-plotter and spymaster was well established, after people had been writing forever about his ability to wait upon men's souls with his eyes, after he had seen the great enemies of the realm to their ends: Mary Queen of Scots to the executioner's block in an ancient castle in Northamptonshire; the invading Spanish Armada to shipwreck and slaughter on the wild coasts of Ireland.

His long, pointed face, and pointed black beard, and dark—or was it just sallow?—complexion made Elizabeth think not of a devil but of a Moor, and that was what she called him: "Moor," or "Ethiopian." It became a standing joke between them: for Walsingham, a self-deprecating way to tell her Majesty exactly what he thought, and turn aside her anger at his temerity in daring to tell her exactly what he thought, as few others did. "The Laws of Ethiopia, my native soil," he once pleaded to the Queen when daring to offer some particularly frank advice, "are very severe against those that condemn a person unheard."

A joke, and yet: there was something undeniably sinister about a man in dark and somber clothes in a Renaissance court filled with velvets and silks and furs and pearls and canary yellows and blood-red scarlets; a man immune to the usual vices of passion and vanity and boastfulness and anger in an age of swagger and lustfulness and sanctimony; a man who kept what he learned to himself; a man who looked enough like a Moor to be called one, even in jest.

Like many who would occupy positions of power and trust in Elizabeth's inner circle, Francis Walsingham was a gentleman rather than a member of the old nobility that once held sway at the court of English kings, that still did hold sway in most foreign lands.

Not that being even a gentleman meant as much as it once had. "As for gentlemen, they be made good cheap in England," Walsingham's old friend and colleague Sir Thomas Smith observed without any particular censure. "For whosoever studieth the laws of the realm, who studieth in the universities, who professeth the liberal sciences, and, to be short, who can live idly and without manual labor, and will bear the port, charge, and countenance of a gentleman . . . shall be taken for a gentleman." The heralds would register anyone who had £10 a year in income from land or £300 in movable goods and—for a suitable fee, needless to say—would produce a coat of arms and a pedigree grafting him on to some supposed ancestor of the same name dredged up from the rolls. The heralds made thousands of these grants in Elizabeth's reign.

There were plenty of jokes and satires about arrivistes braying to be called gentlemen ("I will be a gentleman whatsoever it costs me!" exclaims a character in one of Ben Jonson's plays), but no one lost by it; the heralds got their fee, the Crown got another taxpayer added to the rolls of the taxpaying gentry, and the former town tradesman or country yeoman or sailor or soldier or clergyman who had made some money and bought his way into the countryside got the status and social entrée he coveted. "Gentility is nothing but ancient riches," William Cecil told his son, and by Elizabeth's time not even very ancient riches at that. Francis Walsingham's ancestors a few generations back were shoemakers and vintners and merchants; by his grandfather's generation they had become country gentlemen living off the estates that shoes and wine and trade had bought.

The strident Elizabethan insistence on rank and status and the cult of ancestry was only a nervous reflection of the very eruption of social mobility that was taking place, and the explosion of wealth that propelled it. In an age of invention and expansion, active men found money to be made everywhere: in the woolen trade, in coal, in the new machinery of blast furnaces, in the manufacture of soap and steel and wire, in voyages of discovery and trade and plunder. "Profit," the Spanish Ambassador in London sneered, was to the English "like nutriment to savage beasts": the old hauteur of the noble born to the upstart go-getter. Sir Francis Drake brought back treasure worth £300,000 from his round-the-world voyage, a 4,700-percent return for his shareholders. When Sir Walter Raleigh made a mere 100 percent profit on one voyage, he remarked in disgust that he should have sent his fleet a-fishing instead.

Land was what still made a gentleman, but land was to be had. Dissolving the monasteries and seizing their property, and selling off two-thirds of it for quick cash, Henry VIII had thrown a fifth of the entire productive land of the country onto the market. The rising gentry were the chief beneficiaries. With the land came more new power, for, in the crazy literal-mindedness of English property law, the new owners of monastic properties came into possession of feudal and religious privileges that clung to those lands, notably the right to tithes that had earlier been impropriated by the now dissolved religious orders. Impropriated tithes had originally been the rector's share from the income of the parish that by law was assigned to the church; as the monasteries conveniently found, you didn't really need to supply a rector when a cheaper vicar could do the job just as well out of his own, lesser share of the tithes. And so the rector's share became the monastery's. And what had been good enough for the monasteries was good enough for the new lay impropriators, who now simply pocketed the money, or sold the impropriation to other lay investors. The advowson, the right to name a clergyman to a benefice, was usually sold by the Crown along with the land as well, and this too could be resold by the new lay owner as a valuable commodity—or retained to give the nouveau-riche country gentleman a remarkable say in the character of religious observance in his district.

So the gentry was rising, while the nobility was having its own problems. There were still great feudal lords who lived and acted like medieval princes in their castles with their personal armies and retinues of archaic offices of stewards and bailiffs and constables and castle-greaves, but there was no shortage of hints that past glories were fading. By Elizabeth's accession, the nobility had been pared down to fifty-seven peers, among them but a single duke; half had been created only a generation or two earlier. Elizabeth wanted to keep it that way: she created only eighteen new peers in her entire half-century-long reign, half as many as in the previous half-century.

Some lords still had fabulous incomes from huge landholdings, but with their titles came fabulous expenses: entertaining scores to dinner every night; putting on a show of a hundred retainers in matched livery wherever they went; dropping the amounts that a man in such a position was expected to drop on "hawks, hounds, horses, dice, cards, apparel, mistresses," as the Earl of Northumberland cautioned his son against from his own bitter, or not so bitter, experience; and then finally staging elaborate funerals for themselves when they nobly expired, spending thousands of pounds to outfit all the mourners in new clothes, and on gifts of rings by which all would remember the great late departed. While he was still alive, a nobleman was particularly expected to entertain the Queen on her regular progresses, and to do so in a manner commensurate with his rank; he would be lucky to escape a royal visit £3,000 the poorer. William Cecil, the commoner whose devoted service to the Queen's government she rewarded with a barony, endured a dozen of these visits. He turned down the Queen's offer of an earldom for fear it would ruin him.

The medieval lords with their medieval tradition as men of arms were still the ones to whom the Queen would turn for the command of military expeditions, and when it came to social privilege and entrée to the glittering orbit of the Court, the nobility carried the day as always. The Queen loved ostentation; she loved dancing and gambling; she loved hunting; she loved seeing men who could afford to dress well in crimson satin and velvet and gold lace and loathed those who did not; she loved anachronistic displays of jousting with courtiers got up as picturesque knights with picturesque chivalrous names like the Blue Knight or Knight of the Tree of the Sun, risking life and limb and reciting verses of devotion to her; she loved receiving outrageously costly New Year's Day gifts, a gold jewel in the shape of a pelican sprinkled with rubies, a tiny clock studded with diamonds, an ostrich-feather fan with an engraved golden handle, a dress of white satin embroidered in silk and gold thread and garnished with pearls.

Her notion of society was a hierarchy set in granite, ordained by God from the beginning of time, with the lords in their natural place at the top. She once reproved Philip Sidney for answering back an insult from the Earl of Oxford: the Earl had arrogantly ordered Sidney to get off the tennis court so he could play, Sidney had replied that the Earl ought to ask him nicely, the Earl called Sidney a "puppy," and Sidney called the Earl a liar. When the Queen heard about it, she admonished Sidney that "the gentleman's neglect of the nobility taught the peasant to insult upon both."

But the Queen was no fool; when it came to making the government run, she turned to the sharp, educated, ambitious gentry from the start, not the nobility. Almost all of the key men on her Privy Council were commoners, or peers of her own creation; for the first time in history, the Council was in the hands of university-educated laymen, men of the Renaissance Enlightenment, men more interested in the world than in defending some customary place of privilege in it.

They were capable, efficient, professional, distinctly modern. Parliament, too, was now coming to be dominated by the gentry, and by university-educated men. For a couple of generations, it had been a tradition of sorts for the gentry, and ambitious families of the classes just below, to send their sons after university to the Inns of Court in London. Some became professional lawyers, which took six to nine years of study, but many more stayed for just a few years, to acquire social refinement and valuable contacts and the sort of knowledge that might help them look after their property or assume a county office such as Justice of the Peace. The Inns were said to be the "third university" of the land, with a place alongside Cambridge and Oxford.

Under Elizabeth, they became something more, the place where men seeking a career as a politician or statesman could get their professional start. Being a grandee was fine if one wanted to play cards with the Queen or be invited to dance in her presence. Knowing law, and Latin, and business, and the ways of the world was a better recommendation if what one was after was the real power of government.

✧⊙❀⊙✧

William Cecil had shown the way, the exemplar of the new breed.

His grandfather was a successful yeoman farmer and soldier; his father had made the jump to the ranks of the gentry, purchasing several royal manors and becoming a Justice of the Peace; William was duly sent to Cambridge and Gray's Inn.

Throughout his life, William Cecil remained a scholar through and through, steeped in Latin and Greek, eloquent, a brilliant debater, quick on his feet, ever seeking and storing away any scrap of knowledge that might be of use. At Cambridge he had imprudently concluded a secret marriage with the daughter of an innkeeper: a scandal, but not a simple one, for the girl's brother was actually a great and famous man, already the greatest Greek scholar of his day, a poor man whose native genius had swept away all barriers of class and custom to attain for him a Cambridge education, and then the post of Regius Professor of Greek, and then tutor to no less a person than Prince Edward, the King's heir. When Cecil's young wife died not long thereafter, he remarried; his new wife was herself an accomplished Greek scholar.

Cecil entered Parliament at the age of twenty-three, became Principal Secretary to Edward VI at thirty, survived Mary Tudor's five-year reign by fulfilling a few tactful diplomatic missions abroad and conforming enough to keep his lands and his head, all the while maintaining a discreet contact with the young Princess Elizabeth. When Elizabeth succeeded to the throne, her first act was to name Cecil her Principal Secretary and a Privy Councilor.

Elizabeth's ascension to the throne brought the exiles back, and Cecil, always on the lookout for likely young men, apparently helped see to it that Francis Walsingham—one of the likeliest, who on his return had taken up the life of the country gentleman on the estate at Footscray, in Kent, which he had inherited by his father's will—was elected to Parliament in 1562.

Cecil was the perfect patron and the perfect mentor for a man of Walsingham's inclinations and abilities. Sober, upright, self-controlled, a limitless capacity for work and an unflappable nerve, Cecil was friendly and cheerful to everyone and revealed nothing to anyone. He was no courtier, he said: he shunned the social life of the Court, dressed plainly, lived in his own house, admitting no friend to a footing of true intimacy. His only diversion was pleasant talk at meals; work consumed the rest of his waking hours.

He was no courtier: but he was a master at leading and cajoling a Queen who, ever on guard against the imputation that she was a mere figurehead, a woman pretending to a man's job, spurned cajolery. Elizabeth may not have been schooled to rule a kingdom as other princes were, but she had received a formidable classical education and had taken to hard mental work with enthusiasm; though she loved the pomp and ostentation that were hers to command, she equally prided herself on the mastery of the most complex affairs of state. From the start she made it clear that no decision, however trivial, would be made without her personal consent. Her famous temper was equal parts royal caprice and tactical shrewdness, all the shrewder and shocking for coming from a woman, and she knew it. "When I see her enraged against any person whatever," the French Ambassador once confessed, "I wish myself in Calcutta." As circumstances required, she could be a bully, a coquette, or a wit: whatever it took. But she was not beyond advice, and Cecil could get decisions and answers out of the

Queen as no one else could: "he knoweth her mind," she once said of her chief councilor. She might storm, but she was ultimately loyal to those upon whose efficiency, devotion, and capability her rule depended.

The Queen's nickname for Cecil had none of her usual barbed wit. Her Spirit, she called him, and he was everywhere, the guiding force of her government. He was like a spirit in another way, Elizabeth once reassured him when the intrigues of courtiers began to get to him, in that he was insensible to the "kicks of asses."

Of Cecil's absolute command of detail there could be no possible doubt. He filled hundreds of volumes with dossiers of intelligence scrounged from every corner of the land. He was known to stay up late into the night marshaling facts, writing memoranda to himself, weighing pros and cons: who the important families were, how they were connected, what they were up to, and facts about coinage, and imports, and the size of the fishing fleet, and the fortunes of the Protestant rebels in France and the Low Countries, and the price of French wine. In 1569, when the great lords on the Council, Norfolk and Leicester among them, decided the time had come to put this upstart in his place and hatched a plot to confront him with an accusation of malfeasance and misgovernment and have him thrown into the Tower, Cecil characteristically learned of it first and was ready with a lengthy, brilliant memorandum on the state of the realm and his management of it during his ten years in office. He was ready, too, with the Queen's backing, and her wrath against the would-be conspirators; that was the end of that. The Queen called him her Spirit: others called him the Old Fox.

Francis Walsingham was re-elected to Parliament in 1566. In 1568, thirty-six years old, recently married to his second wife, he bought a house in London. A promising man, acquainted with the world and its tragedies. Walsingham's first wife, Anne Carleill, had died after just two years of marriage, leaving him a young son by her previous marriage to bring up. His second wife was also a widow, Ursula St. Barbe Worseley; her inheritance added to his growing estates, but she had brought her own tragedy, too: shortly after their marriage, the two sons from her previous marriage were accidentally blown up by gunpowder while playing in the porter's lodge at the Worseley estate on the Isle of Wight.

It was around this time, in the year 1568, that Francis Walsingham's mentor William Cecil, the man who knew everything and revealed nothing, began finding little jobs that his promising protégé might take on from time to time in the service of his government.

4

THE QUEEN'S PERILOUS COURSE

They were strange jobs, but, then, England was a strange land; the wonder of Europe, in many ways ungoverned, in many ways ungovernable. The Queen's caution, her famous love for the middle course, was policy and prudence, instinct and necessity, cause and effect: the middle course avoided the shoals, and cut its own narrow way deeper with each traverse.

It was the English themselves who were at heart ungovernable; ungovernable not because they were lawless but because they were just the opposite, a people for whom law was national religion and national sport. The courts were choked with lawsuits over land and inheritances, over ancient rights encroached upon; juries pigheadedly stood on their power to acquit in criminal trials, and did so one time out of three; even armed rebels and rioters, rising up in one of their regular protests against authority, would invariably invoke the law to justify their resistance in the name of some customary privilege, some right to work the land or work their trade in accordance with some obscure, convoluted, but never forgotten grant.

The monarchs of England tried to keep their Parliaments in check, and were not above committing to the Tower members who occasionally spoke too freely; but their increasing dependence upon Parliament for the approval of special taxes, and to confer legitimacy upon such radical social reforms as the reordering of religion, gave voice and power to that same strident demand of the people to be heard and to stand upon their ancient rights and privileges. The Lords and Commons usually in the end gave the sovereign what he or she wanted, but not without some astonishing expressions of independence and will; the Commons especially, for it was the Commons where, by tradition, money bills originated. Though elected only by freeholders who possessed land worth £40, the Commons was universally understood to speak for all: "The consent of Parliament was taken to be every man's consent," wrote Sir Thomas Smith. "The regiment of England is not a mere monarchy, as some for lack of consideration think," a pamphleteer defending Elizabeth in the first year of her reign wrote; "nor a mere oligarchy, nor democracy, but a rule mixed of all these." The Queen ruled, to be sure, the pamphleteer acknowledged, yet "first it is not she that ruleth, but the laws."

A ruler who sought to impose his will by force alone on such an ungovernable, pigheaded, legalistic, outspoken people did so at his peril: not that there was much force to be had. The kings of France had forty thousand officials serving them, an army, a horde of professional bureaucrats and local enforcers. Elizabeth had twelve hundred paid officials in the whole of her realm, and half of those were administrators of her personal estates. It was a tenth the number of government officials per subject that any self-respecting tyrant required: a "government by persuasion," as one later historian would call it.

Most of the burden of local rule in Elizabeth's England fell to unpaid Justices of the Peace, local gentry charged with everything from ensuring church attendance to having vagrants whipped and enforcing the laws against football-playing, swearing, and abducting heiresses. The justices were magnificently amateurish, ridiculously overburdened. London printers, sensing a lucrative market, came out with a whole series of quick-study guides that promised to turn a not always too-bright country gentleman into something that could at least pass for a judge. For other help the J.P. could turn to that other magnificently amateurish and unpaid local official, the constable, whose major contribution to Elizabethan society was to provide the butt of rough humor on the stage for Shakespeare and his fellow playwrights.

Of an army there was almost none because of taxes there was almost none. Many realms of Europe teetered on bankruptcy through profligacy but England managed to do it through sheer penury. A distinction of sorts: the most undertaxed country of the age. Elizabeth inherited a debt of £300,000 and a debased currency, and like her predecessors was expected to foot the entire cost of government out of her own income from Crown lands and customs duties, about £200,000 a year in all. In the first decade and a half of her rule, she borrowed £1 million from abroad. Small military adventures in Scotland and France in the early years of her reign absorbed £750,000; special taxes grudgingly voted by Parliament to cover these extraordinary costs in fact covered but a third. These parliamentary taxes were the only thing England had that ever resembled real taxes, based on a fixed percentage of property or income. But they were viewed, at least by Parliament and ordinary men, as exceptional measures that would be granted only to meet special emergencies. And in practice they never worked as they were supposed to; tradition had reduced the percentages of property and income to a fixed sum to be apportioned among the counties, and even those sums were not met. The local gentry parceled out the actual assessments: they went easy on themselves.

And so the Queen's entire standing army consisted of two hundred royal bodyguards and a garrison of a few hundred men manning the south-coast forces against invasion. In theory, all men between the ages of sixteen and sixty could be called up for militia duty; in practice, they were exempt from foreign service and too poorly trained and ill-equipped to be of much use anyway.

The dearth of government offices and their meager pay bred inefficiency and corruption, a very English sort of inefficiency and corruption, sanctioned by custom, nothing too egregious but impossible to alter. Officers of the Crown supplemented their official earnings with bribes and fees and skimmings and kickbacks and the petty graft needed to oil so creaky a piece of machinery; monopolies were granted on everything from the manufacture of playing cards to the licensing of taverns to the transportation of leather, all a way for the Queen to grant favors without costing herself a penny, only further disabling the machinery of governance. Offices were always for sale, a minor one for £200, a particularly lucrative one for £4,000. A great man like Cecil was above straight bribery, was incorruptible in that sense; but he, like everyone else, accepted the perquisites that more subtly subverted the efficiency and power of government. There were "arrangement fees" from those seeking a profitable wardship, the gift of the Court of Wards over which he presided; there were the presents of plate expected of anyone with private business before the Privy Council. Cecil died with £15,000 worth stashed in his house.

The amateurism and casualness of Elizabethan administration clung to all levels of government, a strange mixing of public and private. Officers hired and paid for clerks out of their own pockets if they wanted them; those who were charged with receiving and spending funds mixed their private and public obligations and freely borrowed or speculated with the government's money; experiments were made in farming out customs collection entirely to private hands. The truly appalling and precarious practices Cecil managed to root out. A bold devaluation of the debased coinage, followed by its immediate recall and reissuance in new coins with full silver value, two-thirds of a million pounds' worth, stabilized the currency and actually returned a small profit to the Treasury; rigid controls on spending erased the government's debt by the 1570s. A long neglect of domestic arms manufacture was rectified: brass and gunpowder industries were hastened into being.

But the merely routine and precarious remained, as always, unchangeable in ungoverned and ungovernable England. If trying to retain power and the security and unity of the nation through so limited a means and so precarious a middle course seemed a dubious formula for success, it at least had the virtue of being a less dubious policy than attempting to impose power and security and unity by force where no force was to be had.

No shoals tested the cautious navigator of the middle course like the shoals of religion.

Religion had cast Elizabeth's very right to the throne in doubt, for as far as Rome was concerned the marriage of her parents, Anne Boleyn and Henry VIII, had never happened. Elizabeth had outwardly professed Catholicism during her half-sister's reign, but enough was known, or thought to be known, about her inner convictions to elate Protestants and grieve defenders of the old faith in the uncertain weeks that stretched between Mary's death, on the 17th of November 1558, and Elizabeth's coronation, on the 15th of January 1559.

At Mary's funeral in Westminster Abbey, John White, Bishop of Winchester, had stood before her coffin to deliver the sermon and a shot across the bow. Mary's coffin was draped in gold cloth and, somewhat grotesquely, surmounted with a lifelike, full-sized image of the late Queen, clothed, robed, sceptered, crowned, bejeweled. The Bishop's text was a verse from Ecclesiastes: "I praised the dead which are already dead more than the living which are yet alive." White did not directly question Elizabeth's legitimacy, and he was cleverly elliptical in explicating those words of the Old Testament decrier of human folly. But he seemed to leave little doubt about what he was getting at when he said, "If ye ask whether it is better for me to be born in this world, and be a rebeller, a murderer, a heretic, a blasphemer, or not to be born at all? In this case I must answer, better is never to be born." The Bishop closed his sermon with a perfunctory expression of hope for a prosperous and peaceful reign for the new Queen—adding portentously, "If it be God's will," implication distinctly not.

Most Englishmen would probably follow sullenly wherever their new Queen led on religion, as they had through the reverses of her sister and brother and father before; so, too, would most of the rank-and-file clergy, good Vicars of Bray almost to a man.

Those who would not were girding for trouble, and were in a position to make it. The hierarchy of the church and most of the nobility were strongly Catholic, or at least conservative. Elizabeth tipped her hand but once: on Christmas Day, in the royal chapel, she walked out of mass when the priest, defying her instructions, elevated the host. It was enough to make every leading bishop of the land refuse to preside at the coronation.

On the other side, the hopes of the hotter Puritans were almost sure to be dashed, so great had they risen and so swiftly; and the reformers' capacity for anger and trouble was almost unlimited. Elizabeth's accession had already unleashed a paroxysm of iconoclasm; mobs set upon churches and made bonfires of relics, roods, banners, vestments, altar cloths, saints' images, "as if it had been the sacking of some hostile city," noted one chronicler. The staunchly Protestant burghers of London greeted the Queen on her coronation procession with five elaborate pageants. None were subtle. In one, a figure representing Pure Religion trampled Ignorance and Superstition underfoot; in another, a child clad as Truth presented Elizabeth with an English Bible; and in the last, the new Queen was portrayed as an English Deborah, rescuing her people from the yoke of oppression.

Elizabeth's middle course had been charted in a secret plan prepared by an adviser to William Cecil before Christmas: "A Device for the Alteration of Religion." It was a profoundly conservative strategy for the reinstatement of Protestantism, a Protestantism of the most circumspect kind, orderly, decorous, uniform, governed by bishops, preserving most of the forms and rituals of the old church, strictly forbidding unlicensed worship and unlicensed preaching. The result, the author admitted, would be dismissed by many Protestants as "a cloaked papistry or a mingle-mangle"; but to acquiesce in the full Puritan vision, every church governed by itself, every man in direct contact with God, free to determine the truth from his own study of the Bible, was to invite chaos.

As it was, it was still too much for the conservative Lords. They boldly rejected the first bill that Cecil submitted. In the end, what came out of Parliament in the spring of 1559 was more a minglemangle than ever. The final act affirmed Elizabeth as Supreme Governor of the Church of England (not Supreme Head: a small theological and diplomatic concession to Catholics, and the Catholic powers abroad); it replaced the Latin mass with the vernacular litany of Edward's 1552 Prayer Book; it left matters of church ornaments and priestly vestment up to the Queen. To assuage the consciences alike of those who believed and disbelieved in Christ's real presence in the Eucharist, a modification was introduced in the service: to the Protestant 1552 version, "Take and eat this, in remembrance that Christ died for thee," commemorative and symbolic only, was added the traditional Catholic formula, "The body of Our Lord Jesus Christ which was given for thee, preserve thy body and soul into everlasting life," which distinctly implied otherwise. Something for everyone: if it baffled the common man, it has baffled theologians ever since. The Queen, for her part, was content to opine, "In the sacrament at the altar, some thinks one thing, some other; whose judgment is best God knows."

The whole package was a formula that could please no one, an attempt to keep a lid on internal pressures while doing nothing to defuse them. It passed the Lords in the end by a vote of only twenty-one to eighteen, with two of Elizabeth's own Privy Councilors voting against.

The Queen's conservatism was honestly come by, at least. The Protestant instruction she had absorbed in her youth left her not with the zeal of a conversion on the Road to Damascus that the pioneers of the Reformation experienced but, rather, with the mild feeling that it was all just rather ordinary common sense. The purpose of reform was just that, ridding the church of its worst abuses and superstitions. Elizabeth's religious defenders always took pains to cast her settlement as no innovation, simply a return to the purity of the primitive church, a stripping away of the accretions and usurpations of popery. The role of the prince as governor of the church in his realm was ordained by God himself; the prince's authority depended neither on the Pope nor on the individual consciences of worshippers over esoteric points of doctrine. A "vain love of singularity" would only lead men to dispute, to undermine the church's authority and provoke schism. Elizabeth liked the trappings of the church that reinforced its majesty, the vestments, candles, ornaments, stone altars; she forbade women to live in cathedral closes and tried to discourage priests from marrying; she distrusted preaching if not strictly regulated.

The deeply religious, Catholic and Protestant alike, were equally unenthusiastic. The Queen blithely insisted to the Spanish Ambassador that the rites of the Church of England were virtually the same as those of the Church of Rome, only a matter of three or four things in the mass, she asserted. True Catholics, needless to say, thought otherwise. The Puritans, for their part, were not about to be mollified until all the myriad remnants of "cloaked papistry" were extirpated.

And as for the common men and women, the mystery and magic that the old church had at least had going for it—the intonations of the Latin mass, the cult of saints and their relics, the pilgrimages to shrines and wells, the ringing of bells for the souls of the dead on All Hallows' Eve, the harvest and Yuletide processions, the blessings of the plows, the anointing of sick cows with holy water, the prayers for rain, all the "Judaical and heathenish rites," as the Puritans scorned them—these were now gone, gone without even the hot evangelical zeal of the new religion to replace them.

The old clergy mostly conformed; no more than a hundred or two were removed for refusing to accept the Prayer Book or royal supremacy. But they were a sorry lot, "loitering lubbers" who "seek not the Lord Jesus but their own bellies"; "some shake-bucklers, some ruffians, some hawkers and hunters, some dicers and carders, some blind guides and can not see, some dumb dogs and will not bark," as one famous Puritan preacher denounced them to be. The Puritans were naturally hard on these holdover priests—"mass-mongers" was the favorite term of opprobrium—but, even discounting Puritan bias, they were a sodden and illiterate bunch. Most priests did not even know the Bible; one bishop a few years before had found that over half of his priests could not recite the Ten Commandments, one in ten could not even name the author of the Lord's Prayer. It was a rather basic failing in a Christian clergyman, given that the author was Jesus himself.

Priests who had just managed to get through the set rites of the Catholic Church, their deficiencies hidden under the aura of magical powers they exercised and the unquestioning obedience the rituals themselves presumed, were at a loss when it came to preaching the word and inspiring congregations. Many did not try; instead—"ill workmen, sleepy watchmen," the Puritans again railed—they resorted to stumbling through preprinted homilies. The services were perfunctory, unedifying: the minister "posteth it over, as fast as he can gallop. . . . They toss the Psalms in most places like tennis balls."

The English-language Prayer Book was supposed to bring congregations closer to the word of God, but there is sometimes something to be said for mystery and incomprehension; most found the new service sterile, dull, tedious, and talked, slept, walked about, or even brawled in church.

In some dioceses, churchwardens were instructed to appoint four to eight large men of the parish to keep order during divine service.

Of course, there was the rather inescapable fact that Protestantism embodied dissent, authorized dissent, *was* dissent: the Queen was swimming against a tide of her own creation. The tide began with religion, but it lapped at farther shores.

Later Protestant triumphalists would credit the Reformation with everything from capitalism to public education to democracy; they exaggerated, but they had a point. Protestant preachers urged both men and women to become literate so they could read the Bible, and literacy blossomed in Elizabeth's reign. People who read the Bible could read other things, too; and, what was more dangerous, write things. "Every gross brained idiot is suffered to come into print," fumed an English scholar. The Queen and her Council were less concerned about the idiots than about the pamphleteers, the propagandists, the *critics:* this was something new.

But she, and her father, had truly brought it on themselves. Henry's very act of securing parliamentary approval for royal authority over the church had authorized people to have an opinion on the right ordering of religion. The Queen might insist on obedience and storm against "vain love of singularity"; she tried to separate the question of inner conscience from outward obedience, doing away with prosecutions for heresy, demanding only that people attend church, not that they stand questioning about their beliefs; but the inner conscience had been recognized and licensed, the door opened to challenging authority in ways unthinkable before.

For Protestantism assumed at its very core that its job was to persuade, not just to command. The Geneva Bible, an English translation begun by the refugees who had fled Mary's reign to that city, and which became the standard household Bible in England for a century, included not just the text but "arguments" and explanatory notes and marginal glosses. The religious debates within Protestantism everywhere were incredible in their passion and violence: hairsplitting points of theology accompanied by an obbligato of personal invective, insult, slander. The English government practiced censorship as a matter of course, as did every government; but twopenny pamphlets poured forth from secret presses that eluded the authorities and their searchers, who combed the back streets and cellars of London. Authors were discovered and thrown in jail; from their prison cells they carried on their work unrepentant.

Some defenders of the conservative order looked to Scotland and the Netherlands, where the full political implications of Protestantism were vividly on display, and saw which way the wind was blowing, and shuddered. "God keep us from such visitation as Knox have attempted in Scotland, the people to be orderers of things," the Archbishop of Canterbury warned in 1559. And another, thinking particularly of the Netherlands: "Unhappy is the country where the meaner sort hath the greatest sway. . . . God keep England from any such confused authority, and maintain us with our anointed sovereign, whose only power under Christ is the safety of us all."

They might as well have tried to stop the wind from blowing. "These heretics neither fear God nor obey their betters," the Spanish Ambassador concluded, after watching Parliament dare to instruct the Queen on the wisdom of her marrying. Public opinion could be watched, and sniffed out, its pulse discreetly taken; it could be shaped and molded subtly, with rumors planted, counterpropaganda deftly insinuated; but once it arose to haunt a society it could never be exorcised.

The divine right of kings was all well and good: a prudent king kept a weather eye to the eddies of this new force that was springing forth from its own divine right.

———————— ❧❧ ————————

The last years of Mary Tudor's reign had been marked by famine and plague, two disastrous harvests followed by a mysterious epidemic. But 1558 and 1559 had brought good, even abundant harvests. The mystery ailment vanished: a good omen, to those looking for good omens. The Bishop of Winchester, now confined to the Tower, had plainly doubted whether God was prepared to grant peace and prosperity to England under Elizabeth; but now peace had seemed to arrive almost as swiftly as prosperity, and by April of the first year of Elizabeth's reign, treaties had been signed ending the seemingly endless small wars with Scotland and France. With Spain, Europe's most powerful empire, England was officially at peace, too.

Yet barely beneath the surface was a gnawing fear in Elizabeth's inner circles, fear born of the certain knowledge that England was powerless, utterly naked against the threat of invasion should any of these ancient enemies and rivals decide once again that war and conquest were more to their interests than peace. England was an eerily empty land, barely three million people in a country that in the fourteenth century, before the great plague, had had twice as many. In sheer numbers Spain and France simply overwhelmed England: Spain's population was three times that of England, France's five times.

Scotland was tiny but a nightmare, Protestant in the lowlands but still Catholic in the highlands, heavily under the sway of France: a French regent—the sister of the Duke of Guise and the Cardinal of Lorraine, no less—ruled; three thousand French troops were there. From London, the Spanish Ambassador reported that "it is incredible the fear these people are in of the French on the Scottish border."

And then there was Scotland's half-French, and all-Catholic, heir, Mary Queen of Scots: betrothed to the heir of the French crown, with a claim to the succession of the English throne better than Elizabeth's as far as the French were concerned. In Paris, the English Ambassador was constantly picking up threads of Guisean intrigues aimed against England through the French foothold in Scotland: he referred to the Cardinal of Lorraine as the "Minister of Mischief."

Peace with Spain had been secured through Mary Tudor's marriage to Philip II—not that it had been much of a marriage, and not that it had sat well with most Englishmen, who in their guts never liked a foreigner, especially a foreigner who had the additional ill-favor of being a Spaniard. Elizabeth's accession had brought pro-forma expressions of continued mutual goodwill between the two realms, but only a fool could ignore the underlying enmity and con-flict of interests between the two seafaring nations. Cecil warned that, with Spain ruler of the Netherlands, and two-thirds of English exports going to Antwerp, Philip's power to "annoy this realm" even short of war was vast and daunting. Nor were the Spanish above dropping hints about what else they could do. Philip's regent in the Netherlands, Cardinal Granvelle, struck a note like that of any none-too-subtle tough when he asked the English Ambassador: "What present store of either expert captains or good men of war ye have? What treasure? What other furniture for defense? Is there one fortress in all England that is able one day to endure the breath of cannon?"

And, as Cecil noted in a memorandum to the Queen in August 1559, the Guises and their intrigues aside, the French Crown had hardly abandoned its ambitions toward England. The French King had recently sought to have the Pope formally declare Elizabeth ille-gitimate, had made certain alarming military and naval preparations, had even served dinner at the French Court to the English Ambas-sador on plates bearing the English arms: a brazen assertion of claim to the title of Elizabeth's realm. Other English envoys warned that England might be reduced to another of those prizes that the two great continental powers, France and Spain, tussled over, as they did various Italian states. Or, worst of all: that they might join forces and divide England between them.

From the very start, Cecil argued that neither open war nor neu-trality would answer. England was too weak to dare provoke a direct conflict; but to do nothing would be to cede to the enemy the license to strike at the time and place most favorable to him. And so Cecil's plan for Scotland, laid out in a long and masterly memorandum, was to secretly aid a group of pro-English Protestant lords who had re-belled against the Regent Mother. To Elizabeth's objection that "it is against God's law to aid any subjects against their natural princes," Cecil chiefly argued necessity. England simply lacked the men or the arms or the military leaders or the money to assemble even a credible deterrent force if the rebels should be defeated and the French lodge a large army in Scotland. It would be far less expensive to spend a bit now than to endure such a calamity later. And if it came to an invasion of England, well, "it will move all good English bloods," but not necessarily in the way she might hope: "some to fear, some to anger, some to be at their wits end."

The Queen gave her reluctant assent, and £3,000 was secretly delivered to the rebels as a first step. She did not like aiding rebels; she did not like the implications that religious rather than national interests might be guiding her policy toward other nations; but just as the weakness of her government to impose its will at home had made the gathering of knowledge and the subtle use of influence the only weapons at her disposal, so the same inescapable logic arose in answer to the problem of Scotland. And so, too, France, where aiding the Huguenot Protestant rebels seemed to offer the best promise of recovering Calais and the other Channel ports that England had lost; and so, too, in the Spanish-ruled Netherlands, where aiding the Dutch Protestant rebels seemed to offer the best hope of keeping Spain occupied.

Keeping Spain occupied, like keeping France occupied, remained a matter of national rather than religious policy throughout the 1560s; but there were straws in the wind of a new alignment of forces between religion and politics that neither Cecil nor Elizabeth could escape. The growing cold war between England and Spain, for now at least, seemed confined to matters of trade and treasure and military threats; rising tensions over English laws favoring English shipping and banning imports of many articles from the Spanish Netherlands had led, in 1563, to severe reprisals in the form of a temporary embargo on English trade with Antwerp. But everywhere there were religious overtones.

There was the Spanish Ambassador in London, Bishop de Quadra, who, Cecil complained, "seemeth to neglect all other affairs and rather serveth, as may appear, like a nuncio of the Pope than the King's ambassador." De Quadra's interference in English domestic matters, in particular his attempts to champion the cause of English Catholics, had led to a formal protest by Elizabeth to Philip, and a warning she would ask for his recall if he persisted. Only de Quadra's unexpected death in August 1563 averted an immediate diplomatic crisis.

And in the Spanish Netherlands the rebels, nobility and merchants chafing under Spanish rule and oppressive taxes, vented their anger with an outburst of iconoclastic attacks on Catholic churches in 1566. Philip had sent the Duke of Alva from Italy to suppress the revolt, and he and his eight thousand "blackbeards," as the fearsome Spanish troops were known, supplemented by forty thousand mercenaries, had done so with especial violence and brutality. Now this menacing army was two hundred miles from London. It didn't help that the new Spanish Ambassador in London, Guzmán de Silva, though in general far more urbane and polished than his predecessor, thought it fitting to celebrate Alva's slaughter of a thousand Protestant rebels with a great bonfire. He also set out two hogsheads of fine claret, and two of beer, for all to drink. Urbane or not, he, too, was soon expressing his revulsion at having to live among so many "heretics" and was asking for a transfer.

When English merchant seamen began trading in Spanish America, that, too, had religious repercussions; Spain protested that it had a monopoly granted by the Holy See; Cecil retorted, "The Pope had no right to partition the world and to give and take kingdoms to whoever he pleased."

And then, finally: an absurd but potentially far more grave rupture over a point of diplomatic protocol occurred in 1567, when the English Ambassador to Spain, Dr. John Man, was forbidden the use of his religion in his own household and forced to attend mass. Shortly thereafter he was expelled from Spain for having remarked at a dinner party that the Pope was "a canting little monk."

5

A MOST UNWELCOME GUEST

It was perfectly fitting, in retrospect, that the events that would cascade toward the sundering of Europe along irrevocable lines of religion, that would force even the most reluctant to identify the cause of England with that of the Protestant faith and her enemies with Catholicism, that would define the personal nemesis whom Francis Walsingham would pursue through most of two decades to come, began with an explosion.

A literal explosion: the astonishing blast of gunpowder that awakened the good citizens of Edinburgh at two in the morning on the 10th of February 1567 reduced to rubble a house known as Kirk o'Field that stood by the city walls.

It was a magnificent but in the end slightly wasted effort, for the intended target of the blast, the increasingly irksome second husband of Mary Queen of Scots, Lord Darnley, had apparently become alarmed by the noise of those coming to light the charge and had managed to clamber out a window and through a gate into the garden by the time the gunpowder went off. The assassins had, in the end, been forced to dispatch Darnley, rather anticlimactically, by strangling him.

Mary had chosen to absent herself that evening from Kirk o'Field. It was she who had selected the house for Darnley's recuperation from a bout of illness—widely rumored to be syphilis; it was she who had entreated him to return with her there from his father's house in Glasgow. But that night the Queen was staying at Holyrood Palace, the official seat of the Scottish monarch, a few miles away in the center of Edinburgh. Brought the news of her husband's death,

Mary immediately declared that the assassins had obviously meant to destroy her as well; she had had a miraculous deliverance.

Within a fortnight, another story reached London. In Edinburgh, placards had boldly appeared accusing Mary of complicity in the murder, and naming the chief assassin: James Hepburn, Earl of Bothwell, a violent, ambitious, vainglorious adventurer who had been on a remarkably intimate footing with the Queen of late. One poster depicted a mermaid and a hare; the mermaid, for which no one could have failed to read the intended meaning *harlot*, wore a crown; the hare, the family crest of the Hepburns, was surrounded by a circle of swords.

Elizabeth, even while surreptitiously aiding Mary's opponents in the miasma of Scottish politics, had carried on a courteous royal correspondence with her sister sovereign; now she sent a stern letter (addressing her coldly as "Madame": not her customary "My dear sister"), warning that if Mary failed to take action against the murderers she would confirm the suspicions of those who thought the worst.

It was likely that anyone who had already lived a life of such melodrama and defiance of the odds as Mary had in her twenty-four years would have acquired a sense of fatalism, if not self-destructiveness. Her father, James V of Scotland, had dropped dead in the throes of a nervous collapse a week after her birth; from infancy she had been a trophy in the rough game of Scottish feuding and factionalism: promised by treaty at age seven months as wife to Henry VIII's son Edward, taken by Catholic lords and crowned Queen of Scots at nine months, shipped off to France at age six (sold to the devil, declared the Scottish Protestant fury John Knox), betrothed to the Dauphin of France at fifteen, Queen of France at sixteen, widowed at eighteen when her young husband the King died, from an abscess on the brain.

No one had expected her ever to return to Scotland, that "arse of the world" as one traveler had called it, not after her upbringing in the magnificently civilized court of Paris, not after having been

Queen of France, not after having been flattered as to her claims to the crown of England. The Scottish Parliament in her absence had made Protestantism the state religion and outlawed the mass. If the Catholic Queen of Scots actually returned to take up her throne, "Here will be a mad world!" said one Scottish lord. But return she did, in August 1561, with reciprocal promises that she would be permitted to exercise her own religion but would do nothing to alter Parliament's religious settlement for the rest of the country.

A mad world indeed. She had then married Darnley, an English nobleman with his own ancestral claim to the English throne: like Mary, he was a grandchild of Margaret Tudor, Henry VIII's sister; the marriage infuriated Elizabeth. She needn't have worried. Darnley, a young and none-too-bright Adonis, was not the stuff great things are made of. He was easily manipulated by a group of resentful Scottish lords—there was always a group of resentful Scottish lords—into believing that Mary's secretary, an Italian singer named David Rizzio, was bedding her, and so led a band that invaded Mary's supper room at Holyrood and stabbed the Italian to death before her. The balladeers had their field day, telling of the Queen's alleged revenge upon her husband:

> . . . for a twelve month and a day
> The king and she would not come in one sheet. . . .

Then the Queen's displeasure with her husband had finally been resolved on a more permanent basis by the explosion at Kirk o'Field, or, rather, would have if it had not also proved necessary to strangle the syphilitic, scorned, and usually drunk Darnley, which was a bit more of a giveaway.

Mary made no move to rebut the rumors about who the murderers had been; by March 1567, it was bruited that she and Bothwell were to marry. In April, when Bothwell theatrically abducted and, presumably, ravished the Queen, everyone assumed it was an act staged with her full foreknowledge and consent. In May they were married.

Self-destruction was not long delayed. Mary's scandalous behavior was both an outrage and an opportunity to the lords of Scotland, and within a month they had risen against her and forced Bothwell's outnumbered army to surrender near Edinburgh. Bothwell fled to Norway: not the best choice, since he had left both enemies and debts from earlier adventures there, and he soon found himself in a Danish prison cell, where he rotted away the rest of his life.

Mary was arrested. As she was led through Edinburgh to be taken to the fortress of Lochleven, soldiers in the streets jeered, "Burn the whore!" On the 24th of July, she abdicated in favor of her infant son, James, whose custody the Protestant lords had made sure of. A Protestant regent, Mary's illegitimate half-brother the Earl of Moray, was appointed.

The following spring, the half-brother of Mary's keeper at Lochleven, in "a fantasy of love" with her, lifted the keys of the castle and let her escape. Again the army she summoned to her aid was routed, this time in a battle near Glasgow. On the afternoon of the 16th of May 1568, Mary made her way to the shores of the Solway Firth, on Scotland's west coast, embarked on a fishing boat with a small band of followers and attendants, and made the four-hour crossing to England.

———————— ⚜ ————————

Elizabeth had for months been expressing her outrage over the Scottish lords' affront against "nature and law" in deposing their sovereign. Whatever Mary's alleged offenses, the lords had certainly acted contrary to what is "ordained by God and received for a truth in doctrine in all Christian governments."

The Queen's affectation of taking her fellow sovereign's part was not pure hypocrisy; she did fear the precedent of acknowledging that it was acceptable for monarchs to be dealt with in such a fashion. She also hoped that, through the feudal chaos of Scottish politics and its quagmire of personal and family alliances, she could find a winding channel that might yet lead to every desired end: nominally restore Mary's right position, or at least her liberty; punish

Darnley's murderers; keep the French out; and secure the safety of the young Prince James, thereby insuring that the real political power in Scotland would remain in the hands of the pro-English Protestant party. Mary's arrival in England was rather an embarrassment to such overcleverness, for it called Elizabeth's bluff.

Cecil, in his usual thorough way, prepared a long memorandum cataloguing the realities of this new and exceptionally thorny situation. It had been one thing to press the lords to grant Mary's liberty while they still firmly held the upper hand, quite another now to support a triumphant return of Mary to Scotland from exile. In so doing the English party would surely be "abased" and the Catholic and pro-French forces immeasurably strengthened. It was equally impossible to allow Mary to go to France; if she regained the Scottish throne with the aid of the French, all of the old dangers of a renewed Franco-Scottish alliance would return with even greater menace. And, finally, it was unthinkable that she should be welcomed at Court, or even allowed to remain at liberty in England, for it was absolutely obvious that here she would become a rallying point for all of those unrepentant Catholics and others within England who backed her claim to the English throne: and did so not merely as Elizabeth's successor, "but afore her."

Those who wished to see Mary replace Elizabeth, Cecil observed, were a disparate lot; some supported Mary "for religion, some for affection to her title, others from discontentation and love of change." But the prize of the English throne would be too much for any to resist; here, as a rival claimant on English soil, Mary would surely be able to draw them all together in common cause: "no man can think but such a sweet bait would make concord betwixt them all."

Mary was no intellectual, no grand strategist. Elizabeth read Latin and Greek, Mary did embroidery. But, like many who were adventurous even to the point of self-destruction, she had charisma and an ability to attract and inspire. They said she was beautiful; they always said that about queens, but what she undeniably had, besides her good points of being tall and auburn-haired and her bad points of sharp and aquiline features, was "some enchantment, whereby men are bewitched," as one who had seen her put it. John Knox accused her of unseemly levity: precisely. She had poise and grace, but also that knack of convincing whomever she happened to be speaking to at any particular instant that she had no greater pleasure in the world than his company. Men, garden-variety egotists that they mostly were, found it irresistible; only a supreme egotist like Knox, who was not to be flattered by intimate chats with a queen since he enjoyed intimate chats with God, was immune.

From the north there were already warnings of the excitement that her arrival had set off among the largely Catholic population of the northern counties. The Earl of Northumberland had hastened across the hills to personally offer his protection to the Scottish Queen; only the government's prompt dispatch of Sir Francis Knollys, a deft courtier but staunch Protestant, had headed him off. Knollys was utterly reliable as her keeper, but even he showed signs of being addled by Mary's charms. "Surely she is a rare woman!" he exclaimed, and driveled on about her "stout courage" joined to "a liberal heart."

Elizabeth maintained the courtly fiction that her dear cousin was a guest in her realm, but the Queen's obvious vexation over this unwelcome presence embarrassed even Knollys when she sent a bunch of her least attractive cast-off dresses as a gift to Mary; Knollys, resourceful courtier that he was, smoothed things over by explaining that it was a misunderstanding, that a servant had picked out the items under the mistaken impression that they were intended as a gift merely for one of Mary's attendants. A small incident, but a telling one; Elizabeth had been forced to bow to the awkward but inescapable logic of the Council's decision regarding Mary's keeping, and she didn't like it, and she took it out in petty petulance. "Her Majesty can neither aid her, permit her to come to her presence, or restore her, or suffer her to depart," the Council had decided, at least not while the matter of the Scottish Queen's guilt in the Darnley murder remained unresolved.

It was Cecil's master stroke to make sure it remained forever unresolved. Mary had sent letter after imploring, affectionate letter to her dear sister sovereign asking that she just be allowed to plead her case in person. In July, Mary finally acceded to a compromise proposal, that agents representing Mary and the Scottish Regent both present their cases before a commission of English councilors and lords that would assemble at York and decide how Mary should be restored to the Scottish crown. To Mary's party, Cecil and Elizabeth offered assurances that the commission would surely uphold her claims. The Regent would be the defendant, called upon to explain his rebellion against his anointed sovereign; if he and the lords refused to be reconciled to Mary, then Elizabeth would "absolutely set her in her seat regal, and that by force."

To Moray a very different message was quietly conveyed. Cecil had carefully set out in a memorandum the legal and propaganda groundwork for what was, in truth, to be an elaborate but extremely deft dirty trick. The Queen's Majesty of course "never meant to have any come to accuse" the Queen of Scots before the commission, Cecil explained. But in seeking to reconcile her and her subjects, Elizabeth was by justice bound "to hear what they can say for themselves." The point was that, the previous winter, Moray had already shown the Privy Councilors copies of letters that were alleged to have been written by Mary to Bothwell, and which thoroughly stained her with the guilt of the Darnley murder. Now Moray was instructed that if he brought them forth before the commission it would certainly be sufficient to absolve Elizabeth of any further obligation to aid Mary.

Whether the letters were real or, as Mary's defenders maintained, clever forgeries was never resolved; not that it really mattered. Moray presented the letters before the commission in late November; they caused the public sensation expected; the commission quickly found itself at an impasse when, as also expected, Mary refused to answer the charges unless she was permitted to do so in person, this request was denied, and Mary's agents withdrew. Elizabeth declared that, given this outcome, she was unable to rule either for or against the Queen of Scots; but while this grievous accusation remained unanswered, she surely could neither restore Mary to her throne nor receive Mary in her presence.

It was the perfect outcome: Elizabeth avoided having to condemn or violate her duty to a fellow queen; what had been mere scuttlebutt the year before was now a matter of formal charges that had been laid before a great body of the realm; and, without actually denying Mary's sovereign rights, her claims to them had been cast into the limbo of perpetual abeyance.

In January 1569, Mary was moved away from the Borders to the far more secure keeping of the Earl of Shrewsbury, whose Midlands domain was safely Protestant; from here her chances of securing local support were greatly diminished. Tutbury was a dilapidated, drafty, damp castle, plagued with "nasty old carpentry," Mary complained. She hated it, as much for the place itself as for the unmistakable message that, whatever pretenses were still respected, she was no longer a guest but a prisoner. From the time of her arrival in England she had been restricted in her movements, accompanied by a guard of a hundred men whenever she wanted to go for a walk or a ride. But Tutbury was dreary, uncomfortable, with foul drains and stinking middens below her very window: it not only functioned as her prison, but had the air and odor of one as well.

A prisoner, but far from a spent force: as Cecil well knew. It would later be known that from the moment the Scottish Queen had arrived on English soil she had begun weaving conspiracies and approaching foreign powers to come to her aid. In September 1568, she had written the Queen of Spain promising that if France and Spain provided the slightest help she would see Catholicism restored in England, or die trying. In January 1569, she sent a message to the new Spanish Ambassador, an arrogant ideologue named Guerau de Spes, who had arrived in September and already succeeded in making himself unwelcome by openly insulting Cecil and Elizabeth; Mary would have the ambassador know that with King Philip's assistance she would be Queen of England in three months, "and mass shall be said all over the country."

De Spes was at that particular moment confined to the embassy by order of the Council: one of the increasingly frequent diplomatic crises between the two countries. French pirates, and a providential wind, had chased four small coasters from Spain into Plymouth Harbor in November 1568. On inspection, they were found to be carrying some chests crammed with £85,000 in gold coins. The money was being sent to the Spanish Netherlands to pay Alva's troops there, but upon further investigation it turned out that the money did not strictly speaking belong to Spain: it was the possession of Genoese bankers who were lending the money to Spain, and the bankers quickly sent word to England that they would be quite happy to lend it to Elizabeth instead, at a suitable rate of interest. While Elizabeth was still thinking that over, de Spes raised a furor, insisted the ships be released at once, and called upon Alva to retaliate by seizing English ships in the Low Countries. In response, the Queen said she would, after all, take the money; and the Council placed de Spes under house arrest for stirring up trouble and, they said, to protect the Spaniard from the uncontrollable and quite understandable fury of the London mobs. Cecil had come in person to deliver the news to de Spes, and had enjoyed the additional pleasure of mentioning in passing, when de Spes protested that he needed to order food and drink, that his predecessor Bishop de Quadra had left his grocery bills unpaid and perhaps the ambassador ought to see to that little matter first.

But despite the isolation from outside communication that both the Queen of Scots and the Ambassador of Spain were at the moment experiencing, there were other, alarming hints of schemes being hatched that tied the two: Mary's fatal and quite undimmed attraction for the forces of opposition, both internal and external, was considerably more than a mere theoretical concern of Cecil's cautious imagination.

And it was here that Francis Walsingham began leaving small traces of the ways in which a literate, well-traveled, multilingual man of discretion could be of use: a wholly appropriate introduction to the world of secret affairs for Walsingham, given the central part that Mary would play in nearly every plot and counterplot that Walsingham the spymaster would be involved in for most of his life and career to come.

It began thus: In August 1568, the English ambassador in Paris warned of reports that the Cardinal of Lorraine was sending some Italians to London to practice against the Queen. He suggested that Cecil get in touch with a certain Italian Protestant now in London, one "Captain François," also known as Captain Thomas Franchiotto, who could look into the matter. Francis Walsingham, fluent in Italian and French, was the man Cecil chose to make the initial contact with Franchiotto.

Franchiotto was but the first of the many slightly shadowy, slightly disreputable characters from whom Walsingham would glean and pass on details of doings that were all but invisible to less shadowy and more reputable men of affairs. Franchiotto had been in the pay of the French Court for forty years, but obviously his services were for sale elsewhere as well. He soon gave Walsingham a list of suspicious travelers who had arrived in England in the past three months and details of a conversation he had had with the Bishop of Rennes, a recently arrived envoy from France, whom Franchiotto skillfully milked for news of the Guises' schemes by goading him into an angry admission: Lorraine was contemplating raising troops to free Mary and launch a rebellion against the English crown.

From other French contacts Franchiotto passed on reports of joint Spanish and French schemes to overthrow Elizabeth and Protestantism. Meanwhile, Walsingham had arranged for the Lord Mayor of London to send him weekly reports of all strangers taking lodgings in the city. Walsingham admitted that Franchiotto's vague reports of "a practice in hand for the alteration of religion and the advancement of the Queen of Scots to the crown" were not much to go on; but "there is less danger in fearing too much than too little"—those words that Walsingham would repeat, again and again.

Walsingham's trail appeared again a few months later, crossing the tracks of rather more dangerous quarry. At the time of the commission at York, rumors had drifted about that some of the Scottish lords had approached the Duke of Norfolk with a startling proposition: that he should marry Mary himself. Rumor also had it that the Duke was extremely enthusiastic about the idea.

Norfolk vehemently denied it, exclaiming to Elizabeth that he would not be able "to sleep upon a safe pillow" lying next to "so wicked a woman, such a notorious adulteress and murderer." But there were safe pillows and there were the glories due a lord who was a direct descendant of Edward I, the only remaining duke in the land, a man widely regarded as the richest and most powerful man in Europe who was not a prince in his own right. Confident of his power, Norfolk began in the spring of 1569 to move openly toward forging so attractive an alliance; even Cecil did not dare oppose him when the Duke sought a Privy Council decision that Mary would be given her liberty if she was safely married to an English lord.

Cecil did not actively oppose the Duke: he had other means at his disposal. Sometime in 1569, a pamphlet appeared, a brilliant, savage piece of propaganda that warned of the evils that would befall the realm and the Protestant cause should the Queen of Scots marry an Englishman. The author was almost surely Walsingham. It purported to be a dispassionate analysis of whether it was better for the Queen of Scots to marry an Englishman or a foreigner, though of course no one was talking about her marrying any foreigner. In fact, it was a wonderful piece of character assassination of both the Queen and the Duke, calculated to provoke the ire of England's Puritans in particular.

In enumerating the sins of the Queen of Scots, the pamphleteer was thorough in appealing to every English prejudice:

> In religion she is either a Papist which is evil, or else an Atheist which is worse. . . .
>
> Of nation she is a Scot, of which nation I forbear to say what may be said, in a reverend respect of a few godly of that nation.
>
> Of inclination, how she is given, let her own horrible acts publicly known to the whole world witness, though now of late certain seduced by practice seek to cloak and hide the same.

Of alliance on the mother's side how she is descended of a race that is both enemy to God and to the common quiet of Europe, every man knoweth, but alas too many have felt.

In goodwill towards our sovereign she hath shewed herself sundry ways very evil affected, whose ambition hath drawn her by bearing the arms of England to decipher herself to be a competitor of this Crown, a thing publicly known. I leave to touch other particular practices that have discovered her aspiring mind.

And as for the Duke, the pamphlet continued, though he was outwardly a Protestant, and though of course his religious belief was a matter to be left between God and his own conscience, there was the undeniable fact that he had once married a papist, had allowed his son to be educated by a papist, had chosen papists for all of the chief men of his house, and was on intimate terms with "the chief Papists of this realm." In short, the "pretended match" between Norfolk and Mary was a threat to religion and to the safety of the Crown. Without coming right out and declaring it to be treasonous as well, the pamphleteer concluded ominously: "I leave to lawyers to define of what quality this presumption is for a subject to seek to match with a competitor of this crown, without making his sovereign privy thereto."

Walsingham had, with considerable accuracy, touched the heart of the case there, for it was Norfolk's failure to inform the Queen of his intentions that would turn out to be the most effective weapon against him. Walsingham's pamphlet was one of just many inspired leaks that Cecil orchestrated throughout the spring and summer; never outwardly confronting or opposing Norfolk, he repeatedly dropped just enough hints to Elizabeth to make it clear that the Duke was up to something.

In early August, Elizabeth encountered Norfolk while walking the grounds at her palace at Richmond; Norfolk had come from London to join the rest of court, and Elizabeth archly asked him if he had any news of a marriage. Norfolk slipped off without giving a straight answer. A few weeks later, she pointedly told him to "take good heed of his pillow," a barbed reference to his earlier denial of any interest in the Scottish Queen. Finally, in September, Elizabeth confronted Norfolk directly and the Duke was panicked into a confession. The Queen responded with "sharp speeches and dangerous looks," and, a bit of a weakling and a bit of a fool, Norfolk fled from Court. Defying the Queen's orders to return, he first pleaded he was too ill to travel, then made for his country estate, where his followers now fully expected him to lead a revolt. The Queen told Leicester that she knew perfectly well that were the planned marriage to take place, she would be in the Tower in four months. But at the moment of crisis, Norfolk gave himself up: it was he who was thrown in the Tower.

Damp powder lit with a wet fuse, a group of Catholic northern earls who had been secretly preparing to join Norfolk's cause once his position was secured through the planned marriage to Mary now went ahead with their revolt anyway, without him, or the marriage. At Durham Cathedral, Northumberland arrived in mid-November with three hundred horsemen, knocked over the communion table, threw Protestant Bibles and prayer books to the ground, and ordered celebration of the mass.

But within a month, the pathetic revolt had fizzled; the leaders escaped to Scotland, the followers were hanged. Mary was moved yet again, farther south.

A stronger guard was ordered placed about her.

Among those swept up in the aftermath of Norfolk's matrimonial plot was a well-known Florentine banker in London, Roberto Ridolfi. He had resided in London for a decade, handling the banking affairs of continental merchants and the Catholic embassies; he was known to receive a regular pension from both France and Spain for his work.

But Ridolfi had also been observed of late delivering considerable sums of money to the Bishop of Ross, Mary's agent in London, as well as to some of Norfolk's servants. Again it was Walsingham whom Cecil now called upon to assist in the matter. On the 7th of October 1569, the Council issued an order authorizing Walsingham to hold the Florentine at his house "without conference until he may be examined of certain matters that touch her highness very nearly."

It would prove to be one of the few times anyone got the better of Walsingham. Ridolfi freely admitted to Walsingham that he had arranged banking matters for Norfolk and the Bishop of Ross and had transferred money for them from abroad; that, after all, was his job. He had even been "made privy to the matter of the marriage betwixt the Queen of Scots and the Duke." But surely this was not a crime. Walsingham was ordered to search Ridolfi's lodgings and did so: nothing incriminating among his papers. So Ridolfi was released on a £1,000 bond and his promise that he would not meddle "in any matters concerning her Majesty or the state of this realm." In January 1570, the bond was returned in full.

In part, Cecil's reason for detaining Ridolfi had been simply to cut off his communication with the Spanish Ambassador, de Spes, while the Norfolk matter was being investigated; that had been accomplished. It was no doubt true, too, that nothing positively incriminating had been extracted from Ridolfi. But Walsingham ended up being beguiled, not just as to Ridolfi's guilt but as to his character; a few months later, Walsingham wrote Cecil urging him to make use of Ridolfi for a sensitive diplomatic mission, praising him as a man who "would deal both discreetly and uprightly, as one both wise and who standeth on terms of honesty and reputation."

It was a mistake Walsingham would scarcely repeat. Ridolfi, for his part, would later boast to friends that the matters Walsingham had interrogated him about were serious enough to have had him beheaded twenty-five times over.

―――――――――⋙⊙⊙⋘―――――――――

Early in 1570, Cecil mentioned to the Queen that he thought Francis Walsingham might be a suitable candidate for her new ambassador to France. By August she had agreed, and Walsingham had already left

England for the Continent when the final act took place in the Norfolk melodrama: it could never quite attain the level of tragedy.

It had quickly became apparent that nothing Norfolk had done strictly fit the definition of treason, and his confinement in the Tower was eased. In August 1570, he was released, having given his word "never to deal in the cause of the marriage of the Queen of Scots."

The following April, of 1571, a passenger arriving at Dover from Flanders became so insistent that certain packages he was carrying be allowed through that the suspicions of the customs officers were, not unnaturally, aroused. The traveler was arrested and his baggage searched.

The man was Charles Baillie, a Fleming of Scottish descent, a servant of the Bishop of Ross. In his possession was a book by Ross, secretly printed in Liège, defending the Queen of Scots. Also in his possession was a packet of letters in cipher. Secretary Cecil—Lord Burghley, as he had become in February—was informed.

Before the letters were turned over to Burghley, however, Ross managed an extraordinarily bold feat: he approached the Lord Warden of the Cinque Ports and explained that, though the letters were perfectly innocent, they would greatly embarrass Norfolk, and surely the Lord Warden did not wish to do that to so great a nobleman. Ross convinced the Lord Warden to deliver the letters to him instead; after opening the packet in the Lord Warden's presence, Ross gave him a packet of old letters to give to Burghley in their place, and so allay any suspicions.

The shoe was on the other foot with regard to the custody of Baillie's person, however: he was thrown into Marshalsea Prison, in Southwark, and practiced upon with every prison confidence trick from time immemorial. A man very convincingly playing the part of an abject fellow prisoner befriended him; Baillie, "fearful, full of words, and given to the cup," let slip that there had been other letters than the ones Burghley had received. The fellow prisoner claimed he himself had found a way to pass cipher messages from Baillie to Ross, should he wish to communicate with his master; these were intercepted and read before being passed on.

Transferred to the Tower, Baillie was then both racked and further practiced upon. In one elaborate ruse, a man appeared late one night in his cell identifying himself as Dr. John Story—a hero of English Catholics who had recently been kidnapped from Antwerp and brought back to England in one of Secretary Cecil's most brilliant secret operations. Though Baillie had never met him before, Story's presence in the Tower was the talk of the prisoners there; Baillie was even placed in the same cell in the Beauchamp Tower where Story had in truth been held, and where the Catholic hero had left an inscription carved on the wall. The "Story" who now slipped in to speak to Baillie, through "the kindness of a gaoler," strongly advised the young man that it would be best, after all, to cooperate with the authorities.

Eventually the miserable man did. He confessed that the two ciphered letters he had been carrying were from none other than Roberto Ridolfi, who had approached him in Flanders shortly before Baillie departed for England. What was more, Ridolfi had told him what was in the letters: they reported on Ridolfi's recent audience with the Duke of Alva in Brussels, during which the Spaniard had agreed to an invasion of England to coincide with a Catholic rising that would free Mary and seize Elizabeth. The letters were addressed to two English noblemen, identified only as "30" and "40." Baillie insisted, apparently truthfully, that he did not, however, know who they were.

Having been wrung dry at last, Baillie was thrown back in his cell, where he was left to scratch his own rueful inscription on the wall, still there to be seen centuries later: "Be friend to no one. Be enemy to none. The most unhappy man in the world is he that is not patient with the adversities they have, for men are not killed with the adversities they have, but with the impatience which they suffer. All things come to he who waits."

Ross was detained and his premises searched. He admitted the charade about the letters but said he had already burned the real ones. But he still maintained they were perfectly innocent: Mary had been seeking Philip's and Alva's aid only against the rebels in her own

Scotland, and that was where the Spanish invasion force was to land. Ross feared, however, that Elizabeth might misunderstand Mary's motives, and that was why he felt it best to get rid of the papers. Asked who "30" and "40" were, Ross insisted they were merely the Spanish Ambassador and Mary herself: again all perfectly innocent.

And so things lay. From her confinement in Sheffield, Mary penned letter after letter to Elizabeth tearfully lamenting her wretched state and protesting her loyalty to "her dear sister"; to Burghley, her "trusty cousin," she insisted with wounded innocence that she could not "conjecture in what manner the Bishop of Ross our ambassador might have offended the Queen our good sister" and pleaded for his release. She would have written in her own hand, she added pathetically, but "the debility of our person would not permit us through sickness we have been vexed with."

From France, Walsingham picked up one thread of the mystery. In May 1571, he wrote Burghley that he had heard of Ridolfi's meeting with Alva and the fact that he was carrying with him letters of credence from the Spanish Ambassador in London; after a long conference with Alva, the Florentine had continued on to see both the Pope and the King of Spain. But what Ridolfi's secret business was, Walsingham had been completely unable to determine.

The break in the case came obliquely, explosively, in August. A merchant reported to Burghley a strange business that he thought his Lordship should know of. The merchant had been asked by the Duke of Norfolk to carry a shipment north. The load seemed unusually heavy; upon investigation, it turned out to be £600 in gold, plus several letters in cipher.

Burghley quickly arrested the Duke's secretary and ordered a search of the Duke's great London house. He was hoping to find the cipher key, but his searchers instead found yet another cipher letter, hidden, with a subtlety well befitting the Duke's skills as a conspirator, under a mat at the entrance to his bedroom.

The Duke's sweating secretary at this point, under further interrogation, suddenly remembered that the Duke had received letters in cipher from the Queen of Scots; it was a point that had slipped his mind until then.

The Bishop of Ross, who had passed a not unpleasant summer in the custody of the Bishop of Ely at his country house, hunting and amiably debating theology, was now brought to the Tower and threatened with more rigorous interrogation himself. He pleaded diplomatic immunity; Burghley countered with a written opinion from the Doctors of Law that "an ambassador procuring an insurrection or rebellion in the Prince's country toward whom he is an ambassador" has forfeited this privilege; whereupon Ross spilled his guts.

Norfolk, he confessed, had been in on the plot from the start. The Duke was in fact the mysterious "40" to whom Ridolfi's progress report had been addressed; "30" was Lord Lumley, a leading Catholic nobleman. Ridolfi had carried letters and money from the Pope to advance the effort. Norfolk had refused to put his name directly to the letters Ridolfi had carried abroad from de Spes, letters that Ross now admitted laid out the whole invasion plan to Alva and the Pope; but Ross and Ridolfi had personally assured de Spes that Norfolk had given his word that he subscribed to the plan, and on that basis the Spanish Ambassador had agreed to lend his support. The plan that Norfolk had endorsed envisioned the Catholic lords assembling 20,000 infantry and 3,000 horse; Alva would supply 6,000 arquebusiers, 3,000 horse, and 25 pieces of field artillery. Harwich was the port most suitable for the invasion force. The plan also called for two diversionary forces, 2,000 men each, to be sent to Scotland and Ireland. Included in Ridolfi's letters were a list of 40 English noblemen likely to stand with the rebellion.

Ross was so terrified of the rack that once he began confessing he could scarcely stop. He dashed off a letter to Mary commending her henceforth to trust only to God; it was obviously His providence that so misguided a plot as this had been uncovered. In a rush of anguish, Ross blurted out to his interrogator, Dr. Thomas Wilson, that Mary had practically murdered all three of her husbands, was unfit to be any man's wife.

"Lord, what a people are these!" Thomas remarked to Burghley afterward. "What a Queen, and what an ambassador."

The plot was ludicrous in many ways; it would much later be known that, although Alva approved of its purpose, he thought Ridolfi a fool and that an invasion made sense only if Elizabeth was first killed or deposed. "A man like this," Alva wrote to Philip of Ridolfi, "who is no soldier, who has never witnessed a campaign in his life, thinks that armies can be poured out of the air, or kept up one's sleeve, and he will do with them whatever fancy suggests."

Realistic or not, it was indubitably treasonous. Norfolk was re-arrested and, "falling on his knees, confessed his undutiful and foolish doings," reported the gentlemen who had been sent to bring him to the Tower. The Duke was carried through the streets of London "without any trouble," his escorts added, "save a number of idle, rascal people, women, men, boys, girls, running about him, as the manner is, gaffing at him."

The realm's last duke was arraigned and condemned by a jury of his peers, and sent to the scaffold on the 2nd of June 1572. The Spanish Ambassador was expelled; in a parting shot, he tried to encourage two glory-dreaming English Catholics to assassinate Burghley, a plot that promptly unraveled when the men sent an anonymous letter to Burghley warning him of it themselves.

Ridolfi dispatched one final letter to Mary from Paris, lamenting that circumstances, alas, did not permit him to return to England. Made a Senator of Rome by the Pope, he peacefully lived out the remainder of his eighty years, dying in his native Florence in 1612.

Ross, and Baillie, were eventually released: All things come to those who wait.

Mary was ordered to reduce the size of her entourage to sixteen servants. She wrote more pathetic pleas to Elizabeth and Burghley bemoaning her "feeble state" and that of her faithful, dismissed servants.

To Walsingham, in Paris, the breaking of the Ridolfi plot merely confirmed his growing convictions that Mary was the enemy, pure and simple, the focus of all of that threatened Elizabeth and her realm; sooner or later she would have to be dealt with, as would the power of Catholic France and Spain. The French Protestants had already seen in Mary the same threat the English had; there were her Guisean connections, her fatal allure, her symbolism as a rallying point for resurgent Catholicism everywhere; if ever Scotland and England were brought back to the old religion, the Protestants of the Continent would be isolated and soon exterminated.

In the wake of the Saint Bartholomew's massacres, which came just two months after Norfolk's execution, all of those points took on a more sinister appearance. If they had not destroyed Mary, recent events now at least gave the Protestants some vivid material with which to tarnish the Scottish Queen's reputation; and in the flood of pamphlets that they now began churning out to tell their side of Saint Bartholomew there was a propaganda opportunity to do some good work against Mary, too. Walsingham almost certainly had a part in the clandestine publication and distribution of a French version of a pamphlet that itemized in lurid but exacting detail all of the sordid charges against her and her lover Bothwell. An English version of the same work had been secretly published in London the year before, in an edition made to look as if it had been printed in Scotland; the French edition similarly bore an Edinburgh imprint, again almost surely a false trail. When the book began appearing in France, the French Ambassador in London was instructed to bring a protest to Elizabeth for allowing the printing of such a slanderous book; Elizabeth innocently replied that it must have been printed in Scotland or Germany, since she certainly would not have permitted it in England. It may actually have been printed in France; but there is no doubt that the English embassy in Paris had a hand in seeing it got to the right people.

But this was a sideshow, as Walsingham well knew.

"So long as that devilish woman lives," he wrote Burghley, neither would her Majesty "continue in quiet possession of the crown, nor her faithful subjects assure themselves of safety of their lives."

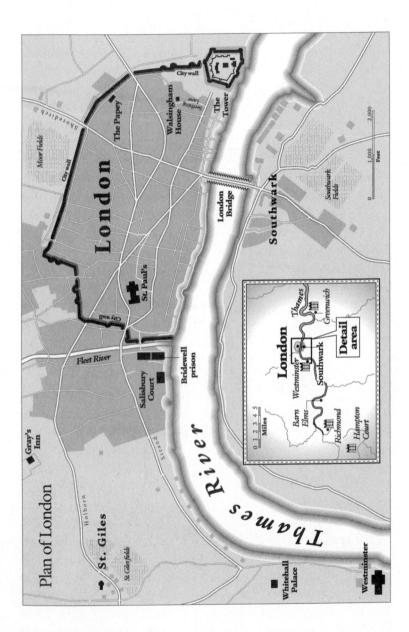

6

INTELLIGENCERS AND SCOUNDRELS

If ever there were a land in need of men adept in the black arts of espionage, betrayal, and subversion, it was England; faction-ridden, ungovernable, outnumbered, hand-tied, outspoken England. It was in London that all the jagged seams of English society and English polity came so jaggedly together, and where such men could surely be found, if one knew the right places to look for them.

The London that Francis Walsingham returned to in May 1573 from his embassy to France was noticeably altered from the city he had left just two and a half years earlier, dramatically altered from the pockmarked urban wreck he had known as a student at Gray's Inn two decades before. In the 1550s, the ruins of the dissolved and demolished religious houses still lay in heaps, an ugly embroidery of gashes and scars across the cramped face of the walled medieval town. Sir Philip Hoby, who was in a position to know since he had traveled far and wide as an ambassador on the Continent, called the London of 1557 "a stinking city, the filthiest in the world."

It had since become a great city, the third largest in Europe, England's unquestioned capital of politics, finance, trade, shipping, society, religion, a city whose fame was known, it was said, in Persia. It still stank: there was no helping that amid the torrent of slops dumped in streets and courtyards and the offal of slaughtered cattle in the marketplaces and the detritus of leatherworkers and the noisome creeks and inlets and the rotting heads of traitors stuck up on the pikes over London Bridge. And then there was the historical and geographical fact that the city walls still stood where the Romans had first placed them, a small circumscribed arc running from the Tower in the east to the River Fleet in the west, lines laid out a millennium earlier by a Roman general to defend a great empire's minor provincial outpost, now the confining bounds to a hundred thousand souls who lived and labored and ate and sweated and defecated and gave birth and died practically atop one another all within 330 acres of meandering medieval lanes. Medieval; and crowded; and cast in perpetual shadows by the overhanging upper stories of their cheek-by-jowl houses.

The plague of 1563 had wiped out a quarter of the city's teeming masses; but England's burgeoning prosperity, carried on a tide of coal and woolens and overseas ventures, and London's unassailable claim to be England's only city worth a fart, counteracted even that collapse with a boom that drew thousands of new dwellers to the capital each year, from across the land and from across the seas. And so the monasteries had at last been cleared, or their better halls kept and taken over for use by the city's wealthy guilds; and to the west, toward Westminster and the royal palace of Whitehall, grand town houses of the nobility now stretched along the Strand, each with its private stairs down to the Thames, for boats were the fastest and least troublesome way to travel about the crowded city, or to get to Greenwich or Richmond when the Court removed to the Queen's palaces there; and Thomas Gresham's Royal Exchange, with its great open piazza and arcaded colonnade and hundred shops for goldsmiths and armorers and financiers, had opened on the east end of Cheapside, heralding London's arrival as the great center of European trade and finance it had become.

And with the grandeur of prosperity came the squalor of prosperity, for each year the city burst a bit more to accommodate the destitute and the adventurers and the ambitious and the refugees drawn by hope or impelled by need. Within the city, hovels and tenements jostled with grand houses and merchants' stalls; just beyond the gates, beyond the reach of the law of the good bourgeois aldermen, the filthy cottages of the poor crowded along the main roads to the north and the east, colonizing the fields where cattle had grazed but a few years before. Farther out, the brick kilns of Islington attracted the more desperate, the homeless unemployed looking for a warm place to sleep while they scrounged for work. And across the river, to the south, the suburb of Southwark teemed with shipwrights and sailors and semi-skilled craftsmen and foreigners and prostitutes, and with the crowds who frequented prostitutes and the bull-baitings and bear-baitings nearby.

The watermen who jammed the Thames calling "Westward ho!" and "Eastward ho!" for fares, and the carriers who carted in water to all who could afford to save themselves from the sickness and death of drinking right from the foul river, and the speculators who divided up some of the old decaying palaces of the wealthy into rude tenements, and the prostitutes, and the bull-baiters, and the butchers, and the tavern keepers, and the prison wardens, all saw little to choose between grandeur and squalor: demand was demand, and prosperity was prosperity.

It was not democracy; but London's hugger-mugger jumbling together of rich and poor, merchants and seamen, aristocrats and tradesmen, cosmopolitans and vagabonds, foreigners and yokels, meant that all kinds of men crossed paths in London's streets and alleys and churches. The parish register of Walsingham's church in London lists them all in their succinct catalogue of baptisms, marriages, and burials: knight, parson, stranger; baker, cobbler, carpenter; gentleman, silkweaver, scrivener; merchant, blackamoor, vintner, broker, sugarmaker, porter. And so they all lived upon and walked upon the same streets, and rubbed elbows in the same taverns, and occasionally even the same prisons; and they heard things, and knew things, well outside the conventional stations that Elizabethan society assigned men to.

The house that Walsingham returned to in London was—suitable irony—known to all as the Papey; it had been a hospital for poor priests before being dissolved by Edward VI. Though the name was actually archaic and had nothing to do with popes, papists, or papistry, everyone believed it did. The house, which had a large courtyard and garden, faced the London wall in the Aldgate Ward at the end of the Saint Mary Axe Street. Walsingham's old friend Thomas Heneage lived across the lane in a great house that had belonged to the Abbots of Bury; Thomas Gresham lived nearby.

Walsingham was still Burghley's protégé, but he was also Leicester's now: Leicester the Queen's favorite, the dashing courtier, expert jouster and equestrian, exactly the sort of man the Queen loved, the man rumored to be her lover indeed; cultured, magnificent physique, master of courtly banter and witty repartee; a man whose recent sudden eruption of Protestant zeal would have been a pathetic disguise for patent political ambition if anyone had dared to point out its craven, neck-saving expediency, coming as it did so hard on the heels of his dabbling in the Catholic intrigue that had landed Norfolk's neck in the noose, but no one did dare. Still, everyone knew. Leicester was the perfect courtier, civil and well mannered to all, self-controlled, never giving sway to his passions, but even that only reinforced the impression of self-serving calculation and guile. He so outrageously, so unscrupulously seized on whatever expedient argument or alliance would advance his own interests that it was a marvel even to his friends. Leicester had thrown in his lot with Norfolk's fumbling attempts to unseat Burghley back in 1569, and had suffered the withering coldness of royal disfavor for it. But he had kept far enough out of it to avoid anything worse than coldness; and now he saw in the Puritans and Walsingham an alliance that might achieve the same end, Burghley's ouster and his own advancement, yet ever more safely.

And so, even while Walsingham was still in France, Leicester had showered him with flattering letters about his influence and achievements. "You know what opinion is here of you, and to what place all men would have you unto," Leicester assured him in January 1573. "The place you already hold is a Councilor's place, and more than a Councilor's place for a time, for ofttimes Councilors are not made partakers of such matters as you are acquainted withal."

On the 20th of December 1573, Elizabeth formally named Walsingham to the post of Principal Secretary, succeeding Burghley, who had become Lord Treasurer; the next day, Walsingham was sworn in as a Privy Councilor.

Neither office, Councilor or Secretary, had powers or duties well defined by law, or even by tradition. Everything in the half-medieval–half-modern, half-amateur–half-professional government of Elizabeth depended upon the personality and influence of the men who held the posts. There were seventeen Privy Councilors, but only thirteen of those had ever shown up for a meeting, and usually only five or six attended. Before long, as the Spanish Ambassador observed, there were only three who really mattered: Burghley, Leicester, and Walsingham. The Queen's trust, and favor, and—at least in Burghley's and Walsingham's cases—their boundless capacity for work, were what determined their true power.

The Council had once been huge, ceremonial, and perfunctory; under Elizabeth's father, Henry VIII, it had become much smaller and more a genuine body of advisers; now, because of both the crush of business and Elizabeth's faith in those three, the Council wielded vast and real executive and judicial powers, meeting every day, Sundays not excepted, often both mornings and afternoons. The Queen never sat at the Council herself, but it was through the Council that royal power was now unquestionably exercised: enforcing the laws; supervising the Councils of the North and the West and Wales, which administered royal authority in the hinterlands; regulating trade and the church; censoring the press; organizing and supplying the army and navy, making war and peace—behaving, as the Venetian Ambassador commented, like "so many kings" themselves.

The office of Principal Secretary depended even more on the man who held it. "All officers and councilors of State have a prescribed authority by patent, by custom, or by oath," wrote a later holder of the post, "the Secretary only excepted." Lord Treasurer, Lord Keeper, Lord Chancellor, Chancellor of the Exchequer, Attorney-General, and so on down to Master of the Horse, Receiver of the Ships, Cofferer of the Household, Foreign Apposer—whose sole job it was to appose a green wax seal upon sheriffs' financial accounts—they all had their duties that no man could challenge. But the Secretary had no power and every power; he could take almost any authority of the government into his own hands, and with it the risk, for his neck was completely exposed: "Only a Secretary hath no warrant or commission in matters of his own greatest peril, but the virtue and word of his sovereign."

Burghley had taken the power and the risk that Elizabeth offered him, greatly expanding the office from that of factotum or clerk in the royal household ·to the chief office of state, the most all-encompassing, the most flexible, and the most dangerous to its occupant. Now Walsingham was prepared to do the same; as his secretary Nicholas Faunt would later describe the post as Walsingham had filled it, "Amongst all particular offices and places of charge in this state there is none of more necessary use, nor subject to more cumber and variableness than is the office of the Principal Secretary."

The very absence of a traditional office of state to handle foreign affairs made the burgeoning of such matters in Elizabeth's reign fall naturally upon the ill-defined, ever-protean secretaryship, and here Walsingham's mark was at once everywhere seen and felt, too. Practically every letter abroad was signed by him and many were written by his own hand. The letters from England's ambassadors abroad all came into his hands as well. No particular law or custom decreed that an ambassador worked for the Secretary; indeed, an ambassador was by custom a representative of the sovereign himself. But Walsingham steadily gathered these reins into his hands, and if he could not always control the appointment of ambassadors, he had a way of having his men in the secondary positions; and if he could not always control what instructions the Queen gave her ambassadors, he had a way of shaping the information that came in from them and seeing to it that some of their letters came to the notice of the Queen and Council, and others somehow never quite did.

Like Burghley before him, Mr. Secretary Walsingham filled book upon book with records of every diplomatic matter, every fact or bit of data that might prove useful in England's dealings abroad. His office was piled high with such books: books of copies of treaties, and records of negotiations, and papers on the necessity of moving England's trading operations from Antwerp to Emden; instructions to ambassadors and to "sundry persons sent into France," and "a memorial for Flanders, with the names of all martial men dispersed through the realm and other gentlemen fit to take charge"; and "sundry discourses" on Flanders, and Germany, and Poland, and France, and Italy, and Spain, and Barbary; and an extract of an ordinance by the King of France concerning the suppression of piracy; and "a small book concerning the values of foreign coins and rates to reduce any foreign coin to sterling, and so & contra"; and so on and on.

And then, on top of all of these foreign papers, there was an even greater heap, an avalanche, of books and papers devoted to all of the domestic affairs that also fell within the Secretary's endless purview. Walsingham's office ledger went on page after page, cataloguing them all: a book of castles and fortifications, and another of the Queen's houses and parks and forests, and a book of expenses and regulations of the army, and plans for which forces should be dispatched to which ports in case of invasion, and a table of all of the costs entailed in putting a navy vessel to sea for one month, and of the provisions needed to feed six thousand men at sea for two months, and treatises on training militiamen, and lists of known Catholics in every county, and reports of the ecclesiastical commissioners on the examinations of priests, and legal opinions from the Attorney-General, and the names of "ill-affected noblemen," and a schedule of expenses for fortifying the town of Berwick.

And then there were still other things that a Secretary had to know: Walsingham's longtime clerk and brother-in-law, Robert Beale, set it all down in a memorandum he wrote years later, shortly after Walsingham's death. A Secretary, Beale stated, had to "understand the state of the whole realm"; he had to know who was who in every shire and city and town, and the affairs of the English trading companies, and the actions of the Justices of the Peace, and the government's sources of revenue and its expenditures, and the operations of the mint; and while he was at it he had better make sure that the post worked as it was supposed to, and take a look each year at the books of the undersheriffs and the coroners of every shire. It was a good idea if he had a complete set of maps while he was at it. And, of course, he had better log every letter that came in or out, and every expenditure he incurred. And, of course, he would be the first to be blamed when anything went wrong. And, of course as bad as it might be to displease his prince, there were even worse fates that a Secretary might incur in shouldering so vast and so grave a set of responsibilities: "Remember there is a higher Lord that will exact an account and is able to lay a more grievous punishment of soul and body than any prince can do."

Like Burghley, Walsingham had so mastered everything, so unquestionably made the duties and responsibilities of the office his, that the man quickly became one with the office. Everyone called him "Mr. Secretary," referred to him in the third person even as Mr. Secretary. Even after he was knighted he was not Sir Francis but Mr. Secretary: it was hard to think of him any other way. He was, in short, a phenomenon, a given, as real and as inevitable a fact of London and life as the stones of the city walls, or the rope of the hangman's noose.

———————————— ✺ ————————————

Beale had one other observation about a Principal Secretary's duties that he had gleaned from his long observation of Mr. Secretary Walsingham's methods.

"A Secretary must have a special cabinet," Beale wrote, "whereof he is himself to keep the key, for his signets, ciphers, and secret intelligences, distinguishing the boxes or tills rather by letters than by the names of the countries or places, keeping that only unto himself, for the names may inflame a desire to come by such things."

This was ground Burghley had also silently but thoroughly trodden before—Burghley, with his relentless hunger for knowledge and his remarkable capacity for keeping it to himself once he got it. It was ground that Walsingham now was equally drawn to by his respect for Burghley's genius, and his own instinct, and his gnawing sense of England's precarious position in a dangerous world.

Knowledge is never too dear: and from places obvious and places strange Walsingham saw to it that he was well supplied. There were the official "searchers" at the ports, who would always be curious about travelers arriving on the packet boats from France, and about any written letters they were carrying; there were patrols of horse along the wilds of the Scottish border, always on the lookout for strangers.

Most of his less official suppliers were men who lived in the fissures of Elizabethan society, but respectably, or at least somewhat respectably: men more unconventional than shady. Travelers, merchant adventurers, Scottish exiles living in Italy, Portuguese exiles living in London, English soldiers of fortune in the pay of the Dutch, ships' captains, expatriate traders, a few famous men of letters and science of the day; the playwright Christopher Marlowe, perhaps; the astrologer, alchemist, and charlatan John Dee, perhaps.

They kept their eyes open and reported news; a fleeting trace of the vast net he threw out survived in a curt memorandum drawn up after his death. "The names of sundry foreign places from whence Mr. Secretary Walsingham was wont to receive his advertisements"; a laconic title, a stark list of names: Paris, Rouen, Bordeaux, Rheims, Lyon, Calais, a half-dozen other towns in France; Hamburg, Frankfurt, Prague, Vienna, and a half-dozen others in Germany; ten places in the Low Countries; five in Spain; Venice, Milan, Genoa, Florence, Rome; Denmark; Barbary; Constantinople, Algiers, Tripoli; "some in Ireland"; "upon the Borders and in Scotland at least 10."

Their letters, some frank, some guarded, came by messengers carried no faster than ships could sail and horses could trot, but they came steadily, week after week, telling of court gossip and trade news and naval preparations and movements of troops. This was no "secret service"; most of these men of affairs and men of the world were not even paid for their troubles; they were less spies than reporters.

———— ⚬☙☙⚬ ————

But there were other men, too, men of a kind Walsingham had already begun cultivating during his time in France, men who lived deeper in the shadows, men who could be bought and sold and flattered into betrayal, men who, out of desperation or vanity or a longing to believe in their own importance—or, the cooler ones, out of simple businesslike calculation of what they possessed and what someone else would be willing to pay for—were prepared to undertake more shadowy tasks.

Some of these were simple enough transactions for a neophyte spymaster. Ambassador Walsingham once sought to bribe one of the French Ambassador's men for news from Spain, a commonplace enough transaction: a good many hangers-on about the courts of Europe were the beneficiaries of such "pensions" from foreign princes. But even in those early days, Walsingham set afoot some more elaborate and dangerous games. There was a charade aimed at neutralizing the intrigues in France of a worrisome Irishman, Maurice Fitzgibbon, the former Archbishop of Casel; Walsingham sought out for the job a certain Captain Thomas, a mercenary who had fought for the King of France in the civil wars, an Irish émigré himself, a man presumed to be a good Catholic, and known to be well connected in the French Court. The deposed Archbishop was plainly seeking the help of the Guises for an Irish rebellion against their Protestant English rulers; Thomas offered his services to Casel in the convincing role of supportive fellow countryman. He then brilliantly poisoned the well, arranging an audience for Casel with the Cardinal of Lorraine, to which he ostentatiously accompanied the Archbishop. "Two days after," Walsingham reported, recounting the tale with obvious satisfaction to Burghley, "the Captain was sent for by the Cardinal; and being demanded, what manner of man the Archbishop was, of what estimation in his country, answered to every point as I required him. Since that time, I learn, that the Cardinal maketh not that account of the Archbishop that he looked for at his hands." So much for the Archbishop and his dreams of glory.

These kinds of services did not come for free; this was new territory, and it was a fight to get the Captain the reward Walsingham had promised him. Captain Thomas "hath been a very good instrument for the discovery of the practices against Ireland, which he hath done with the hazarding of his life, if his dealings with me . . . were known," Walsingham implored Burghley. "Surely, my good Lord, if when we promise in these causes consideration, and no regard be had thereto, neither can those of my calling promise reward; nor they to whom we promise give credit to our words, when no fruits follow. I beseech your Lordship, therefore, deal earnestly with her Majesty in this behalf." In the end, Captain Thomas offered to settle for an office under her Majesty "in Ireland his native country, or elsewhere."

Sometimes Walsingham probably paid such men out of his own pocket and hoped to be reimbursed later, or not even that; any great gentleman maintained a household establishment of servants and messengers and secretaries and clerks, and the line between private and public duties was ever blurred. In France he had had an Italian servant, Jacobo Manucci, who kept working for him for years afterward, doing curious little jobs, keeping in touch with other Italians in Paris, and Milan, and the Azores, traveling to odd places—once to Constantinople, even.

And then some of the more genteel forms of practicing against the Queen's enemies Walsingham could just keep in his own hands. For years he strung along some of the Catholic gentry who, implicated in the 1569 northern rebellion, had sought refuge on the Continent. Most settled in the Low Countries; some became pensioners of the King of Spain; all were a source of vague anxiety and worry, certainly a group of men who bore watching. Walsingham found it an easy enough matter to play them like a trout on a line, giving them just enough slack to keep them from spitting out the hook, all the while reeling them slowly in with vague promises and false hopes that their lands in England might be returned to them; returned to them as long, of course, as they foreswore any more-nefarious schemes for regaining their estates and position. Two of them, Thomas Copley and Charles Paget, apparently quite confused as to which end of the line held the hook, offered the Secretary bribes. A psychological opportunity not to be missed: Walsingham replied with indignation. "If you think me mercenary, you mistake me," he wrote back to Copley. The man then, of course, had to explain and backtrack and apologize; he was distantly related to Walsingham's wife, and was merely proposing to grant "his cousin" as a favor a pension of a hundred pounds per year from the income of his restored property. This was good for another year of backing and forthing, another year when powerful men in exile who might have spent their time plotting revolution and revenge instead spent their time fretting over their future income.

But for the rougher and darker stuff there was no substitute for cash on the barrelhead, and men hungry enough or low enough to do what the more genteel neither would nor could. It was all well and good to rely on merchants and travelers for casual news, but when he wanted specific information about an Irish adventurer seeking Spanish help for an invasion and rebellion, Walsingham sought out a man to pose as a merchant, provided him with a ship and a cargo of corn, and dispatched him to Portugal: not a cheap enterprise. When it came to a scheme to kidnap the papal legate as he traveled to France by sea and interrogate him about papal plots, Walsingham thought that Huguenot pirates might do; in the end, he dropped that idea, but his reading of the men required for the task was right enough.

And though any Englishman abroad might pose as a malcontent Catholic refugee, an easy enough disguise, and thereby hope to work his way into the confidences of the Spanish and French and Italian and English-émigré circles, it was also easy enough to get killed in the process, and in ignoble enough ways that appealed to few idealists or well-born. A man named Best, in Walsingham's service, befriended the Spanish Ambassador's secretary in Paris under such a pretense; one night a suspiciously staged fracas erupted outside the embassy, and when the man went out into the street to investigate he was killed, the perpetrators vanishing into the night.

<hr>

Such men might of course still claim to work for noble purposes; one Thomas Rogers, alias Nicholas Berden, wrote Walsingham's secretary a protestation of his motives that has become famous in the annals of hypocritical high-mindedness. "I profess myself a spy, but am not one for gain but to serve my country," Berden proclaimed.

"Whensoever any occasion shall be offered wherein I may adventure some rare and desperate exploit such as may be for the honor of my country and my own credit, you shall always find me resolute and ready to perform the same." Fine words. On another occasion, Berden was ingenuously describing how he had arranged to shake down two Catholic prisoners in English jails, one for £20, one for £30, if his Honor saw fit to arrange their release: "The money will do me great pleasure, being now in extreme need thereof, neither do I know how to shift longer without it."

Berden, to be sure, displayed a certain genius in his role as scoundrel. An ordinary spy might seek the confidence of his marks by feigning innocence, but Berden instead chose to parade his corruption: he sought to pass himself off as a man who could do them a good turn by knowing the right people to bribe at Court; and so every pound he took increased his credit with them, even as it lined his purse.

But most of Walsingham's paid scoundrels of this ilk had the decency to drop the pretense of high-mindedness; it was money they wanted, and there was not much they wouldn't do to get it. If the exile community abroad offered one route to penetrate the English Catholic malcontents, then the cesspool of the English prisons offered a shorter and fouler one, and there were ever men ready to dive in for a few pounds here and there. One Maliverny Catlyn, a soldier who had gotten in trouble with his commander, fled to France in fear of his life, and was scrounging for his survival, had himself cast into prison in Portsmouth, and then in the Marshalsea in Southwark; from both he sent Walsingham diligent reports of the gossip and confidences of the Catholic prisoners there. Walter Williams, who had been a servant of the very Thomas Copley who had tried to bribe Walsingham, was induced to enter the prison in Rye on a similar errand. "I have been a long time upon bare ground in my clothes and at night lodged among thieves and rovers in a place not fit for men but dogs," he wrote Walsingham, promising results—and pleading for money.

They *all* pleaded for money. "I and mine are like to keep the coldest

Christmastide that hitherto we ever tasted," Catlyn wrote; Walsingham sent him £5. "I owe my host in London above £4 who threatens to have me in prison for the same," begged one Robert Barnard, who boasted he "was never in better credit with the papists" than he was at the moment. A David Jones who haunted various London prisons seeking information about Catholic priests revealed that a Mrs. Cawkin, who had saved him from starvation, was nonetheless a "notorious papist"; he beseeched one of Walsingham's secretaries, "I pray that you desire my master that I may have the benefit of what she doth lose by statute even if it be but the chain she doth wear."

Mr. Secretary had no delusions about the quality of the work such men provided in their venal bargains; he had seen enough of men and their motives to know what money bought and what it did not buy. And so he was never particularly shocked or disappointed. Certainly he took none of it personally: he wasn't looking for friendship or devotion or idealism. His idealism he carried within; from the world, all he looked for was realism.

And so he had no reason to expect subtlety or finesse from these men. The waters needed to be covered, and he covered them with the material available, and he made of it what he could. "Hear all reports but trust not all; observe them that deal on both hands lest you be deceived": those were Robert Beale's words of advice from his observation of the master at work. Mr. Secretary knew the men who would do these jobs; they were lowlifes, they could also be fools, they could also be playing a double game; he took nothing for granted but sought ways to take the measure of each for what he was worth. Walter Williams was one fool: in the prison in Rye, he had been placed in a cell with a Catholic priest he hoped to ferret out, and Walsingham later got his hands on a mock letter of recommendation that Williams's cellmate had smuggled out to warn his fellow Catholics in Paris against him. "His devotion towards the good ale is very substantial," the priest gravely reported; "for his honesty, if it be true as is reported, he never toucheth maid but from the knee upward. His qualities are such as if I should write them, I should be too tedious unto your reverence, whose wisdom is such that you can see, by these few, conjecture and judge of the rest." So could Secretary Walsingham.

This was still no secret service, these scrapings of the dregs of society, but it still took money, and by the end of his first decade in office, Mr. Secretary would be getting the government to provide it, first a drop, then torrents: warrants for £750 on the Exchequer in 1582, increasing year after year until it reached the prodigious sum of £2,000 a year a few years later.

The money, as the Secretary's office ledger simply noted, was to be delivered "to such persons as Sir Francis Walsingham shall name."

7

ADVERSARIES AND MOLES

In the realm over whose depths and breadths Francis Walsingham now bore so heavy a responsibility in his post of Principal Secretary, peace reigned: but an uneasy peace.

From the north came strange reports of omens that were soon on everyone's lips. In Northumberland, a white Saint Andrew's cross was seen in the sky, and on the ground near it a wolf, chasing the largest among a great herd of deer; the wolf was an animal no longer known in England. Though the predator did not reappear after that first sighting, each day the lone deer returned for two or three hours to the same place, where it was seen running about in terror. The general opinion, reported the Spanish government's agent in London, was that these appearances were "portents of some great occurrence."

In Scotland, the regent Moray had been assassinated; the same miasma of clan and family and blood and power sucked in the pro-English and pro-Mary factions alike. Ever unstable, ever venal, ever susceptible to foreign intrigues, an ever shifting coalition of lords sought the mantle of the regency and the personal custody of the very young King James. Scotland, Walsingham had once said, was the "postern gate" from which trouble was always threatening to sally forth; his hopes of shutting it up once and for all now seemed destined to fail.

Queen Elizabeth and the monarch of Spain continued to exchange messages filled with courtly civilities; their ambassadors sent back reports filled with suspicion and bile. Even the outward façade was becoming hard to maintain. Burghley still hoped to preserve amity or at least neutrality with Spain; he worked to keep English aid to the Dutch rebels to a level of plausible deniability, nothing more than an adroit turning of a blind eye to the English "volunteers" who went to fight by their side; he patiently negotiated with the Duke of Alva for three years to smooth over yet another trade war that had erupted between England and the Spanish Netherlands. But it proved impossible even to keep a regular English ambassador in Spain, so palpable was the religious enmity now. Walsingham, dismissing a proposed treaty with Spain in 1575, insisted that no true reconciliation was ever possible as long as the two countries disagreed on religion: "Christ and Belial can hardly agree."

Philip, ordering one more English emissary home a few years later, chose a somewhat different allusion to their religious differences. The man had better leave as quickly as possible, the Spanish King observed, "before he commits some indiscretion which will force us to burn him."

❧⳩⳩❧

In the mid-1570s the stench of Saint Bartholomew still hung in the air, and the poison of the Ridolfi plot; the ground below had meanwhile shifted, too. On the 25th of May 1570, a bill had appeared on the garden gate of the Bishop of London, nailed there anonymously in the night. The text was a papal bull that had been issued by Pius V three months earlier, news of which had not yet reached England.

The title was *Regnans in Excelsis*, "The Lord Who Reigns on High." Its words thundered with Old Testament promises of vengeance; it was, in short, a declaration of war, of religious war, a declaration that aligned the fault lines of religion and politics for England, and for Europe:

> The Lord who reigns on high instituted a Church which should be one, and gave its government to Peter, and his successors. We labor with all our might to preserve that unity, now assailed by so many adversaries. Among them is that servant of infamy, Elizabeth, who styles herself Queen of England, the refuge of wicked men.
>
> Having taken possession of the kingdom, she monstrously

usurps the chief authority in the Church and fills the royal Council with heretics.

We declare the said Elizabeth a heretic, and a fautor of heretics, and that all who adhere to her incur the sentence of anathema, and are cut off from the unity of the Body of Christ.

Moreover, that she has forfeited her pretended title to the aforesaid kingdom, and is deprived of all dominion, dignity, and privilege. We declare that nobles, subjects, and peoples are free from any oath to her, and we interdict obedience to her monitions, mandates, and laws.

The ardent English Catholic who had nailed up the order of excommunication was soon found, and tortured, and executed. The effects of the Pope's words were less easily dealt with. In the wake of the 1569 northern rising, Elizabeth had taken pains to reiterate that, in demanding conformity to the practices of the Church of England, she was not in any way instituting an "inquisition" into "men's consciences in matters of religion." Now the Pope's actions had leapt that gulf: whether this was his actual intention or not, he had equated the religious conscience of England's Catholics with treason against the state.

Elizabeth once hoped, and not altogether unrealistically, that Catholicism would simply fade away in England, that its remnants were no more than a sort of administrative problem that could be dealt with by properly regulating the machinery of the church. Pius's bull, with its savage indictment of the Queen herself, made the problem of recusancy rather more personal, and menacing.

The Puritan faction in Parliament now clamored for sterner measures against Catholicism, beyond the existing statutes that simply required weekly attendance by all at Church of England services. In 1571, the first of a series of ever more repressive anti-recusancy laws appeared. One statute made it treason for anyone to declare that the Queen was not the lawful queen, or to name her a heretic, schismatic, tyrant, infidel, or usurper. A second made it treason to bring into the realm any papal bulls, and also banned the importation of "any to-kens, crosses, pictures, beads or suchlike vain and superstitious things from the bishop or see of Rome." And a third, aimed at neutralizing the Catholic fugitives overseas, declared that any Englishman who went abroad without license and failed to return within six months would forfeit all his possessions and profits from all his lands: if, how-ever, he returned to "fully reconcile himself with the true religion," he might be permitted to recover his lands after a year had passed.

Meanwhile, more alarming reports of Catholic resurgency soon began to filter in to the government. A seminary for training English priests had been founded at Douai, in the Spanish Netherlands, in 1568, by Dr. William Allen, an English Catholic scholar who had re-signed his post at Oxford and fled abroad early in Elizabeth's reign. Now the first of these Douai priests began smuggling their way back into England, sheltering in the houses of secret Catholics, holding stealthy masses and preaching a return to the old religion. The first few arrived in 1575 and achieved a success that immediately sent a chill down Puritan spines. Within a few years, more than a hundred missionary priests had reached English soil.

A seamy fraternity of priest-takers soon had a fine career for them-selves, tearing apart houses in search of hidden priests. But these were not Walsingham's men: Mr. Secretary took a longer and cooler view of the matter. For one thing, the capture, torture, and sadistic execu-tion of priests cut two ways, as Walsingham saw sooner than many of his equally zealous colleagues. It was actually a source of common pride in England—so different from those filthy foreigners—that torture was not the law of the land; it took a warrant from the Coun-cil to authorize it, and generally the rack was reserved for rare cases of state security. Only fifty-three warrants were issued in all of Eliza-beth's reign, but even these caused unease when some of the seamy details leaked out, particularly when it came to the torture of priests, and particularly when it came to the tortures inflicted by one Richard Topcliffe, who was always begging the Queen for permis-sion to practice his artistry. Besides the rack, Topcliffe especially enjoyed suspending prisoners in manacles with their feet just barely touching the floor. He also apparently engaged in embarrassing sexual fantasies while he was at it; one priest who was his victim took the opportunity of his public trial to provide a verbatim account in open court of the monologue Topcliffe had delivered while racking him: Topcliffe had said that "he was so great and familiar with her Majesty that he may putteth his hands between her breasts and paps . . . that he hath not only seen her legs and knees, but feeleth them with his hands above her knees; that he hath felt her belly and said unto her Majesty that she hath the softest belly of any womankind."

Topcliffe was also fond of attending the executions of condemned priests and seeing to it that they were cut down from the rope at once: otherwise, they would not still be alive when they were boweled and quartered by the executioner.

Topcliffe was not Walsingham's man, either. And though Catholic pamphleteers would later seek to vilify Walsingham as being cut from the same cloth—"not content with mocking and bullying and insulting the confessors of the faith of Jesus Christ, but who even went so far as to beat them and kick them," claimed one—he in fact consistently counseled against persecution for persecution's sake. Walsingham's secretary Robert Beale made so bold as to publish a pamphlet strongly denouncing torture of any kind, and under any circumstance, as cruel and barbaric and contrary to English law and liberties. And Walsingham himself argued that it was generally a mistake even to execute priests, "saving in a few for example's sake": the "constancy, or rather obstinancy," shown by the condemned priests, Walsingham warned, who often went bravely to their very public and very gruesome ends, "moveth men to compassion and draweth some to affect their religion upon conceipt that such an extraordinary contempt of death cannot but proceed from above." It was more prudent policy just to imprison the "learned and politic" among the missionary priests, Walsingham concluded, and as for the rest, those with "more zeal than wit or learning," simply to ship them back to France or Rome, where they could do no more harm.

Mr. Secretary Walsingham also had a rather different reaction from most to the fact that idealistic young English Catholics were flocking to Douai to attend Dr. Allen's college (or, later, to a second such seminary for English priests established in Rome in 1579). The influx of these foreign-trained Englishmen was an escalation in the religious warfare; it was also an opportunity. It was not hard for Mr. Secretary to learn from his well-connected spies in English Catholic circles how the priests were smuggled into the country (most came in on French boats that put into Newcastle for coals, each supplied by Dr. Allen with a new suit of clothes and six or seven pounds in cash). Nor was it hard to learn of the internal enmities that were threatening to split the seminaries into rival factions along theological and nationalistic lines (the English and Welsh were at each other's throats). It would likewise not be hard to inflame those feelings and sabotage the missionaries at their source, a more appealing proposition than tracking them all over England. And it would not be hard to infiltrate a more daring man or two into one of these hotbeds of Catholic zeal to penetrate any more nefarious plans they might have afoot beyond simply sending priests to England to say mass in some recusant's attic. (One who would sow dissension and feed information with particular aplomb was Solomon Aldred, the tailor at the English College at Rome, who enjoyed a pension from the Pope and the secret patronage of Mr. Secretary.)

No, the priests were at worst a distraction, a sideshow; at best a means, not an end. It was what the English Catholics might do rather than what they believed that had ever been the real worry to Walsingham, Puritan though he was, political realist that he was. And what they might do in England came down, as always, to what they might do for the imprisoned Queen of Scots.

Secretary Walsingham more than once proposed that the real solution to *that* problem was to arrange to have the lords of Scotland request Mary's transfer to their custody, followed by her prompt execution; but the lords balked at shouldering all the blame themselves for so drastic a step, while Elizabeth was insistent that her hands must be kept at least superficially clean in any such transaction. And so the dangerous limbo had continued.

Mary, for her part, had no doubt where the English Secretary stood: in a letter she wrote in August 1574 to the Archbishop of Glasgow, her ambassador in Paris, she called Walsingham "my mortal enemy."

The knowledge and the feeling, in other words, were now complete, and mutual.

A few months earlier, in May 1574, Mr. Secretary had received a less personal but rather more interesting report regarding the Scottish Queen's correspondence. An eighteen-year-old Scot named Steward had been arrested in Scotland and confessed that he had been employed as a secret courier for Mary. He would meet a man in Doncaster, in northern England, who would hand him packets of letters to be delivered to Mary's friends in Scotland. This man's name was Alexander Hamilton: he was the tutor to the children of the Earl of Shrewsbury, keeper of Mary Queen of Scots.

Walsingham had Hamilton sent to London to be questioned; the man denied everything. Lacking any evidence but the uncorroborated word of a Scottish lad who prudently declined to be interviewed in England, Walsingham was forced to let Hamilton go. The man returned to his position in Shrewsbury's household. But Mr. Secretary was hardly about to let the rest of the matter go so easily.

The Ridolfi plot had made plain the dangers of allowing Mary to communicate freely with her supporters; all of her correspondence was now supposed to be handed to Shrewsbury. That Mary had contrived a clandestine channel of communication presented an ongoing danger; it was also an acute warning in itself that a new scheme for her liberation might be afoot at that very moment. And so Mr. Secretary quietly continued his watch.

In January 1575, another thread appeared: a letter from the Bishop of Ross to one of his servants was intercepted by the Regent of Scotland and forwarded to Mr. Secretary, and it pointed to a far larger network of secret communications. A London bookseller named Henry Cockyn was the hub, and the spokes connected him not only to Mary and Ross but also to a number of prominent men of the country, most notably Lord Henry Howard—the brother of the recently executed Duke of Norfolk.

Cockyn was promptly arrested. He admitted knowing Howard and the other men, but insisted they were just customers of his. Mr. Secretary was named to a committee of three to investigate Cockyn further.

Once again Walsingham preferred subtlety and patience to the cruder methods customarily employed. "I think the show of torture will little prevail, but rather make him more obstinate," Walsingham cautioned. And keeping Cockyn locked up was paying dividends in any event: "The best is that certain Scottishmen lately come over, and having letters to convey, do find great miss of him."

A few weeks of waiting was all it took. On the 22nd of February 1575, Mr. Secretary reported to Elizabeth that Cockyn had made a complete confession:

> Neither by examination nor threatening of torture we could get the party to discover anything. . . . In the end, having great cause to suspect he received some secret pension at the Queen of Scots, which he was loathe to lose, I thought good therefore to run another course with him, assuring him by my letters if that he would discover what he knew (accusing no man wrongfully), I would not only procure your Majesty's pardon, but also send such further consideration as both he and his should be the better for it, and besides that the matter should be handled with such secrecy as he should not be discovered to be an accuser of others.

Cockyn admitted that Ross had approached him in December 1573 to act as a conduit for Mary's letters. He passed and received packets of letters to and from Hamilton; moreover, a number of other servants of Shrewsbury were also involved in the smuggling of Mary's mail.

Four of them were arrested and brought to the Tower, along with two London doctors who had had a part in the matter. But Elizabeth, to Mr. Secretary's distraction, seemed serenely disinclined to take the matter seriously; in particular she refused to pursue the case against Howard (whose letters to Mary, admittedly, seemed innocuous enough). And so the case unraveled.

Warned by the arrests of the others, one Thomas Morgan, who had once been a servant of Shrewsbury's and who was long suspected of having had a key part in many of Mary's conspiratorial doings, made good use of the Queen's repeated delays in deciding how to proceed, and fled to Paris. There he immediately entered the service of the Archbishop of Glasgow and quickly began to assume control of Mary's affairs, her finances, and the more ardent efforts of her growing contingent of powerful friends abroad, English and foreign alike. The others who been taken prisoner were all eventually released.

Walsingham could not conceal his frustration over the way so important a matter had been bungled. As in other moments of crisis, he did not hesitate to tell the Queen exactly what he thought; the steel of inner conviction this time was not even tempered with a self-deprecating joke or a courtly compliment. "Your Majesty's delay used in resolving doth not only make me void of all good hope to do any good therein, the opportunity being lost," he wrote Elizabeth, "but also doth quite discourage me to deal in like causes, seeing mine and other your poor faithful servants' care for your safety fruitless."

To a fellow Councilor he explained that he was not interested in pursuing any vendetta against those who had been named in the matter: "I protest before God I malice none of the parties detected, but rather lament them as one that taketh no delight in another's trouble." Yet: "When I consider that the trouble of a few may avoid a general trouble, I prefer general respects before particular." And, to his colleague Leicester: "Her Majesty's strange dealings in this case will discourage honest ministers that are careful for her safety to deal in the discovery of the sores of this diseased state, seeing her Majesty bent rather to cover them than to cure them."

Walsingham had succeeded in breaking up Mary's secret network of communication but had gotten no further. It was an interesting practical lesson in a dilemma that would vex intelligence chiefs for five centuries thereafter: whether known enemy agents are sometimes better left at large, and watched, and lulled into a false sense of security—rather than exposed and arrested, only to be replaced by others who must then be found afresh.

It was a lesson that Mr. Secretary Walsingham would take to heart the next time he discovered his enemy in secret communication with her friends. On that occasion, *he* would be the one to bide his time.

<hr />

Though it was wrong to speak of "parties" within the Privy Council, Walsingham and Leicester and the younger and more ardent Protestants were increasingly at odds with Burghley and the mostly older, more conservative, and less zealous men who stuck to him. It was becoming personal, too, inevitably: Burghley resentful of the credit that Walsingham, his onetime protégé, now enjoyed on his own.

Politically, the outlines of their differences were becoming ever sharper over policy toward France and Spain. Burghley clung to the venerable English game of balance-of-power diplomacy; playing off France and Spain; drifting to whichever seemed more favorable at the moment. Walsingham wanted to be done with both: a revolution in strategy. He sought to "advance God's glory," he avowed, but there was also a purely pragmatic reason to seek the friendship of Protestant allies: religious ties could be trusted, political ties could not. And in any case, with the Catholic powers drawing together in religious common cause, the Protestant nations had no choice. It was defense of God's will, but it was also self-defense; to fight under these circumstances was to wage a war not of ambition but of necessity, not for aggrandizement but for safety, "not to enlarge but retain," he argued:

> What juster cause can a Prince that maketh profession of the Gospel have to enter into wars than when he seeth confederacies made for the rooting out of the Gospel and the religion he professeth. All creatures are created to advance God's glory; therefore, when His glory is called into question, no league nor

policy can excuse if by all means he seek not the defence of the same, yea, with the loss of life.

Above all, Mr. Secretary wanted Elizabeth to greatly increase support to the rebels in France and the Low Countries, and so vex both of the Catholic powers at once. If "the fire chance to slack," as he once put it, all that would be required would be to "now and then cast in some English fuel which may revive the flame."

Walsingham wanted moral and political clarity; he was an astute enough politician to know what arguments not to try on his own Queen, however. He saved the religious arguments for others. With Elizabeth he concentrated on pragmatism and law. The occasional professions of goodwill that still emanated from Spain, Walsingham warned, were mere ruses to "lull us asleep for a time, until their secret practices be grown to their due and full ripeness." And the Dutch were not "rebels" against their sovereign, he assured Elizabeth, but were in fact loyal countrymen doing nothing more than asserting their ancient and traditional rights that had been unjustly usurped by foreign Spanish governors.

But Elizabeth preferred the temporizing middle course as always; that placed her with Burghley, and a majority of the Council agreed. Walsingham's convictions and desperation for action made an explosion inevitable. He had often tried the Queen's patience with his lectures and his insistent earnestness, but Elizabeth, in recognition of his intelligence and disinterested zeal, tolerated him as she tolerated almost no other councilor who dared speak so plainly. And Walsingham, for all that he confessed he was no expert in handling the Queen the way Burghley was, had known enough to back off prudently at times when he saw he had pressed the Queen too far; when she furiously told him that he cared more about the Puritans than about her own cause, he knew he had to forbear awhile lest he "rather hurt than help" his case.

But now both pressed to the breaking point; and the break came over the ever-volatile matter of the Queen's marriage. In October 1578, Walsingham returned from a mission to the Low Countries that

1. Sir Francis Walsingham

(NATIONAL PORTRAIT GALLERY)

2. The murder of Coligny, depicted in a fresco in the Vatican's Sala Regia

(Art Resource)

3. William Cecil, Lord Burghley

(NATIONAL PORTRAIT GALLERY)

4. Robert Dudley, Earl
of Leicester

(NATIONAL PORTRAIT GALLERY)

5. Elizabeth

(NATIONAL PORTRAIT GALLERY)

6. Mary Queen of Scots

(NATIONAL PORTRAIT GALLERY)

7. The execution of Mary Queen of Scots

8. One of the Ciphers used by Anthony Babington to communicate with the Queen of Scots

9. The Armada

(National Maritime Museum)

10. Walsingham's "platte for intelligence out of Spayne"

(PUBLIC RECORD OFFICE)

11. Sir Philip Sidney

(NATIONAL PORTRAIT GALLERY)

had ended with the usual inconclusive result, the Queen balking at sending her bond for £100,000, which she had earlier promised the rebels. What was worse, Walsingham immediately discovered, was the reason: she was hoping to achieve the same end at less cost and with less chance of directly antagonizing Spain by entertaining the recently renewed marriage suit of Francis, the former Duke of Alençon, who was proposing to lead his own expedition to the Low Countries. Burghley favored the marriage with Francis (who had since succeeded to the title of Anjou, after Monsieur became King of France in 1574): it was marry the Duke or make peace with Spain, he argued. Walsingham opposed it on every possible ground. And, unlike the last time when the Queen's marriage negotiations had so tried his patience, he was now so bold as to make known his views on so personal and sensitive a matter to the Queen.

And so did much of the public: to the Queen's uncontained fury. London bookmakers were laying two-to-one against Anjou's even coming to England to press his suit, three-to-one against the marriage taking place. Preachers in pulpits denounced the very notion of the Queen's wedding a Catholic. Elizabeth threatened to have them whipped. Ballads made the rounds; "A Most Strange Wedding of the Frog and the Mouse," for one, and the one that ended:

> *Therefore, good Francis, rule at home, resist not our desire,*
> *For here is nothing else for thee, but only sword and fire.*

In September 1579, a pamphlet appeared that sent the Queen into a fury that surpassed all her previous outrage and mortification. The author was John Stubbs, a lawyer and country gentleman with strong Puritan ties. The title, unwieldy but unmistakable, was *The discovery of a gaping gulf wherein England is like to be swallowed by an other French marriage, if the Lord forbid not the banns by letting Her Majesty see the sin and punishment thereof.* The text was a masterpiece, combining intimate knowledge of the very arguments that been advanced by opponents of the marriage during secret debates within the Council with a propagandistic appeal to national pride, racial prejudice, detestation of papistry, and none-too-subtle hints that Anjou was syphilitic and the French in general infected with heretical and depraved ideas. "This sickness of mind have the French drawn from those eastern parts of the world, as they did that other horrible disease of the body, and, having already too far westward communicated the one contagion, do now seek notably to infect our minds with the other," Stubbs declared in his slashing prose. The Queen was being "led blindfold as a poor lamb to the slaughter" by "this odd fellow, by birth a Frenchman, by profession a Papist, an atheist by conversation, an instrument in France of uncleanness, a fly worker in England for Rome and France in this present affair, a sorcerer by common voice and fame. . . . This French marriage is the straightest line that can be drawn from Rome to the utter ruin of our Church."

Stubbs and his printer were swiftly discovered and arrested. They were tried and convicted of being "authors and sowers of seditious writings"; on the 3rd of November 1579, each had his right hand stricken off in the marketplace in Westminster. The chronicler Camden related that after the blow fell Stubbs "put off his hat with his left hand and said with a loud voice, 'God save the Queen!'" The crowd "was altogether silent," either out of horror at the punishment, pity toward the man, "or else out of hatred of the marriage, which most men presaged would be the overthrow of religion."

It was never proved, but Elizabeth suspected that some members of the Council were behind Stubbs's work; rumors in Paris certainly linked Walsingham to it; it certainly was his style of logic and invective brilliantly allied, the appeal to both "reason" and "humors." Walsingham's young and close friend Philip Sidney, the brilliant courtier and poet, had also written something that showed familiarity with the inside arguments objecting to the match; though much more tactfully put, it was still highly Puritan and highly provoking.

And so it was upon Walsingham that the Queen's remaining wrath fell. She exploded that the only thing he was good for was to be "a protector of heretics" and bade him "begone." Walsingham left the Court and remained away for the rest of the year. Though he kept his office for now, his future was uncertain.

Walsingham had acquired a country estate, Barn Elms, from the Queen in February of that year, having sold his manor in Kent; it was to Barn Elms he now repaired. Barn Elms stood on a bend of the Thames in Surrey, between London and Richmond: a fine home, surrounded by the elms that gave it its name, glimpses of the drifting river curving along its boundary. Walsingham was a country gentleman by convention; that was what all great men were; but as much as he liked Barn Elms there was unmistakably something of exile in his fate. Though he fussed a bit about his trees, he never had the air of the passionate gardener. And as for other country pursuits, his diaries contain but a single reference to hunting, one day at Windsor. He owned ninety-one horses, sixty-eight of them at Barn Elms, but his poor health often precluded his riding himself. It was exile.

At least his finances had improved considerably since his days of penury doing her Majesty's service in Paris. The office of Secretary carried a salary of £100; his appointment to the ancient and honorable office of Chancellor of the Garter in 1578 brought a pension of £100; and his estates brought in a few hundred more; but he had made something like £17,000 from the sale of licenses to export 108,000 pieces of cloth that the Queen had granted him over the previous five years.

But he could not have been happy at Barn Elms; he had taken ill yet again in August 1579 and was tormented by his obstructed bladder all autumn. A few months into the year 1580, his second daughter, Mary, age seven, died.

In the end, the Anjou courtship became simply a farce, a bit of political theater that dragged on three scenes too long, a joke even to the Queen, as she admitted in moments of privacy and candor.

Elizabeth still coyly hoped to get the French to counterbalance the might of Spain, without actually committing herself to anything; she sadly told the French that she could not proceed with marriage because her subjects opposed it, but she would seek a treaty of friendship and common cause between the two countries.

Mr. Secretary was welcomed back at Court in early 1580; all seemed to have been forgotten. That year, he also moved his London home to a house on Seething Lane, on the northwest boundary of the Tower Ward, where he enjoyed the company of many well-to-do neighbors in "fair and large houses," the Earl of Essex among them.

The following year, Walsingham was sent to Paris to lead the delicate negotiations over the French treaty himself. But it was the same old half-measure. The Queen would entertain a defensive alliance only; any English aid to advance the war against Spain in the Netherlands would have to be completely secret. And, even more infuriatingly, she kept hinting at reviving the possibility of marriage. Walsingham furiously wrote to Burghley from Paris that all of this diplomatic over-cleverness was merely destroying the Queen's credibility; he reported that it was being said that "when her Majesty is pressed to marry then she seemeth to affect a league and when a league is yielded unto then she liketh better of marriage. And when thereupon she is moved to assent to marriage, then she hath recourse to the league, when the motion for the league or any request is made for money then she returneth to marriage."

A weaker or less confident man would have been left chastened and gun-shy by his earlier chastisement and banishment by the Queen, but Walsingham again did not mince words; he boldly told Elizabeth that the French were no fools, that the King of France saw that Elizabeth hoped to goad France into open war with Spain in the Netherlands, and then, when "he should be embarked, your Majesty would slip the collar."

And so Walsingham came home empty-handed: followed hard on his heels by Anjou himself, full of ardent protests of his love for his mistress; the Frenchman also knew how to put the rituals of courtship to good use. It finally cost the Queen £60,000 in promised "loans" to get him to go, and to embark upon his own promised expedition into the Low Countries.

Though Elizabeth affected great tears and lamentations over the departure of her suitor, the Spanish Ambassador, Bernardino de Mendoza, passed on a story he had heard that in the privacy of her bedroom the Queen had danced with joy at the thought of being rid of her "frog" once and for all.

<hr/>

It was not long after Mr. Secretary's return to Court in 1580 that he once again began picking up trails of new Catholic intrigues from his far-flung network of reporters, spies, and purloiners of secret correspondence. The young King James of Scotland was said to be falling dangerously under the sway of his fascinating and dashing French cousin, Esmé Stuart, seigneur d'Aubigny, who had arrived on the scene at the behest of the Guises to assert his claim to the earldom of Lennox. A letter from the Bishop of Ross to Rome was intercepted in Paris; it told of plans by a junta of pro-French Scottish lords to advance the cause of Mary and Catholicism. A Scottish Jesuit, William Creighton, had traveled to Rome and met with the Pope. A letter from Mary to the Archbishop of Glasgow was intercepted and deciphered: she pressed to have the Pope, or the King of France, or the King of Spain, supply the pro-French faction in Scotland with fifteen or twenty thousand crowns in money and five or six hundred arquebusiers. One of the pro-French Scottish lords had been seen in the Low Countries trying to buy arms. The English Catholic refugees abroad were said to be in high spirits. A papal agent in Boulogne got in touch with information to sell, that the Pope and the Duke of Guise were said to be hatching some new scheme for the invasion of England.

In April 1580, a letter was intercepted in France and sent to Mr. Secretary. It was from Rome to a friend of Dr. Allen's, and it reported that two English Jesuit priests had just left Rome "for the English harvest." The appearance of these first Jesuit-trained missionaries, now joining Dr. Allen's seminarians, sent new tremors through the defenders of religion in England; everyone had heard tales of the Jesuits, and Parliament reacted with more draconian defenses of Protestantism. A fine of twenty pounds a year was imposed on Catholics who refused to come to church, two hundred marks on anyone who sang mass, one hundred marks on anyone who heard

mass; penalties of high treason were decreed for the act of withdraw-
ing anyone from the Church of England or securing anyone's obedience to Rome.

In July 1581, the most famous of the Jesuit missionary priests, Edmund Campion, once a distinguished Fellow at Oxford, was tracked
down by a Catholic informer and carried to London, bound hand
and foot with a paper stuck in his hat that declared in great capital
letters, CAMPION THE SEDITIOUS JESUIT. He was mercilessly racked in
the Tower and periodically dragged out to dispute on theological top-
ics at public sessions that were intended to discredit Catholicism but
which, it soon became clear, were only creating sympathy for Campion's pitiful state and calm steadfastness.

Convicted of treason, Campion was taken to Tyburn on the
morning of the 1st of December; called upon to confess, he declared
to the assembled crowd, "I am a Catholic man and a priest. In that
faith have I lived and in that faith do I intend to die; and if you es-
teem my religion treason, then am I guilty. As for any other treason,
I never committed, God is my judge. But you have now what you desire." And so he was hanged, drawn, and quartered.

Walsingham had had nothing to do directly with Campion's interrogation or trial, but he clearly viewed Campion as one of those "few
for example's sake" who ought to be executed. From Paris, where he
had gone on business, Walsingham wrote Burghley, "I pray her
Majesty may take profit of Campion's discovery by severely punish-
ing the offenders, for nothing has done more harm than the over-
much lenity that hath been used in that behalf."

But in the bigger picture, Mr. Secretary was again less concerned
about the role of these invading priests as missionaries than about
their role in more serious threats to the state—and the information
they might be privy to about such threats. And though Campion had
spoken the truth about his innocence of treason, other Jesuits possibly could not make the same claim. And so, when in May 1582 another courier at another border was taken, and was found to be
carrying messages from the Spanish Ambassador Mendoza to the Jesuit Creighton, and the information reached Mr. Secretary in Lon-

don, it was soon clear to him that a new and more dangerous phase in the shadow war had indeed begun.

The courier had been disguised as an itinerant dentist when he was captured by a patrol of the Warden of the Middle Marches on the wild lands along the Scottish border. The "dentist" had promptly bribed the men to secure his release, but he left behind some of his gear, including a looking glass. This was delivered to the Warden, who examined it and found a hidden compartment containing the messages.

Their contents now made clear the full dimensions of the plot whose shadowy outlines only had so far been apparent. It was clear it involved Mary, Philip, Guise, and the Jesuits, all in league together. An invasion of Scotland would be followed by the conversion of the young King James to Catholicism—and then an invasion of England, which would place Mary on the throne.

A few months later, evidence reached Mr. Secretary that the French Ambassador in London had been acting as the key agent in a new system of secret couriers that was once again carrying messages between Mary's supporters and the imprisoned Scottish Queen. Officially, Mr. Secretary was first shown any letters from the French Ambassador to Mary, and they were then sealed up in a packet for delivery. Unofficially, the embassy, it was now apparent, had found some means to circumvent this official inspection to pass along more sensitive correspondence.

The immediate threat in Scotland was dealt with in August 1582, when, prodded by the English government, yet another coup took place, and a group of Protestant lords seized King James yet again and ousted Lennox and his pro-French and pro-Catholic circle.

The problem of Mary's secret correspondence Mr. Secretary now proceeded to tackle with far more subtlety than the last time around. The French Ambassador was an old friend of Walsingham's. Michel de Castelnau, seigneur de Mauvissière, had been one of the French gentlemen-at-arms sent to escort Ambassador Walsingham safely to Court in the terrible days immediately following the Saint Bartholomew's massacres. Mauvissière had been ambassador in

London since 1575. He was a cultured and decent man, now in his sixties; though he did not speak English he liked England and the English, got on well with Elizabeth, enjoyed a wide circle of acquaintances in England. He gave excellent dinners at his residence in Salisbury Court, which stood on the river just outside the western city wall, near the Fleet River and Bridewell Prison. His English friends were many of the leading lights of the age, among them the adventurer Sir Walter Raleigh, the poet Sir Philip Sidney. He was a sincere Catholic who disliked radical Protestantism, but he was also a Renaissance man of the world, an old-fashioned ambassador and a civilized man who cared more about the ennobling friendship of the intellect than the mean divisions of ideology.

He *believed* in friendship: his charm and weakness. He often exchanged courteous notes with Walsingham, assuring his "dear friend" that "you will find me frank and open and ready to do the best offices I can devise." When Mauvissière was beset by scurrilous rumors, "attacking my honor by a gross invention to charge the French in general: inciting a worthless hussy of a woman to make wicked statements about me and of my acts," it was to Walsingham he sent his plea, a plea that bespoke friendship and a bit of injured bewilderment; he, Mauvissière, had served Elizabeth honestly one way or another for twenty-two years, had never complained of anything before, but surely Mr. Secretary his friend could do something to stop these rumors for his sake.

Walsingham did view the ambassador as his friend. Not that that stopped him from at once setting a spy upon the ambassador's household in an effort to penetrate Mary's secret correspondence.

The first attempt went almost nowhere. A Scottish theologian and poet named William Fowler had landed in prison upon arriving from France in the autumn of 1582. The Queen of Scots owed his family money, which gave him a pretext for calling on Mauvissière if he was released from prison, which Mr. Secretary was quite willing to arrange to do on terms. Soon Fowler was haunting the embassy and offering to do the French Ambassador a good turn by keeping him informed of Scottish affairs. But Fowler had turned up nothing of much importance even after six months of this.

It was then, quite out of the blue, that a letter addressed to Mr. Secretary arrived, reporting a small but intriguing tidbit concerning the French Ambassador's affairs:

> 24 April 1583, counting in the French calendar, the ordinary post from the King of France arrived in London at the ambassador's house. In this packet the Duke of Guise sent a letter to the ambassador beseeching him to handle the affairs of the Queen of Scots in England as secretly as he can, and for doing so he will give him a benefice worth 1500 French livres. . . .

Other short reports from this mysterious correspondent followed every few days. The writer was a man who quite assuredly resided in the French Ambassador's house; he wrote in terrible French; and he signed himself—almost surely a jocular pseudonym—Henry Fagot. His reports to Mr. Secretary noted the comings and goings of visitors at the embassy; there were some who came only under dark of night, some only at midnight. They passed on word of money transferred to the Queen of Scots, and of reports received from France that the Duke of Guise himself was intending to be in Scotland "sooner" than anyone expected.

And then, for a few months, nothing more was heard from Henry Fagot; and then a report of a rather different order broke the silence with a crash. Fagot began with some more small matters:

> Monsiegneur I have been a long time without writing to you, the cause of it being that I had not found anything worth writing. But now Monsiegneur that I found something that merits it I would like to let you know. There are two sellers of papist books in the ambassador's house, the cook and the butler. Every two months without fail each makes a trip to France, to

sell church ornaments that they buy in this realm and to bring back papist books. . . .

And then came the bombshell:

> Monseigneur I also tell you that if your excellency wishes I have made the ambassador's secretary so much my friend that if he is given some little bit of money that there is nothing he will not let me know, and all that touches the Scottish Queen and the secret writing in which her letters are written. You should know that after your excellency has inspected any packet of letters addressed to her, he can insert others without anyone knowing at all.
>
> The chief agents of the Scottish Queen are Mr. Throckmorton and Lord Henry Howard, they never come here except at night.

He added a postscript: "Be on guard, if you please, against a Scot by the name of Fowler. He is very treacherous."

1583-87: The Bosom Serpent

8

THE THROCKMORTON PLOT

The government's official account of the incident in English history that would come to be known as the Throckmorton Plot was circumspect when it was published two years later. Francis Throckmorton's apprehension in the matter, the government stated, "grew first upon secret intelligence given to the Queen's Majesty, that he was a privy conveyor and receiver of letters to and from the Scottish Queen: upon which information, nevertheless, divers months were suffered to pass on, before he was called to answer the matter; to the end there might some proof more apparent to be had to charge him therewith directly; which shortly after fell out."

There were advantages in Mr. Secretary's now well-known reputation as the man who believed knowledge was never too dear, for men who thought they had something to sell knew where the marketplace was to be found. There were disadvantages, too: the tides of greed and vanity and mischief-making washed a continual stream of bilge water and refuse along with the much rarer prizes. "Hear all reports but trust not all": the parade of "hired Papists," as Walsingham once termed them, and of disreputable Scotsmen, and of prison conmen who had served Mr. Secretary in his search for privy information were all liars of a lesser or greater sort. They lied to inflate their own importance, or to fill in a slack period when they hadn't found anything genuine to sell; they lied in hopes of playing both sides of the street; sometimes they lied for no reason at all except maybe that they were in the habit of lying and couldn't help themselves or wanted to stay in practice.

And when they weren't lying they sometimes tripped over one

another. Spies watching spies: Fowler was probably not treacherous, as Fagot warned, merely incapable.

Henry Fagot, however, was a spy of a different order. Though he was doubtless seeking reward, there was something of an intellectual game or a jape in the way he wrote. His dislike of Catholicism and the Pope bore none of the vulgarity or perfunctory insults about "notorious papists": it seemed to go deeper.

And his promise of corrupting the ambassador's secretary to betray his correspondence with the Scottish Queen was something else again entirely. By mid-summer of 1583, the French Ambassador's secretary had indeed begun to leak like a sieve, delivering to Mr. Secretary sheaves of copies he had made of the letters secretly passing between Mauvissière and Mary.

The immediate payoff was some useful bits of political intelligence, and counter-intelligence. Mauvissière was greatly optimistic that diplomatic and political pressures were building on the English government to free Mary, with no direct force needed. Mary asked Mauvissière to have a questionable Scottish nobleman in his employ named Archibald Douglas write her a letter praising Walsingham's efforts on her behalf and send it by ordinary post so it would be sure to fall into his hands; this was either a piece of calculated flattery designed to soften Mr. Secretary or a piece of deliberate disinformation designed to embarrass him.

But this was small beer. The very fact that Mary's friends had re-opened a secret channel of communications suggested that something larger was afoot. And so the challenge now was to avoid scaring the prey until they fully revealed themselves. That would also require not scaring the French Ambassador's secretary: for he was already living in constant fear of exposure.

In August, his fear turned to panic after he was slipped a note demanding to know the names of the secret messengers who were conveying Mary's letters. The note appeared to come from Queen Elizabeth herself. But the signature did not quite look right. The man, almost frantic, hastened to his go-between with Mr. Secretary: it was none other than Mr. Secretary's old and none-too-effectual spy

Walter Williams, the one who had received the humorous letter of recommendation from his Catholic cellmate.

Walsingham, unfortunately, was away. And so, on the 31st of August 1583, Williams wrote to the Queen directly, explaining the danger she had placed the ambassador's secretary in by her indiscreet question:

> He is in great fear, as a thing whereon his life dependeth. He sayeth three may keep council if there be two away, meaning thereby if any more be made acquainted, not to proceed any farther in his course begun. He marvelleth why your Majesty should desire to know the messengers who are already known to be but two. . . . If they should be apprehended, then there were but one way with him, for he only hath been employed for this six years in writing all matters of importance and now, especially in the absence of Courcelles, who was acquainted with the delivering of them from time to time, it cannot be but he only must be suspected to be the revealer of secrets.
>
> I therefore beseech your Majesty that it may please you to have a care of such which desire to do you faithful service, and to burn all his writings which shall come to your highness, for he feareth greatly to be betrayed. So fit an instrument is not to be lost. . . .
>
> A fitter time may serve to take the practisers and dealers against your highness's state and quiet with less suspicion for your servant's discovery, and greater confusion and shame to the treacherous and evil-minded against your Majesty. . . .
>
> I most humbly crave of your Majesty to burn this letter.
>
> > Your Majesty's most bounden in this life,
> > Walter Williams

Claude de Courcelles was another secretary in the embassy who handled the ambassador's secret correspondence: he was away in Paris at the moment.

Elizabeth did not burn the letter, but neither did she do anything further to interfere with her Principal Secretary's patient intention to wait this time for more incriminating information to "fall out" before acting, and to keep his manner of discovering it a secret even then.

———————⚜———————

Walsingham was away: gone to Scotland, gone with "as ill a will" as he had ever set out on a mission in the Queen's service, he declared.

In the kaleidoscopic regrouping of factions and alliances, yet another court revolt had taken place in Scotland, led by the Earl of Arran and the Captain of the Royal Guard, one Colonel William Stewart: the usual mix of politics and grudges and venality. But the upshot was that the pro-English Protestant faction was once again out; worse, this time the young King James seemed to have taken an active part in conspiring with the change, and though still professing his friendly feelings for England, he was moving with alacrity to place his trust in France. There were rumors of plans afoot to marry James to a French princess. Arran was nominally a Protestant, but had been the right-hand man—and then the rival—of the leader of the pro-Catholic junta that had been in control several coups back. He was a brutal man, full of power and revenge; Walsingham made clear that if sent to Scotland to remonstrate with the King he would have nothing to do with his new chief counselor.

Walsingham set out early on the morning of the 17th of August 1583 with a large train of horses and eighty men. He was again plagued by ill-health: he had to travel by a "coshe or chariot," really not much easier than riding a horse over rough roads that were barely passable to wheeled vehicles. His colic and pains forced the caravan to halt several times; it was the 26th before he even reached Newcastle. "I hope I shall have more ease in another world than I do in this," he was moved to observe.

It was clearly a hopeless mission, doomed to fail, doomed to have the onus of failure fall on Walsingham. En route, he received a letter from the English Ambassador in Edinburgh that only confirmed he was on a fool's—or a miracle worker's—errand. The passion of this new Scottish ruling faction to take some irrevocable step had become almost unstoppable, the ambassador warned. "I pray God give you might to work some miracle and wonder to alter and assuage this rage, that undoubtedly passeth mine ability and remedy."

At the border at Berwick, the Scottish government subjected Walsingham's party to petty harassments; the safe conduct the King sent provided for only sixty men to accompany the English Secretary, and was made conditional upon the Englishmen's continued good behavior. A diplomatic affront: Walsingham refused to accept the passport under these conditions and demanded that proper forms be followed.

More delays: bookmakers in Scotland were offering attractive odds to anyone willing to bet that the English Secretary would ever make it to the Scottish Court. He finally arrived in Edinburgh on the 1st of September, to be met with still more pretexts and delays about seeing the King.

Walsingham was a man with nothing to lose in the situation; he quickly sought to show he had nothing to fear, either. He told the Scots who called on him that, despite all the rumors swirling about as to the purpose of his mission, he had not come to woo the Scots, or bribe them, or threaten them, or destroy the friendship between the two countries. His mistress the Queen could get along perfectly well without wooing the Scots, he said bluntly. As for bribes, he would advise her Majesty not to spend a sixpence on such a pack of ingrates as the Scots had shown themselves to be. And though the Queen sought the friendship of all her neighbors, "yet hath she not her sword glued in the scabbard."

When Walsingham was finally given his long-delayed audience with the King on the 9th of September, he was equally blunt. A seventeen-year-old sovereign was too young to pass judgment on matters of state. He had chosen badly in his councilors. England could live perfectly well without Scotland; and as far as Walsingham was personally concerned, he could do without the King's friendship, too. And so he left. He declined to meet with any of James's government, on the grounds that his instructions provided for him to deal with the King only.

Two days later, James summoned Walsingham again and professed

himself completely willing to do what the Queen asked of him. Walsingham dictated a long series of conditions: restoring the pro-English
party, respecting the law and the will of the people as expressed in Parliament, avoiding the "great errors upon an opinion of the absolute-
ness of their royal authority" that "young princes" were liable to: for
"as subjects are bound to obey dutifully so were princes bound to
command justly." It was a remarkable statement not just of English
interest but of the Puritan tenets of right governance—and also of
Walsingham's courageous refusal to curry favor with a sovereign who
might, not implausibly, be in a position to exact revenge for such ef-
frontery in the future: more than a few English courtiers were already
seeking James's good graces with an eye to when he might succeed to
the English throne. But now James swore he would do as Walsingham bade him. Then he had his councilors draft a written undertak-
ing full of ambiguities and evasions, and so Walsingham threw up his
hands.

As he had predicted from the start, the effort had been a trial and
was now a failure, personal and professional. He had missed his
young daughter's wedding in September to his good friend Sir Philip
Sidney; he had endured a miserable journey on miserable roads in
miserable health; he had been personally harassed and insulted. Arran
kept up a relentless series of dirty tricks during Walsingham's whole
time at the Scottish Court: issuing orders to refuse members of Walsingham's entourage admittance to the palace; hiring "a common
scold" known as Kate the Witch to sit outside and hurl abuse at the
English delegation as they came and went; and secretly replacing, on
the ring James had presented Walsingham as a parting gift, a diamond worth seven hundred crowns with a worthless piece of crystal.

Mr. Secretary arrived back in London in mid-October 1583 and resumed his vigil upon the French embassy's comings and goings. Still
he stayed his hand. Then, at last, on the 5th of November, the opportunity to strike that he had been waiting so patiently for presented
itself.

The French Ambassador had just dictated a hasty note to his secretary, to be dispatched to Mary at once. It was the very first line that told Walsingham what he needed to know: "Madam, I write this letter to your Majesty in order to send it more promptly to the Sieur de la Tour, who has told me to have a man ready to leave this evening, and that he could not, moreover, keep him." The information appears to have been relayed at once to Walsingham: here was a chance to catch Mary's and Mauvissière's courier red-handed.

Moreover, there was the fact that on the 1st of November the embassy secretary Courcelles had returned from Paris, and that meant two other things of considerable importance: first, that he had probably come bearing a packet of letters for Mary, which would be turned over to the courier for delivery, and these could be seized along with the man himself if Walsingham moved at once; and, second, that with Courcelles back in town, the ambassador's corrupt secretary now had at least some cover for the suspicion that would otherwise fall squarely on him if the "Sieur de la Tour," whoever he was, were to be arrested.

It seems clear that Mr. Secretary knew exactly who the "Sieur de la Tour" was: He was the same Francis Throckmorton whom Fagot had mentioned haunting the ambassador's house at night, along with Lord Henry Howard.

Throckmorton was nearly thirty years old, a member of the staunchly Catholic branch of a well-known family. He had been educated at Oxford and studied law at the Inner Temple; he had passed the last few years on an extended tour of the Continent with his brother. And so, that night, Mr. Secretary ordered certain "gentlemen of no mean credit and reputation" sent to search Throckmorton's houses in London and Kent and arrest him. When Throckmorton was surprised in his London house that night, he was caught in the very act of enciphering a letter to the Queen of Scots. In his possession, too, was a list of Catholic noblemen and gentlemen throughout the country, a list that Throckmorton was apparently in the process of updating and rewriting. The new version pointedly contained notes about which harbors and ports of the country suitable for an invading fleet were situated close to the estates of these friendly men. Throckmorton was also found to be in possession of a dozen copies of the pamphlet published by the Bishop of Ross defending Mary's title to the English crown.

Throckmorton at first denied that he had ever seen the papers before; he insisted they had been "foisted in" among his belongings by the men who had done the searching. Then he acknowledged having seen them, but said they had been left in his chambers by a man named Edward Nuttebie, who had since fled the country. The members of the Council who examined him were scarcely about to credit either story, especially after Throckmorton was caught trying to toss from the window of his cell in the Tower several cards from a pack of playing cards. On their back was a message for his brother, clearly pressing him to corroborate his story: "I have been examined, by whom the two papers, containing the names of certain noblemen and gentlemen, and of havens &c. were written; and I have alleged them to have been written by Edward Nuttebie my man, of whose hand writing you know them to be."

His story now completely fell apart under the persuasion of the rack. During Throckmorton's first interrogation under torture, he confessed nothing. A few days later, on the 18th of November, Mr. Secretary sent word to try again the following day: "I have seen as resolute men as Throgmortin stoop notwithstanding the great show that he hath made of a Roman resolution. I suppose the grief of the last torture will suffice without any extremity of racking to make him more comfortable then he hath hitherto shewed himself."

Walsingham was right: before Throckmorton was "strained to any purpose" the next day, he agreed to tell all. At the behest of Mary's supporters in Paris, he and his brother had, in September, surveyed suitable landing places for a force of five thousand men to be led by the Duke of Guise. From this list, Guise had chosen the port of Arundel in Sussex; Guise had then sent Charles Paget, who handled Mary's affairs in Paris along with Thomas Morgan, to come over to England secretly to make a detailed survey of this port. While in England, Paget had also sounded out his brother Lord Paget and the Earl of Northumberland, the chief magnate near Arundel.

Throckmorton admitted he had relayed many packets of letters between Morgan and Mary. He had also met twice a week in London with Mendoza, the Spanish Ambassador, who was up to his neck in the scheme. Mendoza had canvassed Catholic sentiment in the country and was proposing that a second force, twenty thousand Spanish troops, land in Lancashire, in the Catholic north.

Throckmorton also revealed that when he was arrested he had had under his bed, in a small green-velvet-covered casket, the packet of letters for Mary that had indeed just arrived from Morgan in Paris; but he had managed to have a servant spirit them out of the house—and to Mendoza—under the very noses of the searchers.

On the 19th of January 1584, the Spanish Ambassador was summoned to the Lord Chancellor's house. Walsingham, Burghley, Leicester, and several other members of the Privy Council were present; they rose, bowed, and led Mendoza into a small inner chamber. Walsingham spoke. Her Majesty knew all about his intrigues. He had fifteen days to depart the realm.

The ambassador furiously retorted that Elizabeth should mend her own ways and stop stirring up rebellions in other sovereigns' realms herself before she accused innocent men of the same. Walsingham stood his ground impassively; he suggested that Mendoza might consider himself fortunate to have gotten off so lightly.

And so the ambassador stormed pompously out, hurling a torrent of insults and threats in his wake. "Don Bernardino de Mendoza," he thundered, "was born not to disturb kingdoms but to conquer them!"

Mauvissière was a more delicate matter. The French Ambassador was at the very least guilty of a serious violation of his diplomatic status, for as far back as September 1582 the English government had informed the French that all correspondence with the Queen of Scots must henceforth go through the English embassy in Paris. And if not an active plotter and participant in the conspiracy, as was Mendoza, Mauvissière at least had a general idea of what was being discussed.

In April, the Council prepared a secret list of charges against the French Ambassador:

> He hath had secret intelligence with the Scottish Queen
>
> He hath sought to understand how the Catholics of this realm stand affected in case any foreign prince should seek to invade this realm
>
> There hath been plots delivered unto him to that purpose
>
> He hath sought to draw the affections of her Majesty's subjects unto the Scottish Queen
>
> He hath daily intelligence and is a cherisher of such of her Majesty's subjects as are traitorously affected toward her and her state
>
> He receiveth letters daily from Thomas Morgan, Thomas Throgmorton and other practicing traitors in France: doth convey their packets and letters to the Scottish Queen and hers to them

And then the whole matter was quietly dropped. For there remained the question of the French Ambassador's secretary, who had provided such good value for money, and who still was in precarious risk of being exposed for his troubles; and there was the even greater value that was arguably to be had in keeping Mary and her friends ever guessing just how their secrets had been betrayed.

In late April 1584, yet another large parcel arrived on Mr. Secretary's desk filled with copies of correspondence between Mauvissière and Mary from this still-reliable source. At the top of the heap of two dozen letters was one that had caused the French Ambassador's secretary a new panic. From Mary to the ambassador, dated the 15th of February 1584, it had been sent by a roundabout route, not by the same courier who had brought a recent letter from the ambassador to her, and it expressed her suspicions about a leak in the embassy:

It has not been possible for me to send my reply by the way your letters came because the gentleman has been informed that spies have been set day and night around your house to watch all those who come and go. And also, by the discovery of all my secret contacts with your house many are greatly suspicious that someone among your servants has been corrupted; and in truth I am not without doubts myself. I beg you earnestly that from now on you deal with any others I send you using servants you know to be faithful, and not in your house but rather in or outside the town at rendezvous you can easily set for places and times without any others knowing of it. Otherwise I will never be able to find a man again willing to take the risk on our secret correspondence.

The ambassador's secretary himself had scribbled a frantic note to Walsingham on the bottom of this copied letter:

I humbly beseech you Monsieur to keep all of this as secret as possible, so that Monsieur the Ambassador does not perceive anything of it, which I know you know very well how to do. I would not for all the gold in the world want to be discovered, because of the dishonor I would receive; not only the dishonor but the life which hangs thereby, though of that I do not care as much as the dishonor, since I will have to die sometime.

The ambassador's reply to Mary a few weeks later, also contained in the bundle of copies, contained a reassuring indication, however, that Mr. Secretary's source had *not* been exposed. "I beg you most humbly to believe that there is not a single man in my house who has knowledge of my dealings with Your Majesty," Mauvissière wrote— none, that is, except his secretary, "who never budges from my chamber and who writes everything in front of me and in my presence, and Courcelles who carries the packets from one place to another and speaks to those of your party. Thus neither the Queen of England nor her Council have ever known anything genuine about it, only what has been imagined by various spies who go and come."

From Paris came reports that in zealous Catholic circles there the ambassador himself was the one suspected of having betrayed Mary's cause. A convenient outcome; reinforced when the Privy Council quietly instructed Mauvissière that if the charges against him were not to be pursued further he must mend his ways, cease representing Mary's interests, openly show Mr. Secretary all letters he received for Mary henceforth. Mauvissière hastened to give his assurances. And so awkward publicity was averted, and Mauvissière was quietly but quite completely defanged: blackmailed into good conduct and, for good measure, poisoned in his reputation among Mary's followers.

Thus at Throckmorton's trial in May there was no mention of the secret correspondence or of the French Ambassador; the indictment dropped entire portions of Throckmorton's confessions that had referred to Mauvissière, or that had hinted at his deeper involvement in, or at least awareness of, the plot.

Throckmorton was hanged, drawn, and quartered at Tyburn in July 1584. "I would I had been hanged when I first opened my mouth," he declared at one point that spring. "I have disclosed the secrets of her who was the dearest thing to me in the world and whom I thought no torment should have drawn me so much to have prejudiced."

In November, the French Ambassador's now much-reassured secretary sent Walsingham a brief note confirming that secret communications between Mary and the embassy had indeed ceased in the wake of the none-too-subtle pressure that had been applied: "As for Monsieur the Ambassador, he has received not a thing on this side for a long time."

And as for Fagot, his farewell to Mr. Secretary came a year later, in September 1585, when Mauvissière was recalled and Fagot wrote Walsingham to warn that the new French Ambassador, Guillaume de l'Aubépine, baron de Châteauneuf, was made of much sterner stuff than his predecessor. Immediately upon his arrival, Châteauneuf had closely examined Fagot about various people in the house, demanding to know whether they were spies. "Monsieur Châteauneuf swore to me and promised," Fagot reported, "that he would never tolerate in his house any men who are not of his religion and that he knew perfectly well that Seigneur de Mauvissière had some of them about who were betraying him and this was a great evil and a great scandal for him."

Fagot may or may not have been the same person as a certain lapsed Dominican friar named Giordano Bruno, later to achieve renown as a freethinking philosopher of the Italian Renaissance, and known to have been a resident of Mauvissière's house in London at a time that closely corresponded to Fagot's activity as Mr. Secretary's spy. Much fit in the two men's personalities: both were malcontents, intellectuals, possessors of a sly sense of humor, believers in the clever use of dissimulation for justifiable ends. Bruno throughout his life had a disdain for conventional ways and the conventional threats of authority: he once humorously rewrote the line about turning the other cheek from the Sermon on the Mount to say that if someone strikes your cheek you should strike *his* other one. And when he returned to Italy in 1591, this tactless tendency immediately landed him in the hands of the Inquisition. In February 1600, he was burned alive by the authorities in Rome: simply for heresy, not treason.

The ambassador's corrupt secretary faded smoothly away. Among Mauvissière's three secretaries, Claude de Courcelles, Jean Arnault de Chérelles, and Laurent Feron, the last appears the most likely to have been the spy, since the first two, despite having been suspected from time to time in the centuries since, seem not to have been in London at the relevant time, nor does their handwriting match that of the relevant documents. About Feron little is known; he seems to have been nervously in it for the money, pure and simple, and did his job, and that was an end of it.

And as for Mauvissière, his career was forever ruined by the rumors about him when he returned to France. But he continued to write affectionate letters to Walsingham, his "inseparable friend," for the rest of his life. He was sure to let Walsingham know of his considerable satisfaction, a few years after his return home, when the

King of France finally arranged to have the Duke of Guise assassinated, in 1588.

~⊙⊙~

Mary had been sufficiently circumspect in her own letters to Mauvissière that had fallen into Walsingham's hands. She greatly lamented Throckmorton's persecution for having been a member of her "party"; she did not repeat the mistake, which she had made in her letter to Norfolk a dozen years earlier, of directly endorsing treasonous acts.

It was a few months after Throckmorton's execution, in July 1584, that there came into Mr. Secretary's possession the most complete and authoritative account yet of the Duke of Guise's attempted "enterprise." An agent of Mr. Secretary's in France reported that the Jesuit Creighton was about to sail for Scotland; in September, the merchant vessel upon which he was traveling as a passenger had the remarkable misfortune to run right into a ship that had been dispatched by the Admiral of Zealand, of the Dutch Protestant forces. Creighton, though in disguise, was immediately identified, captured, and brought back to Ostend. The Dutch wanted to hang him on the spot, but instead—as Creighton later wrote in his memoirs—he was "made a gift to the English Queen."

When Creighton was taken, he was found to have about him a "plot set down in the Italian tongue," which he attempted to destroy on the spot. "Although it was torn to pieces and divers parts thereof lost," one of Walsingham's men reported, "we gathered the same thereof which I send you herein enclosed."

The document, when pieced together and translated, proved to be primarily of historical interest, since it dealt with the first iteration of Guise's enterprise, the one from 1582, which had envisioned the dispatch of troops to Scotland to assist Lennox and ensure the ascendancy of the Catholic faction around James. Even so, there were telling points. Already in this first version, the ultimate objective was unmistakably to have been a surprise attack upon England. The eight thousand "good and trained soldiers of strangers . . . so soon as they arrive are to make no stay in Scotland but pass into England before the Queen may suppose." The aim of the enterprise was nothing less than "to depose her Majesty and set up the Scottish Queen" in her place, and thereby reinstitute Catholicism in both England and Scotland. Great importance was laid upon the use of propaganda to prepare the ground; the conspirators had "most infamous and slanderous libels" about Elizabeth "ready made, but not yet printed." It was also "very needful that the Pope do again send forth his Bull of Excommunication against her Majesty," showing how patient and forbearing he had been in the hope that she would mend her ways.

Walsingham's translator noted that the document "was not a discourse only, or devise how such a thing might be brought to pass, but the plot and design set down and agreed upon to be put in execution, whereby the Scottish Queen was made privy, as it is confessed."

Mary's complicity in a conspiracy to secure her freedom by force was not, strictly speaking, news. The involvement of her followers in a plot directly against Elizabeth's life was, however: together these developments represented a sharp escalation in the undeclared war that the Council faced as autumn passed into winter of 1584.

One plot to assassinate Elizabeth had come to light earlier in the year from the zealous efforts of one of Walsingham's least reliable and most unsought agents. Dr. William Parry was not only disreputable but erratic; he had in his earlier life barely escaped hanging for burglary, had squandered the fortunes of two wives, and had then set out for the Continent, where he professed to become a Catholic. He may actually have been sincere in so doing, though he also was in touch with Mr. Secretary at the time.

And then he had returned to England in January 1584 with the rather sensational news that, having befriended Thomas Morgan in Paris, Mary's agent had personally persuaded him to take a holy oath to kill the Queen of England. Parry confessed the matter to the Queen herself, and in March was able to corroborate it with a letter he had by then received from Cardinal Ptolomeo Gallio, the papal

Secretary of State, in answer to one he and Morgan had written. The Cardinal offered the Pope's absolution and encouragement for putting his "most holy and honorable purposes into effect."

The Queen pardoned Parry, accepting his story that he had gone along with the conspiracy only to expose it. Parry met an unfortunate end a year later, when, apparently still hard up for cash, he sought to repeat this successful performance and once again entered into loose talk about killing the Queen; this time his would-be accomplice beat him to the draw and denounced Parry before Parry could denounce him, and no one was quite ready to believe Parry's protests of innocence a second time: he was tried and hanged.

With or without the erratic Parry, assassination was in the air that autumn of 1584. The Protestant leader of the Dutch rebels, William Prince of Orange, had been mortally wounded by a crazed Catholic assassin in July 1584. Against this tightening fear, the Council took an extraordinary, and almost certainly extralegal, step in October to ensure the Queen's safety. The Bond of Association, which all members of the Council signed, pledged that if the Queen was killed the signers would personally "prosecute to death" not only the murderers but "any that have, may, or shall pretend title to come to this crown by the untimely death of her Majesty so wickedly procured." The latter threat was to be made good even if the beneficiaries of the Queen's title were completely innocent of the crime themselves. The Bond was immediately published and a copy pointedly presented to the Queen of Scots. Within days, thousands of men throughout the realm had added their names, some standing in line for hours for the privilege of signing their pledge.

And once again the guard about Mary was tightened. Mr. Secretary had been continually dismayed by her loose keeping. Elizabeth's stinginess in reimbursing the Earl of Shrewsbury for his expenses had been a particular vexation; a few years before, Walsingham had complained directly to Elizabeth, "Pray God the abatement of the charges towards that noble man that hath the custody of the bosom serpent hath not lessened his care in keeping her."

Now the last vestiges of courtly consideration toward Mary were dropped for good. Early in the year 1585, Shrewsbury was replaced with Sir Amias Paulet, a no-nonsense Puritan—certainly no nobleman; indeed, barely a gentleman in some people's book. He had served Mr. Secretary as ambassador to France; he was loyal, tough, and utterly immune to the charms of a Catholic queen. To him Walsingham delivered a meticulous set of instructions: Mary was under no circumstances to be permitted to travel more than two miles when taking the air. She would no longer be allowed to speak to anyone when abroad or distribute alms to the poor. Paulet was to keep a particular watch over Mary's laundresses and coachmen, who "have heretofore been used as principal instruments for the conveying of letters."

Paulet was the man for the job; no doubts on that score. In reply he swore to carry out Mr. Secretary's orders with "preciseness and severity." He assured Mr. Secretary, "I will never ask pardon if she depart out of my hands by any treacherous slight or cunning device." He was preparing to replace Mary's servants with more trustworthy ones of his own choosing; "this alteration will breed (no doubt) great storms and marvelous unkindness," Paulet wrote, "which shall trouble me nothing at all."

A few months later, Paulet reported with satisfaction that the isolation of the Scottish Queen from the outside world was complete. "The residue of this Queen's train watched and attended in such precise manner as they be," Paulet informed Mr. Secretary, "I cannot imagine how it may be possible for them to convey a piece of paper as big as my finger."

9

LETTERS IN CIPHER

Among Thomas Morgan's many duties as Mary's factor in Paris—besides, that is, fomenting conspiracies, suborning murder, and controlling, to his own considerable power and advantage, the 30,000 crown per year "French dowry" to which the Queen of Scots was still entitled—was devising the ciphers that his employer required for her secret communications. Over time he sent out dozens of them; they showed some awareness of the abilities of possible decipherers, but not very much. Morgan's ciphers were all basically of the type known as a nomenclator: letters of the alphabet were replaced by symbols, numbers, Greek letters; a few especially well-used words—proper names, articles, conjunctions, *you, which, my, of, because, say, send, Majesty*—had their own numbers or characters assigned to stand for the whole word. Mary's ciphers usually had more than one possible symbol for each vowel or other commonly employed letter, a standard twist to make things harder for a decipherer; they usually contained a few "nulls," characters that stood for nothing whatever, to throw off the scent; they were generally written in a continuous stream, no breaks between words, to avoid giving away obvious clues.

They were about as good as most ciphers of the day; in other words, not much better than the ones that the Neapolitan scientist and magician Giovanni Battista Porta—but who had ever heard of him?—had dismissed in a treatise on codes he had published in 1563 as fit only for "rustics, women, and children."

No one particularly liked Morgan. He had meddled relentlessly in the English-Welsh feud at the Douai seminary (Morgan was Welsh); the Papal Nuncio in Paris thought he was a "knave." The English government now thought he was patently a criminal, and once his direct involvement in the Throckmorton and Parry plots was clear, Elizabeth demanded of the French with great vehemence that he be arrested and turned over.

A French farce ensued. On the 1st of March 1585, Morgan was arrested at his lodgings in Paris and marched off to the Bastille. His papers were seized, but when the English Ambassador insisted that both Morgan and the documents be delivered up at once, the French King temporized. At last it was decided that Morgan would be held but not turned over to the English; his papers were handed by the French Council to a Court secretary by the name of Jean Arnault de Chérelles: the same who had worked in the embassy in London, who spoke English, who had even recently sent a courteous letter to Mr. Secretary Walsingham from Paris enclosing a gift of quince marmalade and wishing his diplomatic colleague perfect health and long life. Chérelles was instructed to deliver the documents to the English Ambassador, Sir Edward Stafford.

Stafford was a problem. He was well connected, of a family with noble ancestry; his mother was one of Elizabeth's ladies-in-waiting at Court; he was touchy, insecure, full of resentments. He had recently remarried, taking as his wife the Lady Douglas Sheffield, whose major points of distinction were that she had recently been cast off by Leicester, who was rumored to have secretly married her—probably untrue—but by whom he had certainly had an illegitimate child; that, and the fact that she was of the Howard family, which had so distinguished itself of late with its Catholic leanings and involvement in Mary's plottings. There were questions about her religious loyalties and her influence on Stafford; there was no question of her hatred for Leicester, and by extension all of his party.

Stafford himself was Burghley's man for sure; and so when, in 1583, Stafford had been put forward for the ambassadorship, much against Walsingham's desire, Mr. Secretary had coolly, with almost surgical detachment, done his best to slice such a potentially dangerous rival to ribbons. Walsingham, by now a master of bureaucratic back-stabbing, hastened to seek out Stafford, all earnest goodwill, and assure him that he had done his best to put in a good word with the Queen in his behalf, singing his praises more than he deserved, in fact; but he had to confess that the Queen had replied that Stafford was "fit but very poor" for the post of ambassador and she much preferred one of the other names that had been proposed. Nonetheless, Mr. Secretary smoothly continued, he would return and press his case with her Majesty again if Stafford wished. Stafford spurned the opportunity to be beholden to Walsingham, and put his faith in Burghley's patronage instead, and got the appointment; even so, Walsingham had done a bit of brilliant hazing.

Once Stafford took up his post, the hazing only intensified. Stafford's predecessor, Lord Cobham, strangely left Paris without turning over any of his files to the new ambassador. Mr. Secretary ostentatiously neglected to send along to Paris routine reports of developments at home. Stafford complained; Mr. Secretary replied that he had meant to mention one other thing, which was that the ambassador really must stop spending so much money on postage; indeed, Mr. Secretary confessed, he had personally had to conceal from her Majesty some of the ambassador's reports because she was already so vexed at what it must have cost to send them all.

And then there was the matter of the ambassador's wife, and some stories that Mr. Secretary had heard of the ambassador's contacts with the exiled Catholic lords in Paris: "Her Majesty hath willed me to signify to you," Mr. Secretary instructed, "that she is assured that the alliance that my Lady, your wife, hath with them, shall not make you to be more remiss to perform your duty."

Stafford, peevish, now became furious; he became more apoplectic over what happened next, an incident that reflected not only Walsingham's growing distrust of Stafford but, no doubt, his desire to remind the ambassador that a man with Mr. Secretary's resources at his command could not be successfully crossed. Mr. Secretary's searchers at Rye, it appeared, had opened a packet containing the ambassador's private letters, and read them, even those to his wife. "In truth," Stafford protested to Walsingham, "I think it is a thing has never been done to one in my place."

Mr. Secretary smoothly apologized: "The commissioners did so far forget themselves"; it had been a mistake; in the future the ambassador should place "all your letters in a packet by themselves directed to me and subscribe it with your hand, as I will likewise take the same order with those private letters that shall be sent to you from hence, if your man may be directed to bring them unto me for that purpose." Stafford privately fumed to Burghley that Mr. Secretary must "think I am a child" not to see through such an obvious ploy.

And then Mr. Secretary promptly sent another reminder: the ambassador should really *please* try to remember to send dispatches *only* on matters "of very great importance."

So, when Chérelles delivered Morgan's secret papers a couple of months after his arrest in March 1585, Stafford clearly imagined he had an opportunity at last to carry off a coup of his own that would pay Mr. Secretary back, and on his own turf at that. Among the documents were nine cipher keys. The symbols and characters matched those of some intercepted letters of Mary's that Stafford already had in his possession, and with great excitement the ambassador at once set to work attempting to decode them. Alas, he got nowhere. In May, he was forced to admit as much in a letter to Mr. Secretary.

It was only considerably later that Chérelles, in a letter to Mary herself, explained what had happened. There had in fact been thirty-two cipher "alphabets" included among Morgan's papers. Chérelles removed them. In their place he substituted cipher keys of his own devising that used the same symbols but completely scrambled the definitions of which symbols stood for which letters. "After having broken his head for some days upon the said ciphers," Chérelles reported, the ambassador "could never get a word of intelligence" out of the letters. "Meanwhile, having returned to the gentlemen of the council, I laid all these proceedings before them, whereat they laughed very much."

Luckily for the cause of England, there were men available who were more adept in the matter of ciphers than a prickly and proud ambassador of less than completely certain loyalties. The possibilities had been known to Walsingham as early as 1577, when a French Huguenot general, François de La Noue, intercepted in Gascony some coded letters of Don John of Austria, the Spanish governor of the Netherlands. La Noue turned the matter over to a Flemish noble-man who had a reputation for being able to work wonders with such puzzles.

Philip van Marnix, Baron de Sainte-Aldegonde, was William of Orange's right-hand man. He and Walsingham were soon in close contact; the two had much in common. A contemporary called the baron "the most constant anti-Catholic in the world, more than even Calvin himself." He was eloquent in speech; he knew well "the finer points of dealing with people." He was a phenomenal linguist, a scholar of Latin, Greek, and Hebrew, conversant in French, German, Italian, Spanish, English, Scots.

It took Sainte-Aldegonde less than a month to solve Don John's ci-pher messages, even though the Spanish nomenclator that had been used included not only a cipher alphabet but also a vocabulary of some two hundred special words, plus symbols that separately stood for two- or three-letter syllables. In July, Orange presented the results with a flourish to the English envoy in the Low Countries: they re-vealed a scheme by Don John to have his Spanish troops land in En-glish ports under the pretext of seeking shelter from a storm.

Almost as remarkable as Sainte-Aldegonde's way with ciphers was the refusal of the Spanish to believe that their codes could be read by any mortals: they would hardly be the last to be so deluded. Philip, when finally presented with proof a number of years later that the French had broken one of his codes, told the Pope that it must have been done by "black magic." The Pope, whose Vatican cryptogra-phers had been reading Philip's codes for years, presumably smiled quietly to himself.

Soon after the remarkable feat with Don John's letters, Walsing-ham began sending Sainte-Aldegonde other cipher messages to be de-coded. By early 1578, there was a regular traffic back and forth: a letter from the Portuguese Ambassador in March; a whole packet of letters in April; a "letter written in cipher, wherein may be matter of great moment," in June.

In fact, the methods for solving an unknown cipher were perfectly straightforward. No black magic required; all it took was a knack for discerning patterns, a familiarity with language, an endless capacity for concentration, and a bottom made of iron to withstand the long hours sitting at a desk poring over it all. With time and patience there were ways around all the code-makers' dodges. The symbols that stood for whole words could be guessed from context, especially since they were likely to appear repeatedly, even in a single message. The use of different symbols to stand for a single high-frequency letter gave itself away through the appearance of rhymes in the cipher: a decipherer who came upon several occurrences of the ciphered words 8//ε7H and 8+ε7H could conclude they both probably stood for the same common word, with // and + standing for the same high-frequency letter.

Walsingham's secretary John Somers occasionally tried his hand at some of this work; several of the earlier intercepted letters of Mary's in Walsingham's files appear with notes to Somers requesting his services in this matter. But soon Walsingham had a local man more or less dedicated to the job. Thomas Phelippes was one of Mr. Secretary's middling scoundrels: his father was Customer of London, a lucrative enough post; Phelippes himself was well enough educated, proficient in Latin, French, and Italian, passable in Spanish. He was well traveled; he had done the usual sorts of odd and shady jobs in France and elsewhere for Mr. Secretary, carrying messages from informants, delivering money to Protestant rebels, trying to draw out Thomas Morgan with vague hints of offering to serve the Catholic cause. The Queen of Scots herself left the only known physical description of Phelippes from the one time she would meet him later on. Though slanted no doubt from her knowledge by then that he was "Walsingham's man," it was true enough, and ever so slightly unsettling enough: "Of low stature, slender every way, dark yellow haired on the head and clear yellow bearded, eated in the face with small pocks, of short sight, thirty years of age by appearance."

By late 1578, Phelippes was stationed at the English embassy in Paris, and increasingly now it was he to whom Mr. Secretary turned when intercepted letters needed deciphering. The files were soon full of them: proficient, swift copies in a clear hand, lists of symbols and the letters or words they stood for worked out in the margins; and always the neat endorsement, a practice code-breakers would still scrupulously be following five centuries later, noting the date the message was originally written, the date it was deciphered. On his return to England, Phelippes continued his work with the same efficiency and zeal.

For those occasions when it was necessary to return the original without the sender's suspecting its interception, Mr. Secretary had another man now, too, Arthur Gregory. "Ingenious," as he was said to be, he had perfected "the art of forcing the seal of a letter, yet so invisibly that it still appeareth virgin to the exactest beholder."

Robert Poley was another thirty-or-so-year-old scoundrel of the middling classes doing Mr. Secretary's duty. Like so many of the others, he was a dubious but nominal Catholic; like so many of the others he had been cast into prison, the Marshalsea in his case, on Mr. Secretary's orders. Through a year of often harrowing confinement, he ingratiated himself among the four dozen other Catholic prisoners, posing as a fellow sufferer of Anglican persecution. He got information; he also, much more successfully than the hapless Walter Williams, managed to get a genuinely good reference from one of the imprisoned seminary priests he befriended there. Upon his release in May 1584, and with that introduction, Poley wrote to Mary's agent Thomas Morgan in Paris offering his services. He received an encouraging reply.

Walsingham in truth had had his doubts about Poley at first. In early 1585, he ordered Poley rearrested and brought before him; for two grueling hours Mr. Secretary personally questioned Poley about his apparent role in distributing banned Catholic books, among them the brilliantly successful propaganda tract *Leicester's Commonwealth*.

A product of the English Catholic exiles in France, the pamphlet offered enough sexual titillation to ensure wide readership of its slanders against the leader of the English Puritan faction. Among other things, it alleged that there were not "two noblewomen about her Majesty" whom Leicester "hath not solicited to potent ways," and that, having run out of ladies of his own class to rut with, Leicester was now offering £300 a night to the waiting gentlewomen of the Queen's chamber.

A search of Poley's lodgings turned up more seditious books and the encouraging letter from Morgan. Poley explained he had been planning to show the letter to Mr. Secretary in the hopes of being employed by the English government to advance a "plat" against Morgan, the groundwork for which he had already, at so much hardship to himself, laid. Walsingham remained suspicious about both the books and the letter and for now decided not to avail himself of Poley's offers.

Poley was released, however, and now he pressed Leicester himself to employ him where Mr. Secretary would not: "in some course of discovery and service, either abroad or at home, but rather I wish with Morgan, because my plat being laid that way, my credit is both enough with him and also with some of them which were last sent over." By accomplishing something "worthy to her Majesty's and Your Honor's acceptance," Poley pleaded, he hoped he might "countervail and recompense any offences and misbehaviours of my youth past and lost."

In June 1585, he was given his chance by Leicester. Thomas Morgan was still in prison in Paris, but the French authorities were all but openly winking. A steady stream of visitors and messages came and went; the Queen of Scots' business was conducted with scarcely an interruption from Morgan's cell in the Bastille.

Poley arrived in Paris and at once began working the network of Catholic contacts in whose "credit" he stood so well. He said he carried a message from a Catholic gentleman in England who was prepared to re-establish the secret conveyance of letters to and from Mary; he insisted, however, that he could deliver the message to none but Morgan personally. After some initial suspicions, Morgan agreed and "found the means to have him conducted as near as might be to the window of the chamber where I am prisoner." Along with his letter Poley had brought a cipher-key alphabet from the "gentleman" to be used in the correspondence with Mary.

By July, Poley was heading home with a pocketful of gold to cover his expenses and many words of encouragement from Morgan and Charles Paget for his efforts. Early in the new year of 1586, Phelippes was handed the first packet of letters Poley had received from Paris to be delivered to Mary.

Among them was one from Morgan urging Mary to "entertain Poley who . . . by my advice is placed with the Lady Sidney, daughter of Secretary Walsingham, and by that means ordinarily in his house and thereby able to pick out many things to the information of your Majesty."

An extraordinary coincidence.

Walsingham's daughter, Frances, had married Sir Philip Sidney two years earlier, on the 20th of September 1583, when she was barely sixteen. Sidney was Leicester's nephew: a valuable cementing of political alliances. He had first met his future wife eleven years earlier, when he had taken refuge in Walsingham's house in Paris during the Saint Bartholomew's massacres; she was then not quite five years old, he seventeen.

It was probably Walsingham who had first proposed the match to Sidney, and there were advantages to both. Sidney was from a distinguished but financially embarrassed family; Walsingham had no son of his own but had wealth and connections. Sidney had made a name for himself as a sort of dashing Puritan, at once a literary prodigy and a glittering courtier: champion jouster, writer of love sonnets, ambassador to the Holy Roman Empire at the astonishing age of twenty-two. But he was still dogged by some curiously Catholic ties of his youth: Philip II of Spain was actually his godfather, after whom he was named, and his family had offered its protection to Edmund

Campion when the future Jesuit priest had first come under suspicion as to his religious allegiances. Marriage to the family of so firm a Puritan as Mr. Secretary would not hurt an ambitious family desirous of proving its loyalty to the new establishment.

At first the Queen furiously opposed this match of one of the stars of her court to her Secretary's daughter. So did Sidney's father: there had at one time been talk of Philip's marrying a German princess, or the daughter of William of Orange, or some other great prize. But both eventually gave in. For the Sidney family there was the unmistakable fact that, however grand they were, they were also flat broke. Sir Henry, Philip's father, wrote Walsingham a letter of woe in March 1583 in which he denied that he had ever been "cold" to the prospective marriage, and then went on to catalogue his debts and losses and his "decayed estate": if he were to die tomorrow, he would leave his three sons £20,000 worse off than his father had left him. Walsingham agreed to cover £1,500 of his future son-in-law's debts and to provide board and lodging to the married couple—and to leave all of his lands to them.

In October 1585, Frances had given birth to a daughter, Elizabeth; by the time of her christening, a grand occasion that took place on the 15th of November at Saint Olave's church near Walsingham's house in London, the Queen herself present as godmother, Sidney had gone to fight with the Dutch against Spain in the Low Countries. Lady Sidney remained at Barn Elms, Walsingham's estate, where the couple had indeed made their home since their marriage.

Whether it was truly Morgan's "advice" that had originated the idea of Poley's entering Lady Sidney's retinue at Barn Elms, it would have been hard to ask for a better cover for a double agent: it fabulously increased Poley's credit with Morgan while solving the vexatious problem of explaining why he was seen consorting with Mary's self-sworn "mortal enemy."

Among the other news Poley passed on to Mr. Secretary via this ever-so-convenient arrangement was that Morgan had asked him to make contact with the English Catholic party and see that they "be encouraged and put in hope." Morgan was also desirous that some scheme for disgracing or possibly even assassinating Leicester should be put in train; and that Poley should get in touch with Châteauneuf, the new French Ambassador, and see if he had any messages he wished conveyed to the Queen of Scots, or to her supporters in Scotland.

⋯⊙⊙⋯

Poley was a luxury. Mr. Secretary had inherited him from Leicester, but he had his own men already working to the same purpose.

The business of infiltrating Catholic circles was practically down to a routine by now. There was nothing like a spell in prison to establish one's bona fides; it could almost have been a joke now, the way they were mass-producing Catholic spies and shipping them off to Paris and getting them into Thomas Morgan's and Charles Paget's good graces. Close on the heels of Poley came Mr. Secretary's ever-resourceful prison spy Nicholas Berden, who arrived in Paris in August 1585, also bearing a glowing reference from a well-known Catholic prisonmate. He was also soon introduced to Morgan, and Morgan began sounding him out, too, about helping to open a channel of secret correspondence with Mary.

And a third infiltrator: the best yet. It was hard to say exactly when Gilbert Gifford had decided to jump sides. He was a member of a well-known Catholic family; his father had been imprisoned for recusancy; in 1579, Gifford had traveled to Rome and entered the seminary for English priests. It was just at the time that tensions between the Welsh and English students there led to the Jesuits' takeover of the college. Gifford was soon expelled for his unmanageable conduct. He may or may not have hinted to an acquaintance at the time—an acquaintance who undoubtedly was one of Mr. Secretary's agents at the English College—that he would be willing to enter into secret work for the English government at some time in the future. He then showed up penniless at Rheims, where the Douai seminary had moved, and begged to be admitted there. But soon he had fallen out with Dr. Allen, too, and in the end was ordained a deacon by the Cardinal of Lorraine. In October 1585 he was on his way to Paris.

If serving a stint in an English jail cell was a letter of recommendation to Thomas Morgan, then having sparred with the English faction at the English seminaries in Rome and Rheims was an even better one. There were few hatreds that men could work up like the hatred toward a rival in the same cause, and Morgan had effectively become the leader of the Welsh "seculars" arrayed against the Jesuits and the English "religious." From Paris, Berden had sent back to Walsingham reports, penned in invisible ink, full of news of the seething enmities between the two.

Gifford now followed the well-worn trail to Morgan's cell in the Bastille, and came away bearing the best letter of introduction yet to the Queen of Scots. Morgan assured Mary that Gifford was "a Catholic gentleman to me well known for that he was brought up in learning of this side the seas this many years past, where I have been always his friend to my power." He had undertaken to travel to where she was being held, to "practice" with her host, Sir Amias Paulet, his servants, "and such as depend on him or his wife," to "haunt the market towns adjoining the place of your continuance, to see whether he may thereby find any of your Majesty's people." The "said Gilbert" had also been "instructed how to send your letters to my hand to these parts."

Gifford would try to see if he could obtain an actual place of service with Paulet, though if that failed there would be another avenue to try: "It is very likely that one Phelippes hath great access to your host at this time." Phelippes was said to be a "severe Huguenot, and all for that state, yet glorious and greedy of honor and profit. By this means he may perhaps be won to your service." Phelippes himself, Morgan earnestly added, had raised the possibility that he might "serve and honor your Majesty." That Morgan could seriously entertain hopes of corrupting Walsingham's own man to their cause only showed how completely Mary's supporters were entangled in a web woven by Mr. Secretary by this point.

Gifford arrived at Rye in mid-December 1585 and was at once arrested and taken to London. Whether this was when he actually agreed to do Walsingham's service, or whether his arrest was merely a prearranged sham, was never definitely established. In any case, his subsequent cover story was a minor masterpiece of psychological manipulation: Gifford sent word back to Morgan that the story he had told Mr. Secretary while under arrest was that he had come over to try to advance the interests of their Welsh side in the internecine fight of the Catholic factions, and that Walsingham was so taken with the idea that he had let him go, giving him twenty pounds for good measure to carry on his work of agitating the English Catholics against the Jesuits and Dr. Allen.

From Paris, Berden reported that there had been no difficulty in getting Morgan to swallow the story. "Here is great joy that Gilbert Gifford escaped your Honor's hands so easily," Berden informed Walsingham on the 2nd of January 1586.

Gifford spent a few weeks at large in London, being entertained by Catholic noblemen, calling several times at the French embassy to meet the new ambassador's secretary. Finally, Gifford showed the secretary his letter from Morgan and made his pitch: Morgan had told him how Mary's letters were being carried between Paris and the embassy in the diplomatic bag, he confided in the secretary; he was now willing to carry them on their dangerous second leg, between the embassy and Mary. Gifford's father lived near where Mary was now being held in Staffordshire, in a moated manor house called Chartley Hall, so he would have an excuse for traveling there without raising suspicions; even better, since he had been gone from England for nearly a decade but looked much younger than his twenty-five years—he still had no beard—no one would be likely to recognize him anyway.

Châteauneuf was by nature cautious; he had his secretary give Gifford just one letter for Mary, in which he put little of consequence. The letter was enciphered using the last cipher that Mauvissière had used in his communications with Mary, nearly two years earlier.

For most of that time, Mary had been effectively cut off from word from her friends. On the 16th of January, Gifford, having traveled north to Chartley, succeeded in delivering the letters from Morgan and Châteauneuf. Mary replied at once, expressing great pleasure at receiving news; sorrow at Morgan's continuing detention in the Bastille; gratitude "for this bringer, whom I perceive very willing to acquit himself honestly of his promise made to you." But she feared for his discovery: "My keeper having settled such an exact and rigorous order in all places where any of my people can go, as it is very strange if they receive or deliver anything which he is not able to know very soon after." She would accordingly communicate nothing of importance until she was sure the ambassador had received a new cipher, which she was enclosing.

She begged the ambassador also to send the large packet of letters for her that had been accumulating in the embassy since Mauvissière's courier system was blown. She begged him, too, to be on strict guard against the spies who, under the color of the Catholic religion, would be assiduously working to penetrate his house, and her secrets, as they had under his predecessor.

10

THE FINAL ACT

The first time Mr. Secretary Walsingham had discovered Mary in clandestine contact with her allies, he had moved too quickly; he had succeeded in plugging a dangerous breach in her wall of isolation, a wall that he had zealously erected to prevent any collusion with her supporters in and out of England; but in so doing he had thrown away a valuable opportunity to learn more about the plotters who wished to reach her, and the plots by which they hoped to secure her liberation.

The second time he discovered such a clandestine communication system, he had bided his time, having come to recognize in the interval that there was more to be gained by letting a plot mature, and little danger in letting it mature while he was privy to the very confidences exchanged by the plotters themselves. Only after the plot was exploded did he move to plug the breach.

Now Mr. Secretary had simply taken such thinking to its logical conclusion. The advantages of allowing Mary to communicate far outweighed the advantages of maintaining her isolation. And so he would not wait for Mary's friends to attempt the next resurrection of the secret post; he would simply supply it himself, a breach of his own creation, one that would be his from the start.

The means by which Gilbert Gifford delivered his letters to Mary on the 16th of January 1586, and by which he received her replies, was the handiwork of Sir Amias Paulet and Thomas Phelippes, who had traveled to Chartley earlier in the month. Another small psychological masterpiece: completely believable, relying as it apparently did on the venality of a low tradesman; intricate enough in its working to have a certain fascination that was a useful distraction from any suspicion that it was all just a fake.

A local brewer delivered beer to Chartley once a week, taking away the empty barrels at the same time. "The honest man," Paulet facetiously called him. He was first bribed by Gifford to slip packets of letters to and from Mary into a corked tube that could be shoved into the beer barrels through the bunghole. Then he was bribed by Paulet to let him have a look at the parcels before they continued their journey: back into the barrel for the incoming post, to Gifford for the outgoing.

The brewer, like the Scottish Queen herself, assumed Gifford truly was Mary's man; the reason Paulet would take his own look at the parcels was to keep a check on both Gifford and the "honest man," to make sure neither was playing a double, or a triple, game. Once the outgoing letters were in Gifford's hands, Gifford passed them to Phelippes, who deciphered the originals while Gifford made his way leisurely back to London; the originals were then sent by express, restored to Gifford, who showed up at the French embassy and turned them over. Going north, the procedure was reversed: the embassy to Gifford; Gifford to Phelippes; Phelippes back to Gifford; Gifford to the brewer; the brewer to Paulet; Paulet back to the brewer; and so into the beer barrel and so to Mary.

Châteauneuf had his doubts about Gifford; Paulet and Phelippes had their doubts; Mary had none. In her first letter to the French Ambassador, she had eagerly pressed Châteauneuf to entrust the large packet to Gifford at once, placing it in "a strong leather box or pouch": she was clearly taken with the beer barrel scheme. She gave the "honest man" twenty pounds for his good work, then another ten, then various tips of gold "angels," coins worth a half-pound each. Gifford, recognizing an opportunity to make a profit himself while he was at it, managed to convince Morgan that *he* needed money to bribe the brewer, too; Morgan sent along eight angels and a promise of twenty crowns more.

Not to miss a unique chance himself, the "honest man" then raised the price he charged for the beer he delivered to Chartley.

Gifford had returned to London in mid-February to collect from Walsingham Mary's first return post, and had appeared at the French embassy to deliver those letters on the 19th of the month. Châteauneuf, now considerably reassured, turned over the large packet Mary eagerly awaited: it was actually twenty-one packets, virtually every letter that had arrived for Mary since the exposure of the Throckmorton Plot. They were too many to cram all at once through a barrel hole and so would have to be broken into smaller bundles—a convenient excuse for the time it would take Phelippes to decipher them all, and also for breaking the seals on them: no need for the finesse of Mr. Secretary's seal-lifter. They were the last letters to present any real decipherment challenge to Phelippes, too, for henceforth the letters to and from Mary would all be in the new cipher she herself had supplied the ambassador, which had landed in Phelippes's hands along with Mary's very first reply.

⁘

The web that Mr. Secretary had woven about Mary and her friends was now drawn so tight that the flies were colliding with one another on their way to being trapped. For the past year, Mr. Secretary's spy Berden had been sending the occasional news of an English missionary priest named John Ballard. He was traveling about London and the countryside under false names; he had pitched up at the same time as Berden, in August 1585, in Paris, where he enjoyed a great reputation as a leading agitator among the Catholic nobility in England. In May 1586, a letter to Mary from Charles Paget (a letter that Mr. Secretary now read as a matter of course) commended Ballard's efforts to rally the Catholic forces in England to take up arms if the promise of foreign troops could once again be revived.

Yet another spy was on Ballard now, a man named Bernard Maude, another of Mr. Secretary's lowlifes, sprung from prison where he had been serving three years for blackmailing the Protestant Archbishop of York: a satisfactory enough recommendation in

Catholic circles. Maude was Ballard's great friend, haunting the Plough Inn tavern with him every night just outside the Temple Bar in London's legal precincts, securing false passports, traveling with him to Paris in May 1586, clinging to him like the shirt on his back.

Ballard was a priest but a priest with dreams of glory; in the taverns he called himself "Captain Fortesque," treated the young soldiers and gentlemen and various hangers-on to suppers and feasts, wore a cape laced with gold and a hat with silver buttons, presented himself to the world as a gallant swashbuckler.

In Paris that May, Paget had taken Ballard to see Bernardino de Mendoza, who had become the Spanish Ambassador to France following his expulsion from England for his part in the Throckmorton Plot. In his letter to Mary, Paget reported on the state of their efforts to dust off the old plot. Mendoza had asked for a list of the principal noblemen and knights in the north who would support a rising; they talked about the best ports at which to land an invasion force; Mendoza had already "advertised the King of Spain in general terms what Ballard came for." The ambassador had asked him to keep it quiet for now and not inform Mary, but Paget could not resist: "For though to content him I said I would not, yet I know my duty and obedience ever command me to declare to your Majesty what importeth to you; and specially such a matter of importance as this: and therefore am I humbly to beseech your Majesty to direct me in what sort you will have me proceed further."

Ballard returned that month to London, still dogged by the spy Maude, and at the end of May he sought out one of his Plough Inn acquaintances at his lodgings. Anthony Babington was wealthy, handsome, twenty-five years old, Catholic. He had worked as a page in the Earl of Shrewsbury's establishment when the Earl was the Queen of Scots' keeper, had traveled to France and played some part in aiding the missionary priests. His name had a small place in Walsingham's files: he had been mentioned by Henry Fagot among those helping to sell papist books out of the French embassy.

Inevitably, Babington, too, was soon dogged by one of Walsingham's men: Robert Poley, whose work to set up a secret channel between Morgan and Mary had been supplanted by Gifford's far more satisfactory results, and who now had the leisure to resume trolling among the Catholic demimonde of London.

Everyone knew Poley. He kept a house in London with "a table handsomely supplied" where all his Catholic acquaintances could come and go—as one would later recall with the bitterness that comes from betrayal not just of a cause but of one's own emotional gullibility. There was nothing "Robin" would not promise his friends; they could use his house even when he was not there; if they wanted letters or money sent overseas, he could arrange it.

And then there was another hapless conspirator, John Savage, who had been a student at the English seminary at Rheims, where he had, in the presence of none other than Gilbert Gifford, sworn an oath to kill Queen Elizabeth. It was Gifford who now, not unnaturally, attached himself to Savage in London as Mr. Secretary's spy, and a bit of a provocateur as well: Gifford made a point of reminding Savage of his earlier pledge, and Gifford also offered to travel to France to secure theological reassurance on the validity of political assassination in a holy cause. Gifford assured him that, although there was a treatise that had been sent over from Rheims "inveighing against such as should seek her majesty's death," that was merely a ruse to "blind the eyes of the Privy Council here to have less fear of her majesty's person."

------------◦❧ ❧◦------------

The plotters were a slightly dreamy, slightly unbalanced bunch, thirteen eventually, who met at Babington's lodgings in Hern's Rents, or at the Plough Inn, or around Saint Paul's, or in Saint Giles fields, near the city, night after night.

Ballard was the most enthusiastic. At his meeting with Babington in late May, he had excitedly insisted that Mendoza had *promised* to send sixty thousand Spanish troops; they would *definitely* come by September; the job of the plotters was now to organize the English Catholic armies that would rise with them. And Ballard himself raised the necessity of dispatching Elizabeth, proposing Savage as the "instrument" to see it done.

Gifford had by now become one of the inner circle, edging things along as needed, though in truth there was little need. Morgan and Paget themselves, from Paris, kept up a drumbeat of encouragement, urging Savage to make cause with Ballard, seconding Ballard's fantastically exaggerated version of the true state of play with respect to the promised Spanish aid.

By June, Poley was also beginning to pick up hints of a plot from his soundings of Babington. Though Poley did not have anything like the whole picture, he reported to Mr. Secretary that Babington was worried whether it was lawful to murder the Queen of England. Morgan had written Mary in April urging her to send a word of favor and encouragement to Babington; Walsingham had held up that letter, but now, after getting Poley's report, he let it go through to see what hares it might start. On the 25th of June, Mary wrote her young, idealistic supporter, all charming royal graciousness:

> My very good friend,
> Albeit it be long since you heard from me, no more than I have done from you, against my will, yet I would not you should think I have in the meanwhile, nor will ever be, unmindful of the effectual affection you have shewn heretofore towards all that concerneth me.

And so it was put in cipher, and into the beer barrel, and so to London and to Walsingham, and so to Babington.

On the 7th of July, Babington's answer was on its way, this time conveyed by Phelippes himself, who, having been in London of late, was returning to Chartley so he could decipher Mary's letters on the spot. Babington now laid out the entire hazy plan and sought Mary's explicit approval. It was part lament, part boast, part desperate seeking of sanction for so dread a step. He confessed he had been near despair when Mary was placed in the custody of Paulet, "a wicked Puritan and mere Leicesterian, a mortal enemy both by faith and faction to your Majesty and the State Catholic"; he had been preparing to depart the country to spend the remainder of his days in solitary wretchedness until

> there was addressed to me from the parts beyond the seas one
> Ballard, a man of virtue and learning, and of singular zeal to
> the Catholic cause and your Majesty's service. This man in-
> formed me of great preparation by the Christian princes (your
> Majesty's allies) for the deliverance of our country from the ex-
> treme and miserable state wherein it hath too long remained.

And so here was laid out the whole scheme that had been hatched in too many tavern feasts on too many late nights. Babington himself would lead ten gentlemen and a hundred followers to "undertake the delivery of your royal person from the hands of your enemies." And:

> for the dispatch of the usurper, from the obedience of whom
> we are by excommunication of her made free, there be six no-
> ble gentlemen all my private friends who for the zeal they bear
> to the Catholic cause and your Majesty's service will undertake
> that tragical execution.

On the 13th of July, Mary's secretary sent Babington a short reply saying that she had received his letter and would answer in two or three days, when the next chance to smuggle out a letter came.

The next day, Phelippes sent Walsingham a note reporting this, adding: "We attend her very heart at the next."

On the 17th, Mary replied. Phelippes sent the decipher to Mr. Secretary at once with a cover note:

> You have now the Queen's answer to Babington, which I re-
> ceived yesternight. If he be in the country, the original will
> be conveyed unto his hands, and like enough an answer re-
> turned. I look for your honor's speedy resolution touching his

apprehension. . . . I think under correction you have enough of him.

I am sorry to hear from London that Ballard is not yet taken . . .

Mary's letter was long and detailed. She praised Babington for his service; she asked for details of the numbers of forces, the arms and money they would require, what captains they would appoint in each shire, what ports would be used for the invasion. "The affairs being thus prepared and forces in readiness both within and without the realm," she concluded, "then shall it be time to set the six gentlemen to work, taking order, upon the accomplishing of their design, I may be suddenly transported out of this place." She made it clear that it would be a mistake to try to free her before Elizabeth had been taken care of, for in such a case, if the attempt to free her failed, "that Queen, in catching me again," would "enclose me forever in some hole, forth of which I should never escape, if she did use me no worse."

She ended, "Fail not to burn this present quickly."

Phelippes endorsed the packet with a doodle of a gallows.

Babington received the letter on the 29th of July. But in truth, for two months he had been wavering, as Mr. Secretary well knew: for this simple, slightly dreamy soul, who preferred philosophy to action when it came to it, had been confiding his increasingly troubled state of mind to his newfound boon companion Robert Poley.

Not that Babington didn't have his doubts about Poley. In his letter to Mary, Babington had added a postscript to her secretary asking what kind of man Poley was: "I am private with the man and by means thereof know somewhat but suspect more. I pray you deliver your opinion of him." Mary's secretary had replied cautiously. "There is great assurance given of Mr. Poley his faithful serving of her majesty, and by his own letters hath vowed and promised the same," he wrote. But: "As yet her majesty's experience of him is not so great as I dare embolden you to trust him much."

Not much help; though Babington was heading swiftly beyond help. He had begun to look for a way out: in fact, it was his search for an escape that had driven him to make Poley's acquaintance in the first place, for he had suddenly promised Poley a fabulous, a desperate sum, £300, if Poley could use his connections with Mr. Secretary to secure him a passport. Maybe if he went abroad, Babington pressed Poley to tell Mr. Secretary, he could do Elizabeth some service "by way of discovery in his travels."

It was a strange twilight that Anthony Babington now wandered through; actually meeting with Walsingham at Greenwich in the last week of June; Walsingham toying with him, holding out hints that he might save himself yet, urging him to be "open," stretching out his hand and saying, "Come now, act with confidence, do not fear to speak out freely"; then sending word back through Poley that he was now rather disinclined to help, disappointed that Babington "was so close and spare in opening himself and the means of his offered service."

Then offering a second meeting, Babington coming to Barn Elms, Walsingham suggesting he could arrange a meeting between Babington and the Queen herself to discuss his offer. Babington was now unsure who was playing with whom. He confessed to Poley that he was growing uneasy about "the course holden with Mr. Secretary both by him and me"; they seemed to be standing in a limbo between two courses and "not very sincere unto either"; perhaps it would be better if they were both to just give it all up, "to dedicate ourselves to a contemplative life, leaving the practice of all matters of state."

Then the two met with Walsingham a third time, on the 13th of July, again at Barn Elms; Walsingham again pressed Babington to tell everything he might know.

As they were rowed down the Thames back to London, Babington, more doubtful and suspicious than ever, asked Poley how it was that "your credit grows with Mr. Secretary."

Poley replied he had been able to feed some information about the Catholics to Walsingham and allay his suspicions. Babington said this was impossible, since no Catholics trusted Poley and wouldn't tell him anything of importance. Poley said he had been able to get some news from Morgan.

"How is that possible, considering how suspicious Morgan is?" Babington pressed.

"Such points are better imagined, than questioned or resolved," Poley replied, with a small laugh: the endless resources of the double agent to blow layer upon layer of smoke in his twilight world.

Phelippes had urged Babington's arrest at once; Mr. Secretary, however, was not quite finished with him. He had Phelippes add a postscript to Mary's letter to Babington, using the same cipher in which Mary's words had been encoded, asking for the names of the six gentlemen. It was a virtuoso bit of counter-intelligence, but apparently wasted, for Babington had still not answered the letter.

On Wednesday, the 3rd of August, Walsingham told Phelippes to wait one more day but no longer before moving against Babington: it was "better to lack the answer, than to lack the man." Mr. Secretary had already issued a warrant for Ballard, "signed by the Lord Admiral for that I would not be seen in the matter." But he feared Babington was alarmed: a messenger sent to his lodgings for his answer to Mary had found him gone.

Throughout the day, a flurry of messages went from Mr. Secretary at Richmond to Phelippes as the search for Babington continued:

> I look for Poley from whom I hope to receive some light. . . .
> You will not believe how much I am grieved at the event of this
> case. I fear the addition of the postscript hath bred the jeal-
> ousy. And so praying God to send us better success than I look
> for, I commit you to his protection. At the Court the iii of this
> present 1586.
>
> Yr loving friend,
> Fra: Walsyngham

Now Babington cracked—too late. He poured out to Poley a complete confession of the conspiracy, naming Ballard, offering to tell Walsingham all. Poley went down to Richmond with the offer, but now Walsingham put off a proposed meeting with Babington until Saturday—"to the end he may in the meantime be apprehended," Walsingham wrote Phelippes later that day, adding, "Though I do not find but that Poley hath dealt honestly with me, yet I am loath to lay myself in any way open unto him, but have only delivered such speeches as might work. . . . I do not think good notwithstanding to defer the apprehension of Bab. longer than Friday."

On Thursday, the 4th, Ballard was arrested at Poley's garden house, where he had come for a meeting. Poley—a slight comedy of errors—had taken it upon himself to keep Babington close to him, which was why the searchers had not found him at his own lodgings earlier; Babington now probably watched Ballard's arrest from the window of Poley's house. Babington still could not quite grasp Poley's role, or his own situation. He had returned from a walk to find Poley making a copy of the letter from Mary; Poley had torn it up and tried to make a joke out of it; but Babington could see the game was almost up.

That night, he sat in Poley's house and wrote a bittersweet farewell note:

> Robyn,
> Sollicitae non possunt curae mutare rati stamina fusi [Neither worry nor pains can alter the thread of fate]. I am ready to endure whatsoever shall be inflicted. Et facere et pati Romanorum est [Both to do and to bear is Roman]. What my course hath been towards Mr. Secretary you can witness, what my love towards you, yourself can best tell. Proceedings at my lodgings have been very strange.
>
> I am the same I always pretended. I pray God you be, and ever so remain towards me. Take heed to your own part, lest of these my misfortunes you bear the blame. Est exilium inter malos vivere [It is an exile to live amid the wicked].

Farewell, sweet Robyn if, as I take thee, true to me. If not, adieu, omnium bipedum nequissimus [of all two-footed things the wickedest]. Return me thine answer for my satisfaction, and my diamond, and what else thou wilt.

The furnace is prepared wherein our faith must be tried. Farewell until we meet, which God knoweth when.

Thine, how far thou knowest,
Anthony Babington

With several of the other conspirators, Babington now fled to Saint John's Wood, a remnant of a thick forest near the city, and, as the chronicler Camden later told the tale, cut off his hair and "disguised and sullied the natural beauty of his face with the rind of green walnuts." The conspirators had not helped their escape by having vaingloriously posed for a portrait, with Babington in the center; they had even had the painter inscribe a Latin verse, *Hi mihi sunt Comites, quos ipsa Pericula ducunt,* "These men are my companions, whom very dangers draw." On reflection, they had thought that too much a giveaway, and had a new verse put in, *Quorsum haec alio properantibus?,* "To what end are these things to men who hasten to another purpose?" Not that it mattered now. On the 14th of August, Babington and companions, half starved and in rags, were arrested and carried back to London.

On the 20th of September, Babington and his six principal accomplices were hanged—barely—before being drawn and quartered in Saint Giles fields, close to Babington's lodgings at Hern's Rents.

The arrest of the conspirators was a sudden blaze of light cast onto the twilight verge where Mr. Secretary's agents provocateurs and the double agents had been feeding; Poley was momentarily dazzled and was taken with the rest.

Gifford, a wilder or shrewder hare, bolted. From Paris he wrote Phelippes and Walsingham that he hoped his flight would not be taken "sinistrously"; but his situation, however honestly he had served his country in exposing such evil practices, had become precarious in the extreme. "I say, to deal with such treacherous, youthful companions, without any warrant or discharge, in how dangerous a practice: I beseech your Honor to know this to have been the only cause of my departure." Walsingham was eventually convinced; the tracks were covered; Gifford's name vanished from the indictments later officially published; and, a rare token from a parsimonious service, Gifford was granted a pension of £100 a year, enough to set him up for life. He had a bad end: ordained a priest at Rheims in 1587, he was caught in a Paris brothel in December of that year and cast into prison by the Archbishop of Paris; he died, still in prison, in November 1590.

Poley was kept in the Tower for two years; mostly for show. He wrote out a long "confession"; then he went back to doing odd jobs for Walsingham, as a court "messenger." He will "beguile you either of your wife, or of your life," a friend warned the London tradesman in whose house Poley lodged upon his release—and whose wife Poley was indeed bedding. Poley had money to burn, forty pounds to fix up his rooms; he was full of boasts. "Mr. Secretary did deliver me out" of the Tower, he bragged: "There are further matters between him and me than all the world shall know of."

Mr. Secretary now pressed for Mary herself to be brought to trial. For a dozen years or more he had sought her destruction, and now the means were at last at hand. Mary's rooms were searched and all her papers seized. There was some muttering about doing away with her by poison and saving the trouble; Walsingham, with an eye as always toward the public case, wanted an open trial, all of the evidence laid out for the world to see, the endorsement of Parliament to any sentence of death.

Elizabeth dragged her feet but finally consented. In late September 1586, a special commission of forty-two peers, Privy Councilors, and judges, among them Burghley and Walsingham, was named to try the Queen of Scots. On the 25th of September, Mary was brought to Fotheringay Castle, an ancient stronghold in Northamptonshire, near Peterborough, surrounded by a double moat on three sides and the River Nene on the fourth.

Over the next two weeks the commissioners arrived. Mary swore she would have nothing to do with the trial: she would die "a thousand deaths" before acknowledging herself a subject under the Queen of England's jurisdiction. Only when it was made clear to her that she would be tried in absentia did she relent.

The trial opened in the castle's great hall on the 15th of October. The charge was read against her; Mary denied she even knew Babington. Confessions of Babington and the conspirators were read in which they admitted receiving Mary's fatal letter approving their intentions; then the testimony of her own secretaries, who admitted that they had copied and dispatched the letter; Mary blustered that if her secretaries had "written any thing prejudicial to the Queen my sister they have written it altogether without my knowledge, and let them bear the punishment for their inconsiderate boldness." And furthermore, "the majesty as the safety of all princes must fall to the ground if they depend upon the writings and testimonies of secretaries."

A copy of her letter to Babington was produced; she responded that "it was an easy matter to counterfeit the ciphers and characters of others": she was "afraid this was done by Walsingham" to bring her to her end.

At which point Walsingham rose from his place among the commissioners to defend himself:

> I call God to witness, that as a private person I have done nothing unbeseeming an honest man, neither in my public condition and quality have I done anything unworthy of my place. I confess that, out of my great care for the safety of the Queen and realm, I have curiously endeavored to search and sift out all plots and designs against the same. . . .

A careful distinction, but not a disingenuous one: a gentleman's private reputation rested upon his honor and truth in dealing with others, his integrity in office upon his allegiance to the law and to the safety of the realm; but there were times when law and safety demanded, or at least did not forbid, a measure of deception that would be an affront in private affairs. In any case, Mary accepted Walsingham's word, and withdrew her accusation against him.

On the 25th of October, the commissioners reconvened in Westminster and convicted Mary of the "compassing, practicing, and imagining of her Majesty's death."

And now Elizabeth once again began dragging her feet; she cast about for some means to execute sentence while leaving her own hands clean. Parliament at once ratified the commissioners' decision; the Queen responded with regal obfuscation, refusing to answer one way or the other their demand that sentence be executed without delay.

Walsingham prepared a lengthy memorandum arguing the extreme danger of delay; he soon found himself once again out of royal favor for his persistent refusal to indulge the Queen's vacillations. On the 16th of December, he took himself to Barn Elms, leaving behind a note for Burghley displaying a rare burst of self-pity:

> I humbly beseech your lordship to pardon me in that I did not take my leave of you before my departure from the court, her Majesty's unkind dealings towards me hath so wounded me as I could take no comfort to stay there. And yet if I saw any hope that my continuance there might either breed any good to the church or furtherance to the service of her Majesty or of the realm, the regard of my particular should not cause me to withdraw myself. But seeing the declining state we are running into, and that men of best desert are least esteemed, I hold them happiest in this government that may be rather lookers-on than actors.

A week later, Walsingham wrote to Leicester, "The delay of the intended and necessary execution doth more trouble me, considering the danger her Majesty runneth, than any particular grief." In January 1587, he told Burghley that his grief had plunged his health into a dangerous state.

The Queen's vacillations now took an even more duplicitous turn. On the 1st of February 1587, she at last signed the warrant for Mary's execution; she told William Davison, Walsingham's assistant, that on his way to the Lord Chancellor to have the warrant receive the Great Seal she should stop by Walsingham's house and show it to him. "Go tell all this to Walsingham who is now sick, although I fear me he will die for sorrow when he hears it," she wisecracked.

But then she suddenly demanded that Davison and Walsingham write to Paulet and point out how much more convenient it would be if Mary died at the hands of someone other than an official executioner. It was Paulet's finest hour; no one else's. The secretaries did as they were bidden: "We find by speech lately uttered by her Majesty that she doth note in you both a lack of that care and zeal of her service that she looketh for at your hands," they wrote Paulet, "in that you have not in all this time found out some way to shorten the life of that Queen." The Bond of Association, which Paulet himself had signed, was adequate justification for the deed; Elizabeth "taketh it most unkindly" that Paulet should "cast the burthen upon her, knowing as you do her indisposition to shed blood, specially of one of that sex and quality, and so near to her in blood as the said Queen is."

Paulet wrote back at once an appalled but steadfast refusal: "My own good livings and life are at her Majesty's disposition and I am ready to so lose them this next morrow. . . . But God forbid that I should make so foul a shipwreck of my conscience, or leave so great a blot to my poor posterity, to shed blood without law or warrant."

The Queen sneered that Paulet seemed to be a "precise and dainty fellow."

Meanwhile, she gave Davison still more contradictory instructions about whether the warrant should actually be dispatched; Davison, inexperienced in her Majesty's talent for shifting blame upon others, was more bewildered than suspicious that he was being set up for a fall. He nonetheless consulted Burghley, and the Privy

Council agreed to take responsibility for putting the now fully executed and legal warrant into effect at once—before Elizabeth
changed her mind yet again. On the 4th of February, Robert Beale
was sent to Fotheringay with the warrant in hand. An executioner
headed north, too, his axe concealed in a trunk, his way paid by
Walsingham.

On the morning of the 8th, Mary was led to the ground floor of
the great hall of the castle, directly below the room where she had
been tried, mounted three steps to a wooden stage that had been
erected, and placed her head upon the block, where it was severed
with three blows from the executioner's axe.

1584-90: War, at Last

II

OLD FRIENDS AND ENEMIES

Sir Francis Walsingham's public and private muses rarely consulted one another. At the moment when his policy of a dozen years had triumphed, and the bosom serpent at last been slain, he was ill at home, out of favor, broke, bereft.

In one way he was fortunate: it was Davison who bore the brunt of the Queen's fury at the failure of the too-clever maneuvering by which she had hoped to throw the blame for Mary's death on others. Despite the efforts the Council had made to spread the responsibility among themselves, Elizabeth insisted it was Davison alone who had defied her orders not to deliver Mary's execution warrant; she had him thrown in the Tower, threatened actually to hang him.

For a while it looked as if she was really going to do it. She obtained an opinion from a judge that it was within her prerogative to do so, and was preparing to secure the support of the rest of her learned judges; Burghley sent a panicked message to the judges urging them to uphold the law: "I think it a hard time if men, for doing well afore God and man, shall be otherwise punished than law may warrant with an opinion gotten from the judges that her prerogative is above the law."

In the end, a commission found Davison guilty of contempt and misprision and sentenced him to pay a ten-thousand-mark fine and be imprisoned in the Tower at the Queen's pleasure. But the fine was never enforced, and Davison was freed in September 1588, and Mr. Secretary Walsingham managed to see to it that his colleague continued to receive his official salary and financial allowances.

The triumph of Mr. Secretary's policy toward Spain had brought its share of personal grief, too. By the time of Mary's execution in

February 1587, England was at long last engaged in the open war against Spain in the Netherlands that Walsingham had long sought; and Sir Philip Sidney, Walsingham's son-in-law and perhaps his only true friend in the world, had been killed in battle there.

The road to war had been the usual meander through thickets and by-courses, a decade-long series of detours and false starts, frequently driving Walsingham to near-despair. Burghley, ever hopeful of keeping the peace with Spain, had consistently opposed doing anything provocative, and the rift between the two former friends and allies had grown as the grievances between England and Spain had piled up. Besides the rather direct evidence of Spanish evil intentions that had become apparent in Mendoza's plotting on behalf of Mary, there had been many other flash points. Several small bands of Spanish troops had landed in Ireland, in the name of the Pope; Philip disavowed responsibility. In August 1580, Spain had seized Portugal, following the death of the heirless king, a huge shift in the continental balance of power and another menacing step closer to the shores of England; the Queen cautiously extended diplomatic courtesies and a refuge in London to a rival claimant to the Portuguese throne.

The following month, September 1580, Francis Drake, a man scarcely better than a pirate as far as the Spanish—and a good many Englishmen, too—were concerned, returned from a three-year voyage of discovery and plunder. He had circled the world; on his way he had worked up the Pacific coast of America picking off one Spanish treasure ship after another. And so Drake sailed into Plymouth Harbor carrying tons of silver and hundreds of pounds of gold, ingots and coins, worth probably £300,000. Burghley insisted it be returned to Spain; the Queen, who was due a huge share of the booty, agreed with Leicester and Walsingham, both investors themselves in the voyage, that Philip had given her ample reason to keep it. Drake's own huge cut—somehow only £70,000 of what he brought back was ever officially registered—made him fabulously rich, and he quickly bought himself a manor and the respectability he had been lacking. The Queen knighted him and ordered that his ship the *Golden Hind*

be put in dock at Deptford as a permanent memorial to his triumphant voyage. Burghley sourly rejected a gift of ten gold bars, saying he could not in conscience receive stolen goods.

But it was the deteriorating situation of the Dutch Protestants
that had finally begun to force the issue between England and Spain
to a showdown. Anjou's great expedition to champion the Dutch
rebels had been a dud; then he had dropped dead of typhoid just a
month before the Prince of Orange's assassination in July 1584; and
then the Dutch rebels were left holding on by a thread. They had the
provinces of Holland and Zealand in the north; in the south, town
after town had fallen to the methodical and merciless siege-and-
starvation tactics of Parma, the Italian prince and general who now
ruled for Spain in the Netherlands. The besieged towns of Brussels,
Antwerp, and Mechlin were the only rebel strongholds in the south
still in Protestant hands, and not for long by the looks of it.

Walsingham had urged that if ever there were a time for action
this was it; he pressed the Council for a decision, drawing up a list of
precise particulars to be debated and decided:

Matters to be resolved in Council
  Whether Holland and Zealand, the Prince of Orange being
now taken away, can with any possibility hold out unless they
be protected by some potent prince.
  Whether it be likely that the King of Spain, being possessed
of these countries, will attempt somewhat against her Majesty . . .
  Whether if her Majesty enter into the matter it will not
draw on a war.
  What means her Majesty shall have to maintain and continue the war.
  What charges by estimate the said war will amount unto . . .
  By what means it is like the King of Spain, if the war shall
fall out, will attempt to annoy her Majesty, and how the same
may be prevented.
  What way there may be devised to annoy the King of Spain.

He had a brief moment of hope: "Upon thorough debating of the matter . . . it hath grown half a resolution that the peril would be so great in case Spain should possess the said countries . . . it behoove her Majesty to enter into some course for their defense."

And then the usual dithering again. The Queen's long addiction to indecision was both prudence and habit; she had always resisted demands on the Treasury, she was ever wary of committing herself to a course that entailed the risk of failure and blame or that foreclosed the possibility of an easy way out; she had learned from experience that if she temporized long enough many problems just went away. She had long ago perfected the art of tactical delay: if she suspected the Council or her Secretary was preparing to force an issue with her, she would avoid seeing them; if after interminable discussions she at last assented to the drafting of instructions, she would then balk at signing them; if she signed them, she would ask Mr. Secretary to delay sending them.

But what had been policy had increasingly become instinct: now, more and more, whenever anyone pressed her for a decision she simply lost her temper.

Burghley, the master at playing to the Queen's instincts, now held out hope for a complex bit of diplomatic finesse in the Netherlands: a vague promise of English aid to get the French to intervene and carry the burden in the Low Countries, while retaining just enough of an English hand in the affair to keep the French "from acquiring to them the absolute dominion of the countries." Walsingham insisted that there was no time for such maneuvers; the future threat the French might pose, were they to secure such a hold, was "a matter worthy of good consideration," he wrote Burghley, "were it not that time hath wrought the necessity of speedy resolution." The only choices were to back the French wholeheartedly or go it alone wholeheartedly. Even Burghley at this point seemed to go along with the interventionist majority on the Council.

The end of 1584 had found Walsingham once again ill in bed. But he saw some of the dispatches being sent to ambassadors in his absence and began to believe Burghley was playing a double game, in the Council openly supporting Walsingham's arguments for English intervention, privately with the Queen undermining them.

An explosion between the two old friends had long been inevitable; it now came, and cleared the air, and did nothing to alter their fundamental differences. Burghley complained that he had heard reports that made him doubt Walsingham's goodwill toward him; Walsingham wrote back a long and very frank letter admitting it was true, but "so have there the like been made unto me that might have bred the like conceipt." He had been inclined to dismiss these reports as rumors, the work of mischief-makers seeking factional gain. But then he had learned that Burghley had apparently tried to block a personal petition he had made to the Queen for the grant of a customs farm for the outports, a vindictive move that seemed to confirm "the truth of former reports of your Lordship's mislike of me." And so, Walsingham admitted, "thereupon I did plainly resolve with myself that it was a more safe course for me to hold your Lordship rather as an enemy than as a friend": those same words he had used about the kingdom of France following the Saint Bartholomew's massacres.

The two men exchanged another pair of letters, open, frank, thankful of each other's honesty, assuring one another of their friendship: so different from the usual dissimulating obsequiousness or touchy self-pity of the courtier. And so they agreed to disagree.

Burghley continued to drop hints to the Queen that, given the expense and uncertainty of war, it would be best not to provoke the Spaniards, that the best way to protect England was to fortify the coasts and rely on the militia; and Walsingham, beside himself as ever, countered that the militia, its recent improvements notwithstanding, was woefully unprepared to fight a professional army, and that the only sure defense of the realm lay in keeping the Spanish occupied elsewhere. "It is dangerous that by sudden invasions men shall be drawn to the use of his weapons before he hath skill how to use it," Walsingham pointed out; the truth was that the men who were to guard the home front "never saw the face of the enemy and their captains are void of experience."

By May 1585, Elizabeth was coming around, egged on by her fury at Philip's sudden seizure of English merchant ships in Spanish harbors; but then the Dutch had begun balking at the terms of the treaty of assistance, haggling over the Queen's demands that Flushing and other towns be turned over to English control as surety for the repayment of the costs. Walsingham now turned with exasperation on the Dutch commissioners: "You are trying to bring her into a public war in which she is to risk her treasure and the blood of her subjects against the greatest potentates of the world and you hesitate meantime at giving her such security as is required for the very defense of the provinces themselves."

The haggling continued; Antwerp fell; at last, in August 1585, a deal was reached. England would send 6,400 foot soldiers, 1,000 horse, provide £126,000 a year to maintain them; an English nobleman would be placed in command of the army. England would hold Flushing and Brill as security, the Dutch to repay all expenses at the conclusion of the fighting.

"You see, gentlemen, that I have opened the door, that I am embarking once for all with you in a war against the King of Spain," Elizabeth grandly told the Dutch commissioners when all was signed. "Very well, I am not anxious about the matter, I hope that God will aid us and that we shall strike a good blow in your cause."

Mr. Secretary knew her Majesty's ways with doors: there was no door she would ever open very wide, no door even when opened that she could not shut again; so he did what he could to stick his foot in the gap. Or, failing that, keep his own back door open. And so, through the spring and summer of 1585, even as he fought the open battle in the Council, Mr. Secretary pursued a series of secretive stratagems, clever and crude, fair and foul.

The Turks were one back door: a long shot, but a brilliant effort. In April 1585, Mr. Secretary had sent his old and trusted agent Jacobo Manucci to Constantinople for a discreet word with the English commercial agent; perhaps it might be possible to induce the Sultan to divert some of the forces from his current war with Persia and undertake a demonstration against Spain instead. In October, Mr. Secretary sent word to try again, laying out a clever series of arguments, his usual combination of cold logic and appeal to superstition and prejudice. The King of Spain was already the most powerful monarch of Christendom. He was now, under cover of attempting to subdue "the rest princes of Christendom who differ from him in faith," seeking to draw all of Europe under him. Once that happened, there could be little doubt that he would turn next to the empires of the Sultan. Even now the growing reputation of the King of Spain inevitably meant a corresponding decline in the Sultan's reputation as a power to be feared. There were rumors that the Sultan was already so terrified that he was fawning upon the King and "forced to beg his peace." Old prophecies were flying about Europe that the Sultan's empire was soon to be broken.

But with England and Spain at war, now was the time to act; if Spain were assailed from two sides simultaneously, there was no question but that the King of Spain would "sink under so heavy a burden." Even if the Sultan merely made a show of preparing for sea with his naval forces to "hold the King of Spain in suspense," it might serve to good purpose by keeping his forces tied up while her Majesty struck against his might in the Low Countries.

But in the end, the Turks would not be drawn.

More successful by far were several schemes Mr. Secretary advanced for stealthy raids by English privateers and small naval squadrons upon Spanish interests across the breadth of its vast empires. In the early spring of 1585, he outlined the first of these in a paper entitled "Plat for the Annoying of the King of Spain." It proposed sending three warships to snap up the Spanish fishing fleet on the Newfoundland Banks. This time his political timing was fortunate, for Philip's arrest of English shipping provided an undeniable justification for such retaliation. Elizabeth approved the plan, and Sir Walter Raleigh was ordered to send a squadron after the Spaniards. They returned with "a good number of Spanish vessels" and six hundred Spanish seamen prisoners.

At about the same time, a far more audacious bit of stealthy maritime enterprise was moving forward. In 1577, Walsingham had been one of the private subscribers of Sir Francis Drake's fabulously successful voyage. He had since backed and promoted other voyages of discovery that promised to combine private profit, scientific discovery, English interests, and Spanish discomfiture. By the summer of 1585, Drake had had plans for a second voyage in the works for over a year; this would be a raid on the West Indies, with the aim of seizing the Spanish treasure fleet carrying gold from the New World. Preparations had dragged on; investors were slow delivering their promised cash; Elizabeth, keen on profit, had put up £10,000 herself but then hesitated to authorize so provocative an endeavor.

But Philip's actions settled it at last; in July, the mission was on again, and the Privy Council issued Drake letters of marque authorizing him to attack Spanish ships. Then more delays; when Drake finally got away from Plymouth on the 14th of September, he was so fearful Elizabeth would by now have changed her mind again that he threw his stores aboard in disarray so he could be gone on a favorable breeze. Then the winds changed, and it took a week to clear the coast; Drake ordered that if forced into port the fleet should make for Ireland or France, so as to remain out of the Queen's reach.

It was a far less profitable voyage than his last one—Drake missed intercepting the treasure ships—but it nonetheless succeeded in wreaking a satisfying degree of havoc among Spain's possessions in the West Indies, what with landing parties looting churches, seizing cannon and military stores, burning settlements, and extorting ransoms. By the following spring, word had come back to Europe of Drake's exploits, and Mr. Secretary's spies in Italy reported that the news had shaken Philip's credit with the Genoese bankers: they had just refused him a loan of a half million crowns.

Mr. Secretary drew up one other plan in the summer of 1585 to secretly tighten the grip on the policy he had so long sought, which even now kept threatening to slip through his fingers just as it was within his grasp. His truce with Burghley of the previous January notwithstanding, Walsingham now launched a bit of scurrilous intrigue against Burghley himself, aimed at weakening his opposition to the war; or, failing that, to discredit him baldly.

One of Walsingham's venerable agents was William Herle: he had worked for Burghley years ago, as the prison stooge who had offered to help Charles Baillie slip ciphered messages to the Bishop of Ross; he had been Walsingham's go-between with the agent Henry Fagot; he had undertaken more respectable diplomatic missions as well. Now, on Walsingham's orders, Herle turned his talents upon Burghley. Herle wrote the Lord Treasurer warning him that he was being spoken of far and wide as an enemy of the Protestant cause in both France and the Netherlands; that people were also saying that he was looking out only for himself, that he had too many splendid houses and too vast an income, that it was said no one could expect the Queen's smallest favor without going through him.

Burghley was sufficiently rattled that he replied with a long defense of himself. Then Walsingham, through Herle, tried to entangle Burghley in a complex scheme that had been talked of for minting English coins in the Low Countries, where they were trading at a considerable premium over their gold value; Herle said that it could net the Queen £10,000 a month and still leave Burghley a cut of £1,000 a month. Burghley spat out the bait, sternly replying to Herle, "I were to blame if I would not assent to her Majesty's profit. . . . But for any offer to myself, I do utterly refuse either such or less sum. . . . I marvel that any malicious discourses can note me a councilor that do abuse my credit for my private gain."

The autumn of 1585 brought a final bit of political theater from Mr. Secretary. In October, the government published a propaganda pamphlet, *Declaration of the Causes Moving the Queen of England to give aid to the Defence of the People afflicted and oppressed in the Low Countries.* Though ostensibly the word of the Queen herself, it had Walsingham written all over it: the combination of simple logic and appeal to prejudice.

The Queen, it began, was of course a sovereign answerable only to God; yet the suffering of the "natural people of the Low Countries" was so great, and England's motives were so pure, that the Queen was "specially moved" to explain her intentions to her people and her neighbors. England and the Low Countries were tied by ancient connections of trade and commerce, "by which mutual bonds there hath continued perpetual unions of the peoples' hearts together." Far from seeking to remove the Low Countries' allegiance to Spain, England was seeking only the restoration of their ancient rights and liberties. Indeed, had England not come to their aid, the native people of the Low Countries would have been prepared to give their allegiance to some "foreign prince." England, however, had no ambitions of sovereignty or territorial aggrandizement. But the King of Spain—misled by his counselors—had appointed "Spaniards, foreigners and strangers of strange blood, men more exercised in wars than in peaceable government," as the governors of the Low Countries: "These Spaniards being exalted to absolute government, by ambition, and for private lucre have violently broken the ancient laws and liberties of all the countries, and in a tyrannous sort have banished, killed, and destroyed, without order of law, within the space of a few months, many of the most ancient and principal persons of the natural nobility that were most worthy of government." Even Catholics suffered. The Queen of England had sent the King of Spain "many friendly messages and ambassadors" warning him how he was being misled; in return, Spain had sent ambassadors who had conspired to overthrow the Queen's realm with the help of the Spanish forces that it sought to plant "so near to us" in the Low Countries themselves. Thus "no reasonable person can blame us if we have disposed ourselves to change this our former course, and more carefully to look to the safety of our self and our people."

The pamphlet was translated and published in all of the major European tongues: the back door wedged open a bit more.

There had been little doubt that Leicester would be the nobleman chosen to lead the English expedition. He was well known in the Low Countries, hailed there as nothing less than the Prince of Orange come back to life. Now, between his vanity and Elizabeth's meddling and temporizing, they managed to undo almost everything. For months Elizabeth hesitated even to give Leicester his commission; she alternately instructed him to proceed and reversed herself. She regularly went into rages and then bouts of self-pity, at one turn indignant that Leicester was setting himself up as a viceroy, with a court to rival her own, she claimed; at another weeping that she was in poor health and needed her favorite courtier to remain by her side, but that he preferred to abandon her in her time of need. "This is one of the strangest dealings in the world," Leicester complained to Walsingham.

Walsingham had been pressing hard to have his son-in-law, Sir Philip Sidney, appointed to the governorship of Flushing, but here, too, the Queen hesitated; Walsingham's opponents feared having so tight a circle, tied by family and faction, in control of so many key posts. "These changes here may work some change in the Low Countries as may prove irreparable," Walsingham wrote Leicester. "God give her Majesty another mind and resolution in proceeding. Otherwise it will work both honest and best affected subjects' ruin."

It was not until the 8th of December 1585 that Leicester finally took ship. Sidney had left a few weeks earlier, having finally secured his appointment and bidden farewell to his wife and newborn daughter.

When Leicester arrived, he at once found himself in an endless battle for the money Elizabeth had promised. Leicester was said to be spending £1,000 a month out of his own pocket; he had raised a personal loan of £25,000 from the City, but it was disappearing faster than even he could account for it. In January 1586, he wrote Walsingham, "Our money goeth very low"; by February, "All our treasure is gone." Every dispatch from Leicester to Walsingham now mentioned money. Though, as Leicester at one point admitted, "Methinks I hear your answer already, that no man knoweth better than I the difficulty to get money from her Majesty."

Walsingham was rapidly exhausting his favor with the Queen in pressing for the dispatch of the funds now desperately needed to pay the troops. It had left him wide open politically; those who still hoped to abandon the war were muttering that Mr. Secretary was merely working to advance Leicester's personal interests, his policy blinded by factional allegiance. In March, Walsingham confided to Leicester, "The opinion of my partiality continueth, nourished by faction, which maketh me weary of the place I serve in and to wish myself amongst the true-hearted Swiss."

And then there were rumors of secret peace negotiations Elizabeth was already pursuing with Parma, before the first battle had been fought. In the spring of 1586, the Queen had heard reports that Spain was preparing a huge invasion force to send against England; it was obviously folly, she now insisted, to send more troops abroad and risk provoking Philip further at a time like this. Walsingham vainly insisted the reports were untrue: his agents in Spain saw no signs of such preparation in Spanish harbors; one well-informed spy reported that only eighteen ships in the entire Spanish fleet were ready for sea.

Elizabeth chose the moment to act as her own spymaster, never a good idea. A ship sailed past the royal palace at Greenwich and fired a salute; the Queen inquired what ship it was and learned it was a Scottish merchantman come from Spain; she summoned the ship's master and interrogated him. Yes, he had seen with his own eyes a fleet of twenty-seven galleons in Lisbon Harbor making ready; yes, he had heard their intended destination was England.

The Queen summoned Walsingham, berated him, and threw a slipper in his face. Walsingham privately observed that the Queen was "daily more and more unapt to embrace any matter of weight."

Leicester was again left out to dry, pleading as ever for money. Hundreds of men deserted. Thousands lacked supplies. Not that it helped that the great commander of the English forces was engaged in a furious and public feud with his infantry commander, Sir John Norris, a man who, unlike Leicester, actually knew something about fighting a war; or that Leicester's command better resembled a feudal lord's retinue than a field army's headquarters. The Earl had brought with him seventy-five servants to attend to his personal needs: steward, secretary, treasurer, four gentlemen of the chamber, two chaplains, physician, surgeon, apothecary, among the many others. With the other noblemen and knights who had volunteered to accompany the Earl, and their servants, his whole personal entourage totaled some two hundred. Night after night, Leicester lavished hospitality on the ladies and noblemen of the Low Countries: great suppers, music, dancing, fireworks. The military campaign went nowhere; the Earl's grand attempts to meddle in the intricacies of Dutch politics went less than nowhere, breeding resentment and worsening rifts among the factions.

In late June, Lady Sidney had sailed to join her husband: a small bit of cheer amid the increasingly bleak situation that Sidney accurately perceived. By August, Sidney was despairing at the course of the aimless and ill-favored campaign; he wrote to his father-in-law telling of the brink that things had been brought to by lack of money to pay the troops:

> I assure you, Sir, this night we were at a fair plunge to have lost all for want of it. We are now four months behind, a thing unsupportable in this place. To complain of my Lord of Leicester you know I may not, but this is the case, if once the soldiers fall to a thorough mutiny this town is lost in all likelihood. I did never think our nation had been so apt to go to the enemy as I find them.

Leicester meanwhile began to look for scapegoats; he turned even on Walsingham, who had more than any man fought for him, and at greater personal cost. "I think you all mean me a forlorn man as you set me in the forlorn hope," Leicester wrote to Walsingham on the 10th of August, full of mawkish self-pity. "I see all men have friends but myself. I see most false suggestions help other men, and my upright, true dealing cannot protect me. Nay, my worldly protector faileth me."

∽✐☙∾

The morning of the 22nd of September 1586 found Sir Philip Sidney on horseback, in a heavy mist, near the Spanish-held fortress of Zutphen. He was part of a small and hastily assembled force that had been ordered to intercept a convoy bringing provisions to the

Spanish garrison; the English numbered no more than 200 horse and 400 foot. Suddenly the fog broke and the mounted men found themselves, ahead of their infantry, facing an enemy force of some 2,200 musketeers and arquebusiers and 800 pikemen that had been thrown across the highway. The first volley of Spanish fire fell square on the horsemen. Sidney's horse was shot out from under him; he remounted and joined the charge. It was then that a musket ball pierced his left thigh, an inch above the knee.

At first the wound did not seem serious. Leicester wrote to Walsingham on the 2nd of October:

> Good Mr. Secretary, I trust now you shall have longer enjoying of your son, for all the worst days are passed, as both surgeons and physicians have informed me, and he amends as well as possible in this time; and himself finds it, for he sleeps and rests well, and hath a good stomach to eat, without fear, or any distemper at all. I thank God for it.

On the 6th, Leicester wrote again: "Your son and mine is well amending as ever man hath done for so short a time. He feeleth no grief now but the long lying, which he must suffer. His wife is with him."

But within a week the wound was infected and gangrenous. On the 17th Sidney was dead.

Leicester sent an affectionate note to Walsingham that seemed to mend the recent rifts between them:

> Your sorrowful daughter and mine is here with me at Utrecht till she may recover some strength, for she is wonderfully thrown through her long care since the beginning of her husband's hurt, and I am the more careful that she should be in some strength ere she take her journey into England, for that she is with child, which I pray God send to be a son if it be His will; but whether son or daughter they shall be my children too. She is most earnest to be gone out of this country and so I

could wish her, seeing it so against her mind, but for her weakness yet, her case considered.

Not long after that, Frances did return to England. Walsingham wrote Leicester on the 24th of December 1586: "I thank God for it I am now in good hope of the recovery of both my daughter and her child." Frances recovered, but miscarried.

The grief of Sidney's loss lay heavy upon Mr. Secretary. Walsingham had lost one of the few men he loved and admired as a true friend. Sidney had written dozens of letters to Walsingham in the time they were acquainted; he had brought Walsingham into the orbit of many of his fellow young writers; Walsingham, an acquaintance recalled, had often paid an openhearted tribute to how Sidney's star as a poet had risen far above his own as a man of affairs: "Those friends which at first were Sir Philip's for his [Walsingham's] sake within a short while became so fully owned and possessed by Sir Philip as now he held them at the second hand by his son-in-law's courtesy."

There was also the prosaic but nonetheless extremely painful fact that Sidney's death now threatened to ruin his father-in-law financially. Sidney had given Walsingham a power of attorney to sell some lands to satisfy his creditors, but nothing had been done before his death. Walsingham now informed Leicester, "I have paid and must pay for him above £6,000, which I do assure your lordship hath brought me into a most hard and desperate state, which I weigh nothing in respect of the loss of the gentleman, who was my chief worldly comfort."

The next day he had worse news: "I have caused Sir Philip Sidney's will to be considered by certain learned in the laws and I find the same imperfect touching the sale of his land for the satisfying of his poor creditors. . . . His goods will not suffice to answer a third part of his debts already known." It appeared that Sidney was in debt to the extent of some £17,000 to the Flushingers.

Sidney's will gave Walsingham and his wife only a token £100

each, "to bestow in jewels or other things as pleaseth them to wear for
my remembrance." In the absence of a male heir, Frances was left
with a life interest in half his estate; their daughter received £4,000.
But all of the lands were bequeathed to Sidney's brother Robert.
Leicester now refused to pay a penny of Sidney's debts, or even allow
any of the land to be sold to cover the costs. The temporary healing
of the breach that Sidney's death had brought the two former allies
Leicester and Walsingham now hardened into an irrevocable chasm.
It grew only deeper the following spring, when Frances secretly remarried, wedding the Earl of Essex: Leicester's stepson from his first
marriage, a man he openly disliked.

The Queen had given Walsingham an export license for another
hundred thousand cloths in 1582, and in August 1585 he had secured
the customs farm for the ports in northern and western England, but
Sidney's debt was a charge that none of this would bear. The Queen
appeared reluctant to do any more.

And now it was Walsingham's old and long-estranged friend
Burghley who came forth to press the suit in his behalf. Burghley told
Elizabeth that she should consider Walsingham "as one to whom under God she ought to acknowledge the preservation of her life" and
reward him accordingly: Babington's estates were forfeit to the
Crown, and she could make a gift of some of them to the man who,
by exposing the plot, had saved her life. The Queen, however, chose
to give Babington's lands to Sir Walter Raleigh instead.

In the end, Walsingham asked Burghley to leave off, for it seemed
pointless to try further: "My hope is, howsoever I am dealt withal by
an earthly Prince, I shall never lack the comfort of the Prince of
Princes." He expressed himself "infinitely bound" to Burghley for his
efforts, "which I will never forget."

Walsingham's reconciliation with his old friend Burghley was the
one spot of personal comfort that lonely winter. Though Leicester's
personal mistreatment of Walsingham had been part of what had
brought Walsingham and Burghley back together, it was also made
easier by the changing political circumstances. Even Leicester's utter
failure to accomplish anything of tactical value against Spain in the

Netherlands could not undo the larger strategic fact that Spain and England were now openly at war; with England committed to a war policy, the decade-long struggle between Walsingham and Burghley over how to deal with Spain was decided, done with. Several months later, Walsingham sent Burghley a handsome gift of a "very rare coach for ease, strength, and lightness, whereof I made this day a trial upon London stones."

12

A TRAITOR IN PARIS

Walsingham's reconciliation with his old friend Burghley at the end of 1586 was in most ways a blessing, but it complicated one old problem. Sir Edward Stafford, the ambassador in Paris, was still Burghley's man, and he had become considerably more annoying.

For one thing, he had not given up on his hopes of giving one in the eye to his rival and tormentor Mr. Secretary: he was still trying to bring off his own extremely amateurish intelligence coups. Stafford declared to the Queen his intention to infiltrate the Catholic exile community in France himself, or have his wife feign Catholicism to do so; the Queen forbade it. Stafford sulkily interpreted this as more Walsingham harassment. "I never heard of any ambassador being blamed for seeking intelligence any way he could," Stafford wrote back. "Perchance," he added, Mr. Secretary objected because he "can send nobody secretly hither without my being advertised of it." The ambassador then proposed a ridiculous scheme to send false information to the Queen in letters that he would dispatch in such a way that they would be certain to be intercepted and read by the Spanish Ambassador. He would mark the false passages with a special symbol so the Queen would know they were "written for a purpose and not for a truth." He desperately wanted to play spy.

Bad enough that it threatened to undermine Mr. Secretary's painstaking efforts to plant false men on Morgan and Paget and the others in Paris, and bad enough that such an erratic, and meddling, and insubordinate man in the post made it extremely difficult to continue using the Paris embassy as Mr. Secretary had been accustomed to, as a hub for the coming and going of his messengers and a transit point for intelligence from so crucial a diplomatic crossroads; worse was that Stafford, desperate for funds, jealous, miffed, was dabbling in more treacherous shoals. There were reports from Paris that Stafford was up to his eyes in debt, gambling huge stakes "that it passes all reason," heading for certain shipwreck if he were not stopped. Back in October 1584, Walsingham had picked up one of Stafford's servants who had arrived at Court to convey letters; there were hints he had also been secretly conveying letters for the Catholic exiles. (Stafford only learned of the man's arrest four months later, and protested furiously.)

And there were more hints that things were not quite as they should be. A letter, intercepted and deciphered by Phelippes, that had gone from the Archbishop of Glasgow to the Queen of Scots in March 1586 had mentioned that the ambassador was very devoted to her service. Stafford, confronted with this, explained that it was all part of the clever double game he was playing; yes, he had been ordered by Mr. Secretary not to continue with his efforts to befriend the Catholic exiles, but if he had drawn back suddenly from his earlier attempts it would have been obvious that he had merely been practicing against them all along, so he had had to withdraw slowly, continuing to offer vague assurances of his desire to help Mary, and so allay suspicion.

It was about this time that Mr. Secretary decided it might be a good idea to have some of his spies in France turn their eyes on the ambassador. Nicholas Berden had played the part of the former prisoner and Catholic exile in France to perfection: so much so that, upon his return to London in the spring of 1586, he had been tracked and nearly arrested by one of the many English priest-takers. Berden had come back to England as the fully trusted agent of the exiles, supplied with a cipher with which to communicate with Paget and the others, and in particular to send "intelligence from England." Berden wrote Walsingham: "If it be your Honor's pleasure that I shall give them intelligence, then I hope your Honor will procure to be set down unto me such matters as I shall certify." At times Paget complained that the news Berden sent back was "stale," but he never suspected that Berden was in fact Walsingham's man, or that the news he supplied was deliberate chickenfeed.

Nor did he suspect that Berden had been prying into the English Ambassador's affairs while he was in Paris. "Paget is not acquainted that I come by the Lord Ambassador's letters," Berden reported to Mr. Secretary. It was, accordingly, around June 1586 that Berden had delivered to Walsingham's secretary a full report on what he had learned of the English Ambassador's doings. The file, endorsed "secret advertisements," gave Mr. Secretary considerable more reason to believe that his suspicions of Stafford had not been misplaced. The most serious charge was that "the Lord Ambassador, in consideration of six thousand crowns, and in performance of his promise, did show the Duke of Guise his letters and intelligences out of England." Stafford, Berden said, had also revealed to Catherine de Médicis that one of her court officials was a spy in Walsingham's pay; the man had been dismissed. Stafford had promised the Catholic exiles in France that he "can send any man into England" for them that they needed. He had tipped off the Catholics that an English captain who had served in the Low Countries and who had been given a packet of letters to carry from the English seminary at Rheims to Paris had come to him to turn the letters over to the English government; Stafford had instructed the man to carry them to England himself, then had arranged for the Catholics to "procure the letters out of his hands." To cover the ambassador's dealings with the Catholic exiles, it had been "concluded between the ambassador and the rest that the better to increase his credit in England, they would deliver him from time to time such intelligences, or the first fruits of the new books and libels as should first come forth"; but they would pass nothing of actual importance to their cause.

And, finally, the ambassador was consumed with a personal hatred of Walsingham: the past Christmas he had told Berden how gleeful he was when he had heard that Mr. Secretary was ill and "in peril of death."

Not long after came a warning from Henry of Navarre that the

Duke of Guise had learned some things that could have come from no other source but Stafford.

──────── ⁊☙☙⁊ ────────

The evidence of course was all circumstantial—circumstantial or unusable. Even had Mr. Secretary been willing to expose Berden's cover, it would have been the word of a scoundrel against the word of a still-powerful and well-connected gentleman.

Mr. Secretary set other spies on Stafford to see if more could be found out, but these lacked the deftness or luck of Berden. The hapless Walter Williams tried his hand; Stafford got him drunk and managed to get him to reveal what he was up to. Phelippes enlisted Gilbert Gifford to the task; this caused embarrassment a year later, and indeed backfired, when letters from Phelippes were found in Gifford's possession, and gleefully published by the French government, following his arrest in that Paris brothel. The letters also mentioned the names of several other of Mr. Secretary's spies in France. Stafford enjoyed a small triumph: he lorded it over Walsingham, writing to Mr. Secretary sarcastically, "Mr. Phelippes must pardon me, being such a statesman as he would fain to be, for saying that to hazard to write to such a knave as this is, things that may be scanned as these are, is not the greatest discretion in the world."

Walsingham had tried to keep Stafford hemmed in; and watched; and placed on notice that he was hemmed in and watched, but Stafford's cockiness or desperation or both had proved too much even for Walsingham's maneuvers. Then Mr. Secretary began to push hard to have him recalled. Burghley balked; Walsingham managed to have his own candidate to replace the increasingly lame-duck but increasingly dangerous ambassador sent over in October 1586; the man was ostensibly there as a special emissary to the French Court, to explain the arrest and proceedings against Mary, but he had hinted heavily to Stafford that he was merely awaiting the next post to arrive to confirm his permanent commission as ambassador.

Walsingham's renewed political alliance and personal debt to

Burghley at the end of 1586 now put an end even to this maneuver, and the would-be replacement returned to London. By early 1587, Walsingham was writing to Stafford assuring him that the ambassador could henceforth enjoy his "goodwill unfeignedly," and that Walsingham would put aside "all things and jealousies past."

An outward rapprochement: a more subtle problem. Mr. Secretary had failed to contain or deter Stafford; he had failed to remove him; now he would have to use him.

Though it would only be proved for certain a few centuries later, it was precisely at this juncture that Stafford began to sell his services to the Spanish Ambassador Mendoza as well as to the Duke of Guise. But Mr. Secretary had his suspicions even as he was burying the hatchet. For one thing, there was the curious fact that Stafford began to send dispatch after dispatch seeking to portray France as the root of all evil, warning against entering any common cause with the French, while singing the praises of Philip of Spain as a man of peace, restraint, and moral rectitude.

In January 1587, the ambassador sent a wholly ludicrous story that a Spaniard passing through Paris had come to the English embassy and revealed that he had made an offer to Philip's Foreign Secretary to assassinate Elizabeth for four thousand crowns, but had been turned down; Philip's secretary had solemnly explained that, even if it was true that Philip would not weep were Elizabeth to die a natural death, "his conscience was too good to seek it that way." It was a ridiculous story, this unnamed Spaniard suddenly feeling the necessity of calling upon Sir Edward and baring his soul to Elizabeth's representative and testifying to the Christian conscience of the King of Spain: it reeked of amateurish practice.

In the spring of 1587 the war in the Netherlands was still being prosecuted as irresolutely as ever, still undermined by Elizabeth's penny-pinching and peace feelers, now exacerbated by her discomfiture with foreign wrath over Mary's execution and her continuing effort to shift the blame for that. Again Walsingham took up the cause of advocating for the Dutch; again he bore the brunt of her irritation.

He wrote Leicester:

> It appeareth by late letters out of the Low Countries that the foot bands and horse bands in her Majesty's pay there are greatly decayed, insomuch as there remain not of the five thousand footmen above three thousand and of the one thousand horse but five hundred. I have acquainted her Majesty herewith and moved her for a supply, but I find her not disposed to resolve therein, and yet is she given to understand in what readiness the enemy is to march. Her Majesty doth wholly bend herself to devise some further means to disgrace her poor Council that subscribed, and in respect thereof she neglecteth all other causes.

"Subscribed": to Mary's death warrant, that is, at the end of 1586.

Elizabeth berated a commission from the Dutch who arrived: they were ingrates; she had spent £140,000 and had nothing to show for it; she wouldn't send another penny or have more to do with them. Leicester, who had returned to England in December, was pressing to resume the campaign, but he needed a loan of £10,000; the Queen was balking at the terms.

And then there was Drake's latest project: he had been denied a license from the Privy Council to equip a fleet for raid on the Spanish mainland, but Walsingham had privately told him to go ahead and he would see what he could do. Drake already had seven ships of his own making ready and a promise of more from the Dutch. At last, on the 15th of March 1587, the Queen agreed to issue Drake his orders: she would supply several royal ships; the crown would get half of the plunder, private investors the other half.

On the 2nd of April, Drake set sail from Plymouth aboard the flagship *Elizabeth Bonaventure,* 550 tons, twenty-eight guns, accompanied by fifteen other, equally well-armed ships and seven small pinnaces.

Part harassing raid, part pre-emptive strike against Spain's naval potential, Drake's exact mission was but vaguely spelled out in his orders. Only a few knew that one of its possible targets was the harbor of Cádiz, a vulnerable and relatively unguarded merchant port on the southern coast of Spain.

And now Mr. Secretary began to put his newfound friendship with Sir Edward Stafford, and the credulity of the credulous ambassador, to especially good use. In March, the Secretary sent a letter to another English envoy, who was at that moment staying at the embassy in Paris. The letter, sent in the cipher that Stafford himself routinely used, ever so indiscreetly revealed that "the Queen had not yet taken any decisions about sending the fleet because she had been discouraged by the news that the warships promised by the Dutch were not as ready as they thought." Having thrown that tidbit Stafford's way, Mr. Secretary ordered all English ports closed for the next two weeks: no more news would be traveling abroad from England while Drake's final preparations were completed.

On the 21st of April, Mr. Secretary wrote again to the ambassador, sharing the news like one good colleague to another:

> Sir Francis Drake, as I doubt not but you have heard, is gone forth to the seas with four of her Majesty's ships and two pinnaces and between twenty and thirty merchant ships. His commission is to impeach the joining together of the King of Spain's fleet out of their several ports, to keep victuals from them, to follow them in case they should be come forward towards England or Ireland and to cut off as many of them as he could and impeach their landing, as also to set upon such as should either come out of the West or East Indies unto Spain or go out of Spain hither.

However, a cover note explained that he was sorry he had let this letter sit around for another eight days before actually sending it, but her Majesty specifically asked him to wait while she finished a letter to the French King she wished to send along with it. And of course Mr.

Secretary hadn't said anything about what Drake was really going to do, beyond anything and everything that anyone might guess.

A good lead time was given to Drake; he did his best with it. For one thing, he had once again managed to outrun the Queen's change of mind and a hastily dispatched recall order: intelligence had suddenly arrived in London from sources, notably including Stafford himself, that played down the past year's rumors of Spanish naval preparations. The Queen thought it best once again not to provoke Philip; Drake was "to forbear to enter forcibly into any of the said King's ports or havens, or to offer any violence to any of his towns or shipping within harboring, or to do any act of hostility upon the land." He was only to seize Spanish ships he encountered on the high seas.

But the pinnace sent to catch Drake with his new instructions somehow was unable to find him: bad weather, the crew insisted. And so, late on the afternoon of the 19th of April 1587, the sails of a large fleet flying no flags were seen from harbor of Cádiz, and when two galleys were sent out to investigate they were fired on without warning and driven back. A seven-hundred-ton warship and a thousand-ton Genoese armed merchantman that were in the vicinity were quickly captured, looted, and set ablaze. And then the work on the harbor shipping began in earnest. Many of the merchant ships slipped their cables and made for the inner harbor under the sheltering guns of the fort; the next morning, Drake followed them in. Four large Spanish ships were captured intact with huge stores; some two or three dozen others were burned to the waterline. Drake crammed his ships with captured provisions and wine; thirty hours after arriving, he was at sea again.

Over the next month, he snapped up dozens more ships and barks; Walsingham followed his progress in a series of dispatches that Drake sent back, addressed to him personally: no mistaking who his chief supporter and patron was. Drake had burned vast quantities of cargoes, "oars for galleys, planks and timber for ships and pinnaces, hoops and pipe-staves for cask, with many other provisions for this great army" of Spain. He had also seen signs that preparations for a Spanish fleet capable of moving against England were not to be discounted; he wrote Walsingham, "I assure your honor the like preparation was never heard of nor known, as the King of Spain hath and daily maketh to invade England." Ships were coming through Gibraltar to rendezvous with others preparing in Lisbon: "I dare not almost write unto your honor of the great forces we hear the King of Spain hath out in the Straits. Prepare in England strongly, and most by sea. Stop him now, and stop him ever. Look well to the coasts of Sussex."

On the 2nd of June, he sent another report to Walsingham, hoping for one more great coup before heading home:

> I assure your honor our sickness is very much, both of our soldiers and mariners. God mitigate it. Attending to his goodwill and pleasure, we are not yet thoroughly resolved what service we shall next take in hand. And for that there is as yet no supplies come out of England. But if God will bless us with some little comfortable dew from heaven, some crowns or some reasonable booty for our soldiers and mariners, all will take good again, although they were half dead.

It came a week later. A fine ship had been spotted at nightfall as the fleet lay off São Miguel, in the Azores. The next morning, Drake made straight for it; the ship approached, dipping its flag to ask Drake to identify himself; Drake waited until he was within range, broke out the English flag and battle streamers, and opened fire from ships that surrounded the enemy from every direction. Token return fire; then surrender.

She proved to be the *San Felipe,* the King of Spain's own ship, an East Indiaman laden with china, silk, spices, gold, jewels, and slaves. On the 26th of June, Drake sailed into Plymouth with his prize. Drake, former pirate that he was, was never too careful about his books; the *San Felipe's* cargo was officially valued at £114,000, of which £40,000 would to the Queen. The Spanish said it was worth more than £250,000.

If Drake had not struck a direct blow at the Spanish naval might, he at least tied it in knots; in his felicitous phrase—by now Drake had men better with words than he penning letters and proclamations in his name—he had "singed the King of Spain's beard." Unaware that Drake had returned to Plymouth, Philip's naval commander, the Marquis of Santa Cruz, chased across the Atlantic in search of him with his fleet of forty ships until October, when, battered, out of supplies, and running out of good sailing weather before winter, he returned to Lisbon.

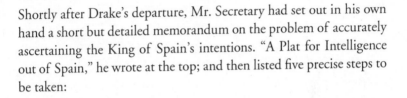

Shortly after Drake's departure, Mr. Secretary had set out in his own hand a short but detailed memorandum on the problem of accurately ascertaining the King of Spain's intentions. "A Plat for Intelligence out of Spain," he wrote at the top; and then listed five precise steps to be taken:

1. Sir Ed. Stafford to draw what he can from the Venetian Amb.
2. To procure some correspondence of the Fr. K. agent in Spain.
3. To take order with some in Rouen to have frequent advertisements from such as arrive out of Spain at Nantes, Newhaven [i.e. Le Havre], and Dieppe.
4. To make choice of two especial persons, French, Flemings or Italians, to go along the coast to see what preparations are a making there. To furnish them with letters of credit.
5. To have two intelligencers in the court of Spain
   one of Finale
   another of Genoa
   To have intelligence at Brussels, Leyden, Bar.

Since at least the autumn of 1586, Mr. Secretary had known the general outlines of Spanish hopes for mounting a seaborne assault upon England, for he had in his hands nothing less than a verbatim copy of a letter that Santa Cruz had written to Philip in March 1586 describing his strategic plan, listing every ship and its location, numbers of sailors and soldiers, stores, and wages and expenses.

There had also been a regular tidal wave of leaks coming through the diplomatic corps in Italy: In July 1586, Philip had decided that Santa Cruz's plan should be modified to have his ships sail to the Channel and there join a huge flotilla of barges that would carry Parma's troops across from Dunkirk, and strike at Kent; Philip had told his son-in-law the Duke of Savoy, and one of the Duke's ambassadors had told his Venetian colleague, and soon everyone in Italy seemed to know about it, and so the news came back to Mr. Secretary. And so, when Philip sought Pope Sixtus's backing, and his promise of a million crowns in money for the enterprise, and a secret treaty was signed promising Philip that the Pope would recognize any Catholic he chose to bestow the crown of England upon, that, too, was soon known in London—in part because Philip was so fearful that Sixtus would die and his successor would renounce the deal that he had insisted the entire College of Cardinals pledge to uphold the treaty as well, and the College of Cardinals leaked like a sieve. The ten independent Italian states all had ambassadors in Madrid, and the Spanish possessions in Italy always had money and troops and diplomats of the Spanish empire passing through, and everyone talked about everything.

But there were details for which a pair of human eyes or someone who knew where and how to get his hands on certain documents could not be substituted. The Santa Cruz plan had come by way of a particularly well-placed and prolific correspondent of Mr. Secretary's in Florence. He signed his name Pompeo Pelligrini and his letters to Walsingham were addressed to Walsingham's servant Jacobo Manucci in England; written in a style affecting to be that of one zealous Catholic to another, they were full of the most acute observations about the movements of ships out of ports and the number of soldiers being levied: six galleys and fifteen ships were seen in the harbor of Lisbon with 1,000 Spaniards and 3,500 Italians aboard; eighteen galleys arrived in Genoa from Spain with 1,500 Spaniards aboard, new soldiers to put in garrisons there, and 40,000 crowns in money; a regiment of 4,000 Neapolitans embarked upon galleys that, according to the word publicly proclaimed, were heading for Spain, though instead they had gone to Milan, where they were now.

Pelligrini's real name was Anthony Standen. An English Catholic gentleman who had worked for Mary's cause since sometime around 1565, traveling to Spain, Flanders, and Constantinople, he was now in the service of the Duke of Tuscany. He was extremely well connected; he was also quite interested in seeing if he could perform some service that might bring him back into the good favor of his country, now that the cause of Mary had come to an end. And so he had been in touch with Mr. Secretary, and he was soon to receive one of those rare £100-a-year pensions that were reserved only for the best and most efficient of Mr. Secretary's agents; indeed, he had been quite surprised and gratified to find, upon returning from his own investigative journey into Spain, that waiting for him back in Florence was his entire first year's pay.

Among Standen's contacts was his good friend the Tuscan Ambassador in Madrid, who kept him very well informed. And then there was a certain Fleming in Madrid to whom Standen had given a hundred crowns, and whose brother worked for the Marquis of Santa Cruz, and for whom the ambassador was quite happy to extend the courtesy of sending documents in the diplomatic bag back to his good friend Standen in Florence. There were others, too: Englishmen traveling about Italy (there were always Englishmen traveling about Italy); and Italians and Flemings and Frenchmen in Spain; and the spies in Parma's army in the Low Countries; and the merchant sailors who kept their eyes open in the ports of Flanders and Italy; and the disaffected Portuguese who fed a steady stream of reports from the Iberian coasts.

As early as June 1587, Standen had been able to confirm that the Spaniards were so thrown into disarray by Drake's raid on Cádiz that they were unlikely to do anything for the rest of the year against England. "My Fleming writeth flatly," Berden reported to Mr. Secretary, "that this next year is undoubtedly holden they intend to visit us in England with a mighty force and that presently this year they mean no other but to secure their fleet that cometh so sick." Walsingham at once shared this news with Burghley: "Your Lordship by the enclosed from Florence may perceive how some stay is made of the foreign preparations," he wrote in a cover note. "I humbly pray your Lordship that Pompey's letter may be reserved to yourself. I would be loath the gentleman should have any harm through my default." Shortly after that, Standen reported for certain that the fleet heading out from Lisbon under Santa Cruz was bound not for England but for the Azores, in pursuit of Drake; this information had come directly from the King's orders to Santa Cruz, which "was only known to the one and the other."

But it was clear this was but a reprieve. Mr. Secretary was now spending Treasury money on agents like never before; it would amount to some £3,300 from the spring of 1587 to the spring of the next year. And so, throughout the summer and autumn of 1587, the reports from what was now something considerably more than a few "paid Papists," something that indeed looked very much like a network of professional intelligence agents, flowed into Mr. Secretary's office as he watched and waited for signs of the gathering Armada.

13

FOREARMED

Fifteen eighty-eight: another year of portents and omens. The fifteenth-century mathematician and astrologer Regiomontanus had predicted that the year would bring "either an universal consummation and final dissolution of the world, or at least a general subversion and alteration of principalities, kingdoms, monarchies and empires." Everyone had heard that and talked of it; that, and the strange sightings that had already occurred, the thirty porpoises that had come up the Thames and gathered at the water gate of the Queen's court, the vast number of fleas that had collected on the window of the Queen's Presence Chamber. The Privy Council commissioned its own scholar to write a book disputing Regiomontanus's prophecies: all based on a misreading of the position of the planet Mars, the Council's expert explained.

From Venice and Florence and Madrid and Brussels and Paris the reports kept coming in about Spanish naval preparations. They were full of contradictions, but then other reports suggested that the reason for this was that the King of Spain was himself uncertain how and when to proceed: a maddening position for an intelligence officer trying to read his enemy's mind, when the enemy did not know his own mind himself. Toward the end of 1587, reports had come in that Philip decided to launch his attack at once. Other reports said he was considering an assault on Scotland instead, or would suddenly send Parma's barges across the Channel without any escort, or might try to seize the Isle of Wight. Burghley and Walsingham wanted to mobilize the fleet at once; Drake proposed another strike against the Spaniards in their ports. Elizabeth balked at the expense: she had heard too many cries of wolf before. The Council was permitted to alert the Lord Lieutenants of the counties to have their trained bands ready for service at one hour's notice, and they were permitted to requisition merchant ships for the royal service, but Drake was not to sail. "The manner of our cold and careless proceeding here in this time of peril and danger maketh me to take no comfort of my recovery of health," Walsingham wrote Leicester, "for that I see apparently, unless it shall please God in mercy and miraculously to preserve us, we cannot long stand."

Mr. Secretary took refuge in planning as best he could, putting in place a system and organization to do whatever England had to do but had never had to do before. He wrote a lengthy memorandum, "A Consideration What Were Fit to be Done When the Realm shall be Assailed":

> The defence to be made by sea and land
> The defence by sea committed to the Lord Admiral
> *Defence by land—*
> To be considered
> What number of men are put in readiness throughout the realm, horse and foot.
> How they are directed to assist upon any invasion.
> Who be the lieutenants of the shires and captains of the men both trained and untrained.
> What pioneers appointed for every band and what carriages.
> What powder appointed for every band.
> What field pieces and munition is placed in certain of the maritime counties.
> *These being done*
> (*a*) Where is it likely that the enemy will attempt anything against this realm.
> (*b*) How may he best be withstood—whether by offering a fight when he has landed or in avoiding a fight (which it is likely the enemy will affect) and to make head against him with the use of the pioneers and withdrawing of victuals.

What men of sufficiency meet to be sent to those places where
the descent is likely to be made.

What engineers there are in this realm meet to be used for the
direction of the pioneers.

What forces were meetest to be about her Majesty's person both
of horsemen and footmen.

If anything should be attempted against the city of London
which way it would be attempted and how it may be best
withstood.

Stafford was still assiduously muddying the waters: he now sent a
barrage of reports disparaging the Spanish threat. In January, he insisted in a letter to the Queen that the Armada had been disbanded.
The report was passed on to Stafford's brother-in-law, the Lord Admiral, Charles Howard of Effingham; Howard reacted with in-
credulity: "I cannot tell what to think of my brother Stafford's
advertisement; for if it be true that the King of Spain's forces be dissolved, I would not wish the Queen's Majesty to be at this charge that
she is at; but if it be a device, knowing that a little thing makes us too
careless, then I know not what may come of it."

Stafford sent other reports, each more unlikely than the last. The
Armada was headed for Algiers; it was bound for the Indies; an out-
break of plague had driven it back to Spain; Paris bookmakers were
laying odds of six to one that it would never reach the English Channel. Stafford claimed he had seen in the Spanish Ambassador's study
a paper mentioning an enterprise against England, but it was obviously a ruse, Stafford explained: Mendoza must have left it out on
purpose to deceive him; therefore, the Armada was surely headed
anywhere *but* England.

Mr. Secretary had Howard feed some bilge back to his brother-in-
law: a detailed report in which he exaggerated the firepower of English ships by 40 percent.

In fact, by April there could no longer be any doubt as to Spain's
true intentions, nor as to how utterly bogus Stafford's reports were.

Pinnaces sent to look into Spanish harbors could see the preparations; an intercepted and deciphered letter from the Count of Olivares in Rome to Philip spoke confidently about the "investiture" of the new sovereign of England after the conquest was complete.

On the 30th of April 1588, specific orders for the defense of the realm at last went out. Local commanders were advised of points on the coast where the water was deep enough to admit enemy vessels; at these points ramparts were to be erected, defended by trenches. At Lynn, where the Channel was narrowest, causeways were to be broken up, parapets built, and cannon emplaced. Instructions were given for the destruction of bridges across the Ouse River on the approach of the enemy. Signal beacons were prepared.

And so the waiting and watching continued. Mr. Secretary's men in Spain, still swiping the letters and orders of the Spanish commanders, continued to send meticulously detailed accounts of the Spanish force and its war plans. In May came a report from one of them, Nicholas Ousley, who had seen a dispatch from the new commander of the Armada, the Duke of Medina-Sidonia: Santa Cruz had died suddenly in February. Medina-Sidonia had twenty-five thousand men, four thousand of them mariners; victuals for six months, except for cheese, which was in only four months' supply; fourteen galleons had departed Sanlúcar for Lisbon; four argosies, three carrying coin and one munitions, had departed from Cádiz.

In mid-May, Standen reported that a ship from Dunkirk had arrived in Lisbon carrying pilots sent by Parma to guide the invasion force.

From Rome came word that Pope Sixtus V had reissued the Bull of Excommunication against Elizabeth; from France, word that Dr. Allen had penned a violent attack on Elizabeth, printed and prepared for distribution once the Spanish invasion began, *An Admonition to the Nobility and People of England*. A copy of it came into Burghley's hands, and Burghley sent it to Walsingham. Elizabeth, Dr. Allen wrote, was "an incestuous bastard begotten and born in sin of an infamous courtesan." She was "an infamous, deprived, accursed, excommunicate heretic; the very shame of her sex and princely name;

the chief spectacle of sin and abomination in this our age." She had taken part in an "unspeakable and incredible variety of lust." Her kingdom had become "a place of refuge and sanctuary of all atheists, Anabaptists, heretics, and rebellious of all nations." The Catholic King had undertaken to deliver the people of England "from the yoke of heresy and thralldom of your enemies."

Then, on the 29th of May, Standen wrote again to Walsingham, from Sanlúcar:

> The army departeth this day 11 days, I say 11 days for I saw a letter that the Duke directed to one of his Council, was written that same day 10 leagues in the sea, and caused a caravel which the army met to come aboard and receive the packet. Their purpose is The Groyne, and there to remain upon further advice, as the same Councilor my very friend shewed me in secret, who believes me to be a greater friend to his country than I hope in God ever to be.

In the midst of the racking anticipations of the Armada, a delegation of Dutch Calvinists arrived: slight comic relief. Hoping to induce the Queen to accept sovereignty over the Low Countries and suppress all other worship but the truly reformed faith, they had prepared a lengthy discourse that they pressed upon Mr. Secretary; it was, in Walsingham's words, "filled with astounding parallels between their own position and that of the Hebrews, Assyrians, and other distinguished nations of antiquity." Walsingham suggested that they cut it down, as the Queen did not like to read papers more than one page long.

Drake had pleaded all spring to be allowed to sally forth against the Spaniards. He had won over Howard, who had originally opposed the idea as too risky; he bombarded the Queen with letters. "If your Majesty will give present order for our proceeding to the sea . . ." "With fifty sail of shipping we shall do more good upon their own coast than a great many more will do here at home. . . ." "The advantage of time and place in all martial actions is half a victory, which being lost is irrecoverable. . . ." "These great preparations of the Spaniard may be speedily prevented . . . by sending your forces to encounter theirs, somewhat far off and more near their own coast, which will be the better cheap for your Majesty and people, and much the dearer for the enemy. . . ."

Now, at last, the Queen assented. On the 30th of May, the fleet sailed from Plymouth—only to be driven back by fierce winds. "We have danced as lustily as the gallantest dancers in Court," Howard quipped to Walsingham, determined to make light of the battering they had just weathered, determined to try again. But the Queen now again forbade it, ordering Howard to "ply up and down" in home waters instead, lest the Armada slip past him at sea.

Howard retorted sarcastically, "I must and will obey; and am glad there be such there as are able to judge what is fitter for us to do than we here; but by my instructions which I had, I did think it otherwise."

The Queen relented again; again the fleet was blown back.

Then, on the 19th of July, the Spanish fleet was spotted off The Lizard, the southwestern tip of England. A hundred and thirty sail in all, a staggering force: for all of the strategic warning that Walsingham had so painstakingly gathered, the Spanish had achieved tactical surprise. The Armada threatened to catch Drake and Howard bottled up in Plymouth Harbor; the following day, with the wind against them, they warped their way painstakingly out: a small boat carrying the anchor ahead, dropping it, the ship's cable drawn up on the capstan to heave forward.

Then beating tack upon tack into the night, westward, until, at two in the morning of the 21st, the English had the weather gauge, the wind behind them, the Spanish before them.

Howard was a man of Walsingham's own stamp, tactful, free of vanity, concerned more with results than glory; there had been worries how the vain and hotheaded Drake would take to being placed under his command, any man's command; Howard had pulled it off with near genius. In May, he had sailed into Plymouth flying the flag of an admiral and vice-admiral; in full view of Drake and all his cheering men, he had lowered the vice-admiral's flag, sent it across by his pinnace, and bidden Drake to send it aloft on his ship. Howard had reported to Walsingham, "I must not omit to let you know how lovingly and kindly Sir Francis Drake beareth himself and also how dutifully to her Majesty's service and unto me, being in the place I am in." The English navy had Howard and Drake; it also had ships that were weatherly and fleet; the largest of them mostly no more than five hundred tons, half the size of the Spanish galleons; they could maneuver and turn to fire two broadsides in the time the big ships could manage but one; they carried light culverins on wheeled carriages that could fire fast and far compared with the older, heavier, and clumsier Spanish guns.

And so there began a week's running battle up the Channel; the Spanish trying to get close enough to grapple and board with their hordes of men, the English nimbly keeping out of range and playing long bowls with their guns.

Chivvied like a flock of sheep they went: a keg of gunpowder went off in one Spanish galleon; another lost its bowsprit in a collision, fell behind, and was snapped up by Drake, its crew taken prisoner and sent to London to be interrogated by the Privy Council. On the 27th, the Armada anchored off of Calais.

Early the next morning, in a high wind and heavy sea, the English set ablaze eight merchant ships packed with combustibles and sent them drifting toward the Spanish. Their cannon had been loaded, double-shotted, so they would go off as the heat of the flames reached them: more a psychological threat than real, it did its work. As the fire ships approached, the Spanish in a panic cut their cables, left their anchors on the sea bottom, and fled. In the ensuing confusion, the flagship of the galleases suffered a wrenching collision that damaged its rudder and sent its mainmast crashing by the board; seeking to evade capture, the Spanish admiral ordered his ship grounded at the entrance to Calais. Howard sent in an assault party on boats and carried the ship in a violent hand-to-hand struggle, the Spanish admiral shot in the head in the fight.

The following day, the 29th, the scattered Spanish were set upon in earnest. Medina-Sidonia managed to gather thirty-two of the Armada's ships together as he sought to cover Parma's embarkation ports; the English came on at closer range than ever, so close the crews could shout insults at one another, yet still not so close that the Spanish could use their grappling hooks. "Cowards!" "Lutheran chickens!" the Spanish crews cursed. The Spanish flagship was struck by more than a hundred cannonballs. Two other galleons were battered and ran aground on the Zealand shoals. A third Spanish ship, crippled but still afloat, sank suddenly, taking her crew of 175 to the bottom with rescue ships in sight.

The surviving Spanish ships had lost so much leeway that now they, too, were in danger of being broken apart on the sandbanks; only a last-minute change in the wind saved them, but now they were flying north, and all hope of making their way back to the Channel gone. Parma and his invasion force and barges were bottled up in Dunkirk by the wind and the English and Dutch forces.

Though Howard did not know it, the battle was over. That evening he cautiously wrote to Mr. Secretary: "I will not write unto her Majesty before more be done. Their force is wonderful great and strong; and yet we pluck their feathers by little and little." Howard pursued the Spanish as far as the Firth of Forth in Scotland, then returned, sick at heart for the suffering of his men, who were dying by the thousands of typhus and scurvy. "Sickness and mortality begins wonderfully to grow amongst us," he wrote, "and it is a most pitiful sight to see, here at Margate, how the men having no place to receive them into here, die in the streets, I am driven myself, of force, to come a-land, to see them bestowed in some lodging; and the best I can get is barns and outhouses. It would grieve any man's heart to see them that have served so valiantly to die so miserably."

But it was victory; though the realization took time, it came with savage glee when it did. Two months later, the news filtered back of the Spaniards' ultimate fate. They had rounded Scotland, the long way home; they had then wrecked on the coasts of Ireland in violent storms. Half of the ships were lost, thousands drowned, and then a thousand or more who had survived shipwrecks and made it ashore simply butchered, several hundred after they had surrendered. The massacre had been egged on by fantastic yet widely believed rumors that the Spanish prisoners in London had confessed they had been ordered to kill every Englishman over age seven, that their ships were supplied with special whips of cord and wire for flaying alive the English heretics.

On the 24th of November, the Queen attended a service of thanksgiving at Saint Paul's, making her way there through cheering throngs in streets bedecked with blue cloth, riding upon a chariot throne with a canopy supported by four pillars, drawn by two white horses. A commemorative medal was struck: a time for mocking humor. It bore the motto *veni, vidi, fugit;* I came, I saw, I fled.

And to Mr. Secretary, from Vice-Admiral Lord Henry Seymour, a more subtle tribute.

"I will not flatter you," Seymour wrote when it was all over, "but you have fought more with your pen than many have in our English navy fought with their enemies."

─────────────◦❧◦─────────────

As was ever his fate, Walsingham had been healthy in times of adversity and crisis; now, almost as soon as the danger to the nation was gone, the danger to himself returned; in mid-September, he was again ill and subjecting himself to the crude torments of physic in search of a cure.

Leicester died that same month. The loss of his old ally and recent enemy saddened few people besides the Queen (public joy in the victory over the Armada, Camden recorded, was not "anything abated by Leicester's death"); but it could not have failed to add to Walsingham's growing intimations of his own mortality.

The Queen paid Walsingham visits at Barn Elms in 1588 and 1589—an honor, but a mixed blessing given the crushing cost of each royal visit. Walsingham's finances were still a wreck; the customs farm was a bust. In the spring of 1589, he petitioned the Queen to be forgiven the £12,739 he still owed the Exchequer for its lease over three years. The disruptions to trade and the war with Spain had so cut into revenues that his original pledge to pay £11,000 a year had proved impossible to meet. The Queen agreed; but the books were so convoluted, and then there were various other official expenditures he had made and licenses he had received, that it was hard to tell by the following year whether he owed money to the Crown or was owed money.

In November 1589, Francis Walsingham prepared a will that provided for an annuity of £100 to his daughter, in addition to an earlier one of £200 he had provided her. He had already conveyed most of his remaining lands to her, retaining a life estate to himself and his wife, but these amounted to only £70 per year in income. "And I will that my body, in hope of a joyful resurrection," Walsingham instructed, "be buried without any such extraordinary ceremonies as usually appertain to a man serving in my place, in respect of the greatness of my debts and the mean state I shall leave my wife and heir in; charging both my executor and overseers to see this duly accomplished, according to the special trust and confidence I repose in them."

In late March 1590, he was still attending the meetings of the Privy Council: two weeks later he was dead. The chronicler Camden wrote that he had "died of a carnosity growing intra testium tunicas"—a fleshy growth within the membrane of the testicles; that, "or rather through violence of medicines."

It was an age when stories of how men died and with what pious last words on their lips carried great weight, and Mr. Secretary had made more than most men's share of enemies in his life; the Catholics were quick to spread a story that was anatomically improbable, but just vile enough to be repeated, of the death of the man they saw as their tormentor: "The Secretary Walsingham, a most violent persecutor of Catholics, died never so much naming God in his last extremities. And yet he had his speech, as he showed by telling the preacher that he heard him, and therefore he needed not to cry so loud—which were his last words. In the end, his urine came forth at his mouth and nose, with so odious a stench that none could endure to come near him."

Walsingham died late on the night of the 6th of April; the following night, Camden recorded, he was buried as he had instructed, "by dark in Paul's Church at London without any funeral solemnity."

———————— ⚬⚬⚬ ————————

The men who had served Mr. Secretary the most faithfully landed more or less on their feet. Thomas Phelippes had been awarded a pension of one hundred marks for his role in the Babington case. Nicholas Berden, his cover having finally been blown from his work in Paris, was granted the sinecure in the Queen's household that he sought: Purveyor of the Poultry. Anthony Standen learned of his patron's death from a prison cell in Bordeaux, where he had been arrested: supposedly as a Spanish spy, for he had apparently assumed the role of double agent as his cover for earlier spying for the English government. But Standen was able to make contact with Burghley, get himself released from prison, and take up where he had left off, sending reports to his new patron on Spanish shipping and troop movements. In 1593, he at last returned to England to enter the service of the Earl of Essex.

But others were lost—lost along with the knowledge of secret methods that Walsingham had so painstakingly assembled and so jealously carried with him to his grave. His secretary Robert Beale tried to salvage some of it in the guide he assembled for Walsingham's possible successor; Beale lamented that Mr. Secretary himself, perhaps "more private than were fit for her Majesty's service," had scrupulously neglected to provide for the "instruction and bringing up others in knowledge to be able to serve her Majesty."

Some other of the pieces of Mr. Secretary's secret service were gathered up by Burghley and by the increasingly ambitious Essex, Frances Walsingham's second husband; but though Burghley had experience and Essex enthusiasm, their growing political rivalry inevitably meant a loss of much that Walsingham had built. Essex had money and youth, but he was no Walsingham. Determined to make his mark in secret affairs, he claimed to have discovered that the Queen's physician, a Portuguese Jew named Roderigo Lopez, was in the pay of Spain and had been offered fifty thousand crowns to poison her. Burghley's son Robert Cecil defended Lopez, and the man himself insisted that all he had done was to make contact with some Spanish officials, and that only at Walsingham's behest to draw out useful information; but with Walsingham gone and Essex determined to give the Cecils one in the eye, he prosecuted the matter with relentless zeal and saw Lopez convicted and hanged.

Essex did at least lavish money on the support of many of Mr. Secretary's old agents in their old work, Phelippes included; yet all that ended for good in 1601, when, half mad and driven by jealousy of the Cecils, Essex attempted a bizarre coup against the Queen's ministers that ended in his execution.

Frances Walsingham had three sons and two daughters by Essex, the most famous being Robert Devereux, the 3rd Earl of Essex, who inherited something from both his Essex and Walsingham forebears: becoming the Puritan parliamentary general of the seventeenth-century civil wars.

There had been much talk of making Sir Edward Stafford the next Principal Secretary, but somehow he never quite got the job: another of Walsingham's subtler legacies, no doubt. The post lay vacant for several years and finally was given to Robert Cecil. But the office itself soon decayed; with Cecil's successors, its holder became little more than a clerk who handled routine business.

And yet: something had been born that could never die. Mr. Secretary had not only won the war, he had won the battle. England's star had risen to heights none had dared imagine possible; England had defeated the Armada of the mightiest empire in the world, had made Elizabeth's prestige soar throughout the courts of Europe, had heartened Spain's enemies, had placed England irrevocably on the side of Protestant Europe in a political and military struggle against Catholicism. And in an age when violence and brute force were still the only things most men understood, there were now—in the memories and experience of at least some select band of men who knew, and buried away in the files of state papers however disordered and obscure and picked over and expunged—the traces of another way of looking at things. Knowledge is never too dear: not a thought most sixteenth-century men of action would have subscribed to, but an idea that would never again quite disappear from the halls of power, especially the halls of power of outnumbered nations with democratic leanings facing the power of tyrants.

———————— ⚬⚬ ————————

Two days after Walsingham's death, the Spanish agent in London sent King Philip a letter bearing the news. "Secretary Walsingham has just expired, at which there is much sorrow," he wrote.

"There, yes!" Philip jotted in the margin when he read it several weeks later. "But it is good news here."

CHRONOLOGY

		ENGLAND AND THE WORLD	WALSINGHAM'S LIFE AND CAREER
1532			Francis Walsingham born
1533	Sep	Elizabeth, second daughter of Henry VIII, born	
1534	Jan	Parliament renounces papal authority over English church	
1547	Jan	Henry VIII dies; Edward VI becomes King	
1548–50(?)			attends King's College, Cambridge
1552			enrolled as law student at Gray's Inn
1553	Aug	Edward dies; Mary Tudor becomes Queen of England, reinstates Catholic religion	
1555–56			student of Roman civil law in Padua
1558	Nov	Mary Tudor dies; Elizabeth proclaimed Queen	
1560	Aug	Scottish Parliament establishes Protestantism	

1561	Aug	Mary Stuart returns to Scotland from France	
1562			marries Anne Carleill; Member of Parliament for Lyme Regis
1564			wife, Anne, dies
1566			marries Ursula St. Barbe Worseley
1567	Feb	Darnley, Mary Stuart's husband, murdered at Kirk o'Field	
	Aug	Alva arrives with army in Netherlands, suppresses rebellion	
	Sep(?)		daughter Frances born
1568	Mar		purchases London house, the Papey
	May	Mary flees to England	
	Aug		employed in secret work by Mr. Secretary Cecil
	Dec	Spanish pay ships seized	
1569	Oct		examines Roberto Ridolfi
	Nov–Dec	Catholic rising in north fails	
1570	Jan	Moray, Protestant Regent of Scotland, assassinated	
	Feb	Pope issues *Regnans in Excelsis* deposing Elizabeth	

	Aug		sent on diplomatic mission to France
	Dec		appointed ambassador to France
1571	Aug–Sep	Norfolk caught sending money and messages to Mary's agents and arrested	
	Dec	Spanish Ambassador de Spes expelled	
1572	Apr	renewed rebellion in Low Countries Treaty of Blois signed with France	
	Jun	Norfolk executed	
	Aug		witnesses Saint Bartholomew's massacres
1573			daughter Mary born
	Mar		recalled from France
	Dec		named Principal Secretary and Privy Councilor
1575	Jan		uncovers Mary Stuart's secret contacts via London bookseller Henry Cockyn
1577	Jul		Receives deciphered letters revealing Don John's invasion plot
	Nov	first Catholic missionary priests executed in England	

	Dec		knighthood conferred
1578	Apr		named Chancellor of the Garter
	Jun– Oct		diplomatic mission to Low Countries
1579	Feb		granted Barn Elms by Elizabeth
	Oct		opposes Alençon match and is dismissed from Court
	Nov	John Stubbs punished for seditious libel	
1580			daughter Mary dies; moves to house on Seething Lane
	Jan		returns to Court
	Jun	first Jesuit priests arrive in England	
	Aug	Spain seizes Portugal	
	Sep	Drake returns with plundered Spanish treasure	
1581	Jun	Scottish Regent executed by Lennox's pro-Catholic faction	
	Jul– Sep		diplomatic mission to France
	Oct		Alençon arrives to press marriage suit

	Dec	Jesuit Edmund Campion executed	
1582	Aug	Protestant faction in Scotland seizes James and ejects Lennox	
	Sep		receives reports of secret contacts between Mary and French embassy
1583	Apr		approached by Henry Fagot, spy in French embassy
	Summer		mole in French embassy begins leaking copies of Mary's letters
	Aug–Oct		diplomatic mission to Scotland
	Sep		daughter Frances marries Sir Philip Sidney
	Nov	Francis Throckmorton arrested in invasion plot	
1584	Jan	Spanish Ambassador Mendoza expelled	
	Feb	Mary expresses fears of leak in her correspondence	
	Jul	William Prince of Orange assassinated	
1585	Feb	William Parry arrested for conspiracy to kill Elizabeth	

	Apr	Amias Paulet takes charge of Mary	
	Aug	English troops land in the Netherlands	
	Sep	Drake sails to attack Spanish West Indies	
	Dec		arrests Gilbert Gifford; arranges sham system to convey Mary's letters
1586	Jun		receives spy's report on treason of Stafford, ambassador to France
	Jul		receives decipher of Mary's incriminating letter to Babington
	Aug		arrests Babington plotters
	Oct	Mary convicted of treason	Sidney killed in Low Countries
	Dec		reconciliation with Burghley
1587	Feb	Mary executed	
	Apr	Drake attacks Cádiz Harbor	writes plan for intelligence from Spain
	Jun		receives intelligence that Armada will not sail on England in 1587
1588	Jul	Spanish Armada attacked and dispersed off Calais	
	Sep	Leicester dies	
1590	Apr		dies

NOTES ON SOURCES

The indispensable starting point for any treatment of Walsingham is Conyers Read's three-volume *Mr. Secretary Walsingham*. Based on an exhaustive study of manuscript sources, it has stood the passage of eighty years remarkably well. Though many today would quibble with some of his interpretations, his research remains unsurpassed. And no one could possibly improve upon the perfect anecdote that Read found to end his account of Walsingham's life, so I have not tried to—and merely acknowledge my debt here.

I have included here a brief survey of the key sources I consulted for each section. A complete list of these sources, with full citations, is found in the bibliography.

1572: MURDER IN PARIS

Key documents relating to the Saint Bartholomew's massacres, including the accounts of Sassetti and the Venetian and papal ambassadors, are found in Potter, ed., *French Wars of Religion;* Soman, ed., *Massacre of St. Bartholomew;* Layard, *Massacre of St. Bartholomew.* Knecht, *French Wars of Religion*, provides a very useful summary of key events and sources.

Noguères, *Massacre of Saint Bartholomew,* and Erlanger, *Saint Bartholomew's Night,* have reconstructed the events in narrative form; though they provide many important and colorful details, their depiction of the inner councils of the French Court are based on sources that recent scholarship has for the most part dismissed as later propagandistic inventions. Kingdon, *Myths About the St. Bartholomew's Day Massacres*, and Sutherland, *Massacre of St. Bartholomew,* provide a careful assessment of the sources taking into account this well-founded skepticism. Kingdon, along with Strype, *Annals of the Reformation,* also documents the reaction to the massacres across Europe.

Digges, ed., *Compleat Ambassador,* reprints a large collection of Walsingham's official correspondence with the English government during these critical events and his later missions abroad. Important original drafts of several of these letters are in the BL Cotton MSS, notably Vespasian F vi ff. 163–64, Walsingham to Sir Thomas Smith, 2 September 1572; and Vespasian F vi f. 169 and following, Walsingham to Privy Council, 24 September 1572. Catherine de Médicis's correspondence with the French Ambassador to England, recounting her meetings with Walsingham following the massacres, is in Fénélon, *Correspondance,* vol. 4.

1532–72: MAKING OF A SPYMASTER

Most of what is known about Walsingham's family background and early life is found in Webb, Miller, and Beckwith, *History of Chislehurst,* with some additional details (culled from a variety of impressively miscellaneous sources) in Read, *Mr. Secretary Walsingham.* Read also reprints in full Walsingham's advice to his nephew, a manuscript that has since been destroyed by fire.

The chroniclers—Camden's *History,* Naunton's *Fragmenta Regalia,* and Lloyd's *State Worthies*—offer the earliest published character sketches of Walsingham. His paradoxical role in establishing a troupe of stage players for the Queen is discussed in McMillim and MacLean, *Queen's Men.* The *Calendar of State Papers, Simancas* is the source for the Spanish agent's comments on Walsingham as a "heretic" (De Guaras to Zayas, 7 November 1574).

The demographic and social background of Tudor England and the nature of Tudor law, government, and taxation are developed in rich detail in Rowse's classic *England of Elizabeth;* Palliser, *Age of Elizabeth,* updates this perspective with more recent research, notably the rigorous study of the demographics of the Elizabethan age by the Cambridge Group. Guy, *Tudor England,* is another excellent survey full of insights and remarkable facts. The records of Walsingham's London parish, *Registers of St. Olave, Hart Street,* provide an interesting snapshot of the social milieu of sixteenth-century London, as well as the dates for a (very) few events in Walsingham's personal life, notably the baptism of his granddaughter.

Somerset, *Elizabeth I,* a solidly researched as well as extremely lively and readable work, has the wonderfully vivid details of the Queen's character, her tastes, her attitudes toward religion, and her swearing. William Cecil's background and role in Elizabeth's government are covered in Read, *Mr. Secretary Cecil.*

The English Reformation and the religious settlement of 1559 is an immense and complex subject with an immense and complex literature to match. I have relied mainly on the above-mentioned works by Rowse and Palliser, and also on MacCaffrey's *Queen Elizabeth and the Making of Policy* and *Shaping of the Elizabethan Regime;* Guy, *Tudor England;* and McGrath, *Papists and Puritans.* John White's funeral sermon for Mary Tudor is in Strype, *Ecclesiastical Memorials,* with additional details recounted in Starkey, *Elizabeth.*

The life and character of Mary Queen of Scots is choked with romance and legend; Somerset, *Elizabeth I,* is a superb guide through this morass, as is Guy, *Queen of Scots;* Fraser, *Mary Queen of Scots,* has a lot of reliable detail and a lot of debatable interpretation.

Walsingham's warning to Cecil that there is "less danger in fearing too much" is in PRO SP 12/48 no. 61. His propaganda pamphlet against the Norfolk marriage is reprinted in full in Read, *Mr. Secretary Walsingham.* Norfolk's marriage plot and arrest in 1569 and Cecil's quiet role are discussed in Read, *Mr. Secretary Cecil.* The orders from the Privy Council to Walsingham to detain and interrogate Ridolfi, and Walsingham's letter mistakenly expressing confidence in Ridolfi, are in PRO SP 12/59 nos. 3 and 11, and SP 12/74 no. 12.

All of the key documents concerning the Ridolfi plot and its discovery are reprinted in Murdin, ed., *Burghley Papers;* Mary's correspondence with Ridolfi is in Labanoff, ed., *Lettres;* the acidic views of de Spes, Alva, and Philip are found in *Calendar of State Papers, Simancas,* for this period; and Plowden, *Elizabethan Secret Service,* offers an exceptionally clear and straightforward narrative of the events of the plot. The case of Charles Baillie is recounted in the *Dictionary of National Biography* entry under his name, and the prison ruse with Dr. Story in Pollitt, "Abduction of Doctor John Story."

1573–83: MR. SECRETARY

Walsingham's town houses are mentioned in Stow, *Survey of London*.

The office of Principal Secretary and its duties are described in Faunt, "Discourse," and in Robert Beale's memorandum reprinted in Read, *Mr. Secretary Walsingham*. Rowse, *England of Elizabeth*, has a short but excellent discussion of the role of the Privy Council and the Secretary; Read, *The Tudors* and *Government of England*, also provide much helpful background. Walsingham's "table book," which lists all of the books and documents in his charge is in BL Stowe MS 162. The "Journal of Walsingham," which covers 1570 to 1583 (with some notable gaps, particularly the St. Bartholomew massacres), lists Walsingham's official correspondence and extremely brief accounts of his activities; "Journal of the Secretary's Office 1585," BL Harley MS 6035, is even more cryptic but has some important clues about his secret doings; "Entry Book of Letters and Papers Kept for Sir Francis Walsingham," PRO 12/45, is a random grab bag of official correspondence and memoranda.

The list of places from which Walsingham received reports is in PRO SP 12/232 no. 12. The ruse played on the Archbishop of Casel in France is recounted in Digges, ed., *Compleat Ambassador*. Read, *Mr. Secretary Walsingham*, contains numerous examples of the men recruited by him and the work they did. The record of secret funds approved for Walsingham's use is in PRO SP 12/229 no. 49.

The report of the white cross and wolf are in *Calendar of State Papers, Simancas,* 7 Nov. 1574. The translated text of *Regnans in Excelsis* is given in Pollen, *English Catholics*. McGrath, *Papists and Puritans,* thoroughly covers the anti-recusancy laws and the missionary priests; Challoner, *Missionary Priests,* tells many of their individual adventures and gruesome ends.

The documents relating to the Cockyn case are in PRO SP 53/10, nos. 10–16.

Read, "Walsingham and Burghley," discusses the growing rifts between the two on the Privy Council. Stubbs's *Gaping Gulf* and some of the ballads about the Anjou match have been reprinted in the modern edition edited by Lloyd E. Berry. Walsingham's personal finances are discussed in the last two chapters of Read, *Mr. Secretary Walsingham;* the estimate of the profit he made from the sale of his cloth-export licenses is based on the Earl of Sussex's sale to a trading consortium in 1577 of licenses for twenty thousand cloths for the sum of £3,200, noted by Somerset. A reference to the death of Walsingham's daughter Mary is in a letter of condolence from Paulet in July 1580, BL Cotton MS Titus B ii f. 345.

Mauvissière's character is discussed in Bossy, *Giordano Bruno* and *Under the Molehill,* which are also the source for the exhaustive case identifying Fagot and the leaker in the French embassy. Although these books make for demanding reading, and some of his interpretations and conclusions have been disputed, Bossy's research into this matter is without parallel, a tour de force of meticulous detective work and analysis, drawing together an extraordinary range of sources and evidence. Copies of Fagot's first reports to Walsingham are in PRO SP 52/31 no. 26 and SP 53/12 no. 61.

1583–87: THE BOSOM SERPENT

The official account of the Throckmorton Plot was published in *A Discoverie of the Treasons.* Bossy, *Under the Molehill,* reprints many of the key documents in the secret correspondence and is now the definitive authority on Walsingham's behind-the-scenes role in the affair.

The parcel of Mary's copied letters turned over to Walsingham in April 1584 are all mostly in BL Harley MS 1582; many of the important ones are also reprinted in Labanoff, ed., *Lettres.* Especially interesting are the Feb. 1584 letter from Mary expressing fears of a leak in the embassy, with the mole's panicked postscript to Walsingham (BL Harley MS 1582 ff. 311–13), and Mauvissière's reassuring reply, ff. 370–73. Walsingham's order for the torture of Throckmorton is in PRO SP 12/163 no. 65. The list of charges against Mauvissière is reprinted in Bossy, *Under the Molehill*. The note from the leaker to Walsingham in Nov. 1584 reporting that no letters from Mary had been received for some time is in BL Cotton MS Nero B vi ff. 371–72. The translation and summary of Creighton's seized papers, and the account of his capture, are in SP 12/173 no. 4 and SP 53/13 no. 61.

Chérelles's trick upon Stafford is documented in *Calendar of State Papers, Scotland*, vol. 6, no. 315. A number of letters in *Calendar of State Papers, Foreign*, refer to the deciphering work of Sainte-Aldegonde and others (e.g., vol. 10, nos. 714 and 768; vol. 13, no. 52); Sainte-Aldegonde's career and the contemporary history of codes and decipherment is excellently covered in Kahn, *Codebreakers*.

The key documents in the Babington case have been collected in Pollen, ed., *Babington Plot*; Poulet, *Letter Books*, and Labanoff, ed., *Lettres*. Nicholl, *Reckoning*, has an excellent study of Robert Poley. Poley's reports to Walsingham on what he picked up from Morgan, Paget, and Châteauneuf are in PRO SP 53/6 no. 9 and SP 53/7 no. 2. His "confession" detailing his relations with Babington is in *Calendar of State Papers, Scotland*, vol. 8, no. 685.

Copies of the ciphers used by Babington are in PRO SP 12/193 no. 54; the forged cipher postscript inserted by Phelippes is in SP 53/18 no. 55. Walsingham's letter to Phelippes regretting the suspicion aroused by adding the forged postscript is in BL Cotton MS Appendix L f. 144. One of the several copies of Babington's farewell letter to Poley is in BL Add. MS 33938 f. 22.

1584–90: WAR, AT LAST

MacCaffrey, *Queen Elizabeth and the Making of Policy*, and Read, *Mr. Secretary Walsingham*, cover in detail the negotiations leading to the Leicester expedition. The *Declaration of the Causes* is reprinted in *Somers Tracts*, vol. 1, pp. 410–19. Duncan-Jones, *Sir Philip Sidney*, is a solid work of modern scholarship on Sidney's life that strips away much of the legends of centuries. Walsingham's rapprochement with Burghley is discussed in Read, "Walsingham and Burghley."

The story of Stafford's treason is well covered in Read, "Fame of Sir Edward Stafford," and in Leimon and Parker, "Treason and Plot"; the latter builds an exceptionally powerful case against Stafford by matching the reports filed by Mendoza with details about Stafford's activities and information he received. The full text of Berden's report on Stafford is in *Calendar of State Papers, Foreign*, vol. 21 (pt. 1), pp. 34–36; his comment about reading the ambassador's letters and supplying the Catholics with false reports is in PRO SP 12/187 no. 81.

Drake's expeditions are well covered in Kelsey, *Sir Francis Drake*. Walsingham's "Plat for Intelligence out of Spain" is in PRO SP 12/202 no. 41.

Many of the intelligence reports from Standen and Ousley are in BL Add. MS 35841. Parker, "Worst-Kept Secret," is an excellent summary and analysis of the intelligence on Spanish preparations received in London. English preparations to resist invasion are detailed in Bruce, *Report on the Arrangements*.

The events of the Armada have been told countless times; I found Kelsey, *Sir Francis Drake;* Rowse, *Expansion of Elizabethan England;* Martin and Parker, *Spanish Armada;* and Martin, *Spanish Armada Prisoners,* particularly useful.

Walsingham's will is reprinted in Webb, Miller, and Beckwith, *History of Chislehurst.*

The fate of Standen, briefly discussed in Birch, *Memoirs,* is reconstructed in fascinating detail in Hammer, "Elizabethan Spy."

BIBLIOGRAPHY

PRINCIPAL MANUSCRIPT SOURCES

British Library (BL)
  Additional MSS
  Cotton MSS
  Harley MSS
  Stowe MSS
Public Record Office, Kew, U.K. (PRO)
  SP 12 State Papers, Domestic, Elizabeth I
  SP 52 State Papers, Scotland, Series I, Elizabeth I
  SP 53 State Papers, Scotland, Series I, Mary Queen of Scots

PRINTED PRIMARY SOURCES

Birch, Thomas. *Memoirs of the Reign of Queen Elizabeth from the Year 1581 till Her Death.* London, 1754.

Bruce, John. *Report on the Arrangements which Were Made, for the Internal Defence of these Kingdoms, when Spain, by its Armada, Projected the Invasion and Conquest of England.* London, 1798.

Calendar of Letters and State Papers Relating to English Affairs, Preserved Principally in the Archives of Simancas, Elizabeth. London, 1892–99.

Calendar of State Papers, Foreign Series, of the Reign of Elizabeth. 23 vols. London, 1863–1950.

Calendar of the State Papers Relating to Scotland and Mary, Queen of Scots, 1547–1603. 13 vols. Edinburgh, 1898–1969.

Camden, William. *The History of the Most Renowned and Victorious Princess Elizabeth*. London, 1635.

Challoner, Richard. *Memoirs of Missionary Priests*. Edited by John Hungerford Pollen. 1924. Reprint. Farnborough, U.K.: Gregg, 1969.

Digges, Dudley, ed. *The Compleat Ambassador*. London, 1655.

A Discoverie of the Treasons Practised and Attempted Against the Queen's Majestie and the Realme, by Francis Throckmorton. 1584. Reprint. *Harleian Miscellany*, vol. 3. London, 1809.

Faunt, Nicholas. "Discourse Touching the Office of Principal Secretary of Estate, &c. 1592." *English Historical Review*, vol. 20 (1905), pp. 499–508.

Fénélon, Bertrand de Salignac, seigneur de La Mothe. *Correspondance diplomatique*. 7 vols. Paris and London, 1838–40.

"Journal of Sir Francis Walsingham from December 1570 to April 1583." *Camden Miscellany*, vol. 6. London: Camden Society, 1870.

Labanoff, Alexandre, ed. *Lettres, instructions et mémoires de Marie Stuart, reine d'Écosse*. 7 vols. London, 1844.

Lloyd, David. *State Worthies*. 2 vols. London, 1766.

Murdin, William, ed. *Collection of State Papers . . . Left by William Cecill Lord Burghley*. London, 1740–59.

Naunton, Robert. *Fragmenta Regalia; or Observations on Queen Elizabeth, Her Times & Favorites*. Edited by John S. Cerovski. Washington, D.C.: Folger Shakespeare Library, 1985.

Pollen, John Hungerford, ed. *Mary Queen of Scots and the Babington Plot*. Publications of the Scottish History Society, third series, vol. 3. Edinburgh, 1922.

Potter, David, ed. *The French Wars of Religion: Selected Documents*. New York: St. Martin's, 1997.

Poulet, Amias. *The Letter Books of Sir Amias Poulet, Keeper of Mary Queen of Scots*. Edited by John Morris. London: Burns and Oates, 1874.

The Registers of St. Olave, Hart Street, London: 1563–1700. London, 1916.

Somers Tracts. 13 vols. 1809–15.

Stow, John. *Survey of London; Reprinted from the Text of 1603*. Oxford: Clarendon Press, 1971.

Strype, John. *Annals of the Reformation*. 2 vols. London, 1725.

————. *Ecclesiastical Memorials*. 7 vols. London, 1816.

Stubbs, John. *The Discoverie of a Gaping Gulf*. Edited by Lloyd E. Berry. Charlottesville: University Press of Virginia, 1968.

SECONDARY SOURCES

Bossy, John. *Giordano Bruno and the Embassy Affair*. New Haven, Conn.: Yale University Press, 1991.

————. *Under the Molehill: An Elizabethan Spy Story*. New Haven, Conn.: Yale University Press, 2001.

Duncan-Jones, Katherine. *Sir Philip Sidney: Courtier Poet*. New Haven, Conn.: Yale University Press, 1991.

Erlanger, Philippe. *Saint Bartholomew's Night: The Massacre of Saint Bartholomew*. Translated by Patrick O'Brian. New York: Pantheon, 1962.

Fraser, Antonia. *Mary Queen of Scots*. 1969. Reprint. New York: Dell, 1993.

Guy, John. *Tudor England*. Oxford: Oxford University Press, 1988.

————. *Queen of Scots: The True Life of Mary Stuart*. Boston: Houghton Mifflin, 2004.

Hammer, P.E.J. "An Elizabethan Spy Who Came In from the Cold: The Return of Anthony Standen to England in 1593." *Historical Research*, vol. 65 (1992), pp. 277–95.

Kahn, David. *The Codebreakers*. Revised edition. New York: Scribner, 1996.

Kelsey, Harry. *Sir Francis Drake: The Queen's Pirate*. New Haven, Conn.: Yale University Press, 2000.

Kingdon, Robert M. *Myths About the St. Bartholomew's Day Massacres, 1572–1576*. Cambridge, Mass.: Harvard University Press, 1988.

Knecht, R. J. *The French Wars of Religion, 1559–1598*. London: Longman, 1989.

Layard, Henry Austen. *The Massacre of St. Batholomew and the Revocation of the Edict of Nantes.* London, 1888.

Leimon, Mitchell, and Geoffrey Parker. "Treason and Plot in Elizabethan Diplomacy: The 'Fame of Sir Edward Stafford' Reconsidered." *English Historical Review*, vol. III (1996), pp. 1134–58.

MacCaffrey, Wallace T. *The Shaping of the Elizabethan Regime.* Princeton, N.J.: Princeton University Press, 1968.

———. *Queen Elizabeth and the Making of Policy, 1572–1588.* Princeton, N.J.: Princeton University Press, 1981.

———. *Elizabeth I.* London: Edward Arnold, 1993.

McGrath, Patrick. *Papists and Puritans Under Elizabeth I.* New York: Walker, 1967.

McMillim, Scott, and Sally-Beth MacLean. *The Queen's Men and Their Plays.* New York: Cambridge University Press, 1998.

Martin, Colin, and Geoffrey Parker. *The Spanish Armada.* New York: W. W. Norton, 1988.

Martin, Paula. *Spanish Armada Prisoners: The Story of the "Nuestra Señora del Rosario" and Her Crew, and of Other Prisoners in England, 1587–97.* Exeter, U.K.: University of Exeter, 1988.

Nicholl, Charles. *The Reckoning.* New York: Harcourt, Brace, 1992.

Noguères, Henri. *The Massacre of Saint Bartholomew.* Translated by Claire Elaine Engel. New York: Macmillan, 1962.

Palliser, D. M. *The Age of Elizabeth: England Under the Later Tudors, 1547–1603.* Second edition. London: Longman, 1992.

Parker, Geoffrey. "The Worst-Kept Secret in Europe? The European Intelligence Community and the Spanish Armada of 1588." In *Go Spy the Land: Military Intelligence in History*, edited by Keith Neilson and B.J.C. McKercher. Westport, Conn.: Prager, 1992.

Pollen, John Hungerford. *The English Catholics in the Reign of Queen Elizabeth.* New York: Longmans, Green, 1920.

Pollitt, Ronald. "The Abduction of Doctor John Story and the Evolution of Elizabethan Intelligence Operations." *Sixteenth Century Journal*, vol. 14 (1983), pp. 131–56.

Read, Conyers. "Walsingham and Burghley in Queen Elizabeth's Privy Council." *English Historical Review*, vol. 28 (1913), pp. 34–58.

————. "The Fame of Sir Edward Stafford." *American Historical Review*, vol. 20 (1915), pp. 292–313; vol. 35 (1930), pp. 560–66.

————. *Mr. Secretary Walsingham and the Policy of Queen Elizabeth*. 3 vols. 1925. Reprint. Harwich Port, Mass.: Clock & Rose Press, 2003.

————. *The Tudors: Personalities and Practical Politics in Sixteenth-Century England*. New York: Henry Holt, 1936.

————. *Mr. Secretary Cecil and Queen Elizabeth*. New York: Alfred A. Knopf, 1955.

————. *The Government of England Under Elizabeth*. Washington, D.C.: Folger Shakespeare Library, 1960.

Rowse, A. L. *The England of Elizabeth*. 1950. Reprint. Madison: University of Wisconsin Press, 2003.

————. *The Expansion of Elizabethan England*. 1955. Reprint. Madison: University of Wisconsin Press, 2003.

Soman, Alfred, ed. *The Massacre of St. Bartholomew: Reappraisals and Documents*. The Hague: Martinus Nijhoff, 1974.

Somerset, Anne. *Elizabeth I*. New York: St. Martin's Press, 1991.

Starkey, David. *Elizabeth: The Struggle for the Throne*. London: Chatto & Windus, 2000.

Sutherland, N. M. *The Massacre of St. Bartholomew and the European Conflict, 1559–1572*. New York: Harper and Row, 1973.

Webb, E. A., G. W. Miller, and J. Beckwith. *The History of Chislehurst*. London: George Allen, 1899.